ARIS & PHILLIPS CLASSICAL TEXTS

LUCAN
Civil War VIII

Edited with an Introduction, Translation and Commentary by
Roland Mayer

Aris & Phillips is an imprint of Oxbow Books

Published in the United Kingdom in by
OXBOW BOOKS
10 Hythe Bridge Street, Oxford OX1 2EW

and in the United States by
OXBOW BOOKS
908 Darby Road, Havertown, PA 19083

Paperback Edition: ISBN 978-0-85668-176-9

First printed 1981. Reprinted with corrections and addenda 2007, 2014.

A CIP record for this book is available from the British Library

For a complete list of Aris & Phillips titles, please contact:

UNITED KINGDOM
Oxbow Books
Telephone (01865) 241249
Fax (01865) 794449
Email: oxbow@oxbowbooks.com
www.oxbowbooks.com

UNITED STATES OF AMERICA
Oxbow Books
Telephone (800) 791-9354
Fax (610) 853-9146
Email: queries@casemateacademic.com
www.casemateacademic.com/oxbow

Oxbow Books is part of the Casemate Group

Printed and bound by CPI Group (UK) Ltd, Croydon, CR0 4YY

For Ted & Anne Kenney

Nur der Freundschaft Harmonie
Mildert die Beschwerden;
Ohne diese Sympathie
Ist kein Glück auf Erden

Die Zauberflöte

CONTENTS

PREFACE

This book is founded upon a dissertation submitted in 1976 for the Ph. D. degree in Cambridge University. The commentary has been much revised, and the introduction has been enlarged in scope. In both cases the refashioning has been carried out with a view to the needs and interests of the reader (perhaps an undergraduate) who wants to sample a representative piece of Lucan. But it is inevitable that some of the material is addressed to professional scholars. It has been my aim to elucidate the poet's use of language and rhetoric, and to show how the present book is structured. Since Lucan is not a poet of the first rank, it also seemed important to point to his influence and to show to what degree his preoccupations are those of his own age. For advice on both the general plan of revision and on details of notes I am most grateful to Professor R.D. Williams of Reading University and to Mr R. Coleman of Emmanuel College, Cambridge. It is also a pleasure to acknowledge my debt to several institutions which have enabled me to carry on my studies. In 1969 the University of California at Berkeley gave me the Amy Bowles Johnson Traveling Fellowship in Classics. In 1972 Peterhouse, Cambridge, gave me the Lady Mary Ramsey Studentship. Birkbeck College, London University, has made a grant towards expenses. I am especially grateful to an enterprising publisher, who is ready to take his chance on the unproved student of a difficult poet. But all these debts of gratitude do not equal the one which has already been acknowledged.

ABBREVIATIONS

The complete title and date of publication of works cited only once is given at the place of citation. Works more frequently cited are designated by the author's name, or by initials in the case of standard works of reference. The following is an alphabetical list of these books.

In preparing this commentary I also consulted Housman's own interleaved and annotated copy of *Lucan* which is deposited in the library of Trinity College, Cambridge, as well as the three copies of Lucan used by Bentley for his proposed edition of the poem, and the two copies of the poem which belonged to Markland, all in the British Library.

adn.	*Adnotationes super Lucanum*, ed. J. Endt, 1909
Ahl	F.M., *Lucan: An Introduction*, 1976
Auerbach	E., *Mimesis*, 1953 (Eng. trans.)
Axelson	B., *Unpoetische Wörter*, 1945
Bell	A.J., *The Latin Dual and Poetic Diction*, 1923
Bentley	R., Lucan, 1760
Bonner	S.F., *AJP* 87.1966.257-89
Borneau	D., *La Crue du Nil*, 1964
Burman	P., Lucan, 1740
Butler	H.E., *Post-Augustan Poetry*, 1909
Caspari	F., *De Ratione quae inter Vergilium et Lucanum intercedat quaestiones selectae*, Diss. Leipzig, 1908
comm. Bern.	*Scholia in Lucanum I.*, ed. H. Usener 1869 (all published)
Cortius	G., Lucan, 1828-9 (notes posthumously published by C.F. Weber)
Ehlers	W., *Der Bürgerkrieg*, 1973
Fraenkel	Ed., *Kleine Beiträge zur Klassischen Philologie*, 1964, 2 vols
Fraenkel Pathos	'Lucan als Mittler des Antiken Pathos' included in the

Kleine Beiträge and in *Lucan,* Wege der Forschung 235
(1970), ed. W. Rutz

Francken	C.M., *Lucan,* 1896-7
Getty	R.J., *Lucan I,* 1955 (ed. 2)
GLK	*Grammatici Latini,* ed. H. Keil, 1855-78
Håkanson	L., *Statius' Silvae,* 1969
Haskins	C.E., *Lucan,* 1887
Heinsius	N., *Adversariorum Libri IV,* ed. P. Burman, 1742
Heitland	W.E., 1. Introduction to Haskins
	2. Lucan in J.P. Postgate's *Corpus Poetarum Latinorum,* 1900
Hellegouarc'h	J.H., *Le Monosyllabe dans L'Hexamètre Latin,* 1964
Herescu	N.I., *La Poésie Latine,* 1960
Hosius	C., *Lucan,* 1913 (ed. 3)
Housman	A.E., *Lucan,* 1927 (corr. ed.)
Housman Papers	*Collected Classical Papers,* edd. J. Diggle and F.R.D. Goodyear, 1972
Hübner	U., *Hermes* 100.1972.577-600
KG	R. Kühner and B. Gerth, *Ausführliche Grammatik der Griech. Sprache* (1.1898, 2.1904)
KS	R. Kühner and C. Stegmann, *Ausführliche Grammatik der Latein. Sprache* (1.1912, 2.1955)
Lejay	P., *Lucan I,* 1894
Leo	F., *De Senecae tragoediis observationes criticae,* 1878, (ed.2)
LHS	M. Leumann, J.B. Hofmann, A. Szantyr, *Lateinische Syntax und Stilistik,* 1965
Löfstedt	E., *Syntactica,* 1.1942 (ed.2), 2.1933
Löfstedt comm.	*Philologischer Kommentar zur Peregrinatio Aetheriae,* 1911 (repr. 1970)
Löfstedt Studien	*Vermischte Studien zur latein. Sprachkunde und Syntax,* 1936
Lundqvist	N., *Studia Lucanea,* diss. Holmiae, 1907
Mooney	G.W., *Index to the Pharsalia of Lucan,* 1927
Morford	M.P.O., *The Poet Lucan,* 1967
Müller	L., *De Re Metrica,* 1894 (ed.2)
Nisard	D., *Etudes de Moeurs et de Critique sur les Poëtes latins de la Décadence,* 1888 (ed.5)
Norden	E., *P. Vergilius Maro Aeneis Buch VI.,* 1970 (ed.5) –

	generally cited by page number
Neue	F., and C. Wagener, *Formenlehre der latein. Sprache*, ed.3, 1892-1905
OLD	*Oxford Latin Dictionary*, 1968-
Ollfors	A.O., *Studien zum Aufbau des Hexameters Lucans*, 1967
	2. *Textkritische und Interpretatorische Beiträge zu Lucan*, 1967
Oudendorp	F., *Lucan*, 1728
Pichon	R., *Les Sources de Lucain*, 1912
Pichon Histoire	*Histoire de la Littérature Latine*, 1897
Plessis	F., *La Poésie Latine*, 1909
Postgate	J.P., *Lucan VII*, 1913 (ed.2), rev. by O.A.W. Dilke 1960 and 1979; *Lucan VIII*. 1917
RE	*Real-Encyclopädie der classischen Altertumswissenschaft*, 1893-
Ribbeck	O., *Geschichte der römischen Dichtung*, vol.3, 1892
Riley	H.T., Translation for Bohn Library, 1853 (often reprinted)
Roby (cited by section, not page)	H.J., *Grammar of the Latin Language*, Pt. 2, Syntax, 1892
Schnepf	H., *Untersuchungen zur Darstellungskunst Lucans im 8. Buch der Pharsalia*, in *Lucan*, Wege der Forschung 235 (1970), ed. W. Rutz
Seitz	K., *Hermes* 93. 1965.204-32
Shackleton Bailey	D.R., *Propertiana*, 1956
Strand	J., *Notes on Valerius Flaccus' Argonautica*, 1972
Summers	W.C., *The Silver Age of Latin Literature*, 1920
Syme	R., *Roman Papers*, 1979, 2 vols, ed. E. Badian
TLL	*Thesaurus Linguae Latinae*, 1900-
Vahlen	J., *Opuscula Academica*, 2 vols, 1907-8
Wackernagel	J., *Vorlesungen über Syntax*, 1.1926, 2.1928 (ed.2)
Weber	C.F., *Lucan*, 1821-31
Weinstock	S., *Divus Julius*, 1971
Weise	C.H., *Lucan*, 1835
Wight Duff	J., *A Literary History of Rome in the Silver Age*, 1960 (ed.2)
Winbolt	S.E., *Latin Hexameter Verse*, 1903
Woodcock	E.C., *A New Latin Syntax*, 1959

This book was noticed in *Greece and Rome* 29 (1982) 200, and reviewed by M. Coffey, *JACT Bull.* Rev. 62 (1983), O. Dilke, *C R* 33 (1983) 201–3, W. Rutz, *Gnomon* 55 (1983) 22–7, S. Hedberg, *Eranos* 80 (1982) 34, J. Beranger, *Museum Helveticum* 40 (1983) 26, E. Fantham, *Echos du Monde Classique/Classical Views* 27 (1983) 374–6, R. Verdière, Latomus 42 (1983) 912, M. Morford, CJ 80 (1984) 70–1, G.W.M. Harrison, *AJP* 106 (1985) 138, and J. Oroz, *Helmantica* 39 (1988) 249–50. Dilke especially offered some plausible alternative interpretations.

For discussions of the eighth book, in whole or in part, see:

Dilke, O. 'Lucan's account of the fall of Pompey' in *Studi su Varrone, sulla retorica, storiografia e poesia latina : scritti in onore di Benedetto Riposati* (Rieti and Milan, 1979) i.171–84.

Johnson, W.R. *Momentary Monsters: Lucan and his Heroes* (Ithaca, 1987) 79–83.

Leigh, M. *Lucan: Spectacle and Engagement* (Oxford, 1997) 118–25, 183 n. 36.

Tremoli, P. *Figure retoriche lucanee alla luce dello strutturalismo (Luc. bell. civ. VIII 484–535)* (Trieste, 1970).

Introduction:

p. 2. 'he was also made an augur': at such an early age this was a signal mark of imperial favour.

'Neo-Augustanism': see now 'Neronian classicism', *AJP* 103 (1983) 305–18

p. 8. 'Nile excursus': this is a typically 'sublime' theme, for which see D.C. Innes, 'Gigantomachy and natural philosophy', CQ 29 (1979) 165–71.

p. 9. Text: there is a crisp account by R.J. Tarrant in L.D. Reynolds (ed.), *Texts and Transmission* (Oxford, 1986 corr. ed.), 215–18. There is an indispensable new edition of the whole poem by D.R. Shackleton Bailey (Stuttgart, 1997, ed. 2), in which there is much helpful interpretation, often correcting my own, e.g., at 132, 447.

p. 14. 'inadvertant prosy turns': *uelamenta* 368 is perhaps another such.

p. 15. The reference to Aristotle, *Poetics* is based on misunderstanding and should be ignored.

p. 21. For the ancient belief in apparitions see A.D. Nock in *Gnomon* 33 (1961) 586 n. 1, and cf. Acts of the Apostles 16.9.

Translation:

p. 65, l. 621: *probat* 'wins approval' (*OLD* s.v. *probo* 6) is also possible.

Commentary:

p. 91, l. 62: in fact the ancients did like beaches, see Cic. *Pro Caelio* 35 *actas*, with Austin's n., or *OLD* s.v. *acta*.

p. 112: *pietas*: see W. Heyke, *Zur Rolle des Pietas bei Lucan* (Diss. Heidelberg, 1970).

p. 115, l. 222: possible locations of the *Caspia claustra* are canvassed by J. F. Standish, 'The Caspian gates', *GR* 17 (1970) 17–24.

p. 116, l. 223: *Alanos*: see R. Syme, 'Exotic names, notably in Seneca's tragedies', *Acta Classica* 30 (1987) 59–60 = A. R. Birley (ed.), *Roman Papers* (Oxford, 1991) vi.282–3

p. 127, ll. 334–5: add *Anth. Lat.* 415R, 40 *pueri regis adire pedes*.

p. 127, l. 335: *transfuga* is in fact found in Hor. *Carm.* 3.16.23.

p. 128, l. 341: *potes*: see now *OLD* s.v. *possum* 3.

p. 135, l. 398: for the promiscuity of beasts see Pease on Virg. *Aen.* 4.551.

p. 148, l. 537: *rex puer*: see addendum to p. 127, ll. 334–5 above.

p. 165, ll. 692–711: Plutarch paired his biography of Pompey with that of Agesilaos.

p. 167, l. 711: *umeris* has fallen out of the second line of the Virgil citation after *caput*.

p. 167, Intro. to ll. 712–872: see E. Burck, 'Epische Bestattungsszenen' in *Vom Menschenbild in der römischen Literatur: ausgewählte Schriften* (Heidelberg, 1966) ii.429–87.

p. 175, l. 740 suttee: see W. Heckel and – J. C. Yardley, 'Roman writers and the Indian practice of suttee', *Philologus* 125 (1981) 305–11.

p. 181, l. 801 *vacant*: see now *OLD* s.v. 4a.

INTRODUCTION

I. THE POET AND THE POEM

Marcus Annaeus Lucanus, who has always been called Lucan by English speakers, was born on 3 November AD 39 at Corduba in the Spanish province of Baetica. His maternal grandfather was Acilius Lucanus, an orator of some renown even after his death. Lucan's paternal grandfather was the elder Seneca, a devotee of rhetoric who has left us in his ten books of *Controuersiae* and one book of *Suasoriae* a vivid record of the sort of display pieces which professed rhetoricians recited in Augustan Rome. This Seneca had three sons. The eldest, Novatus, was adopted by the orator L. Junius Gallio; so he took the name Gallio, and by it he is known to S. Luke in *Acts* 18.12-17. The next son, who is called the younger Seneca, was a man of parts. He forged a prose style that rivals Cicero's; he also wrote tragedies, prose satire, moral essays and letters, and a work on natural history. He was also a millionaire, and the guardian of Nero until he retired from public affairs in AD 62 (Tac. *Ann.* 14.52-6). Only these two brothers sought public careers, and both ennobled the family by reaching the consulship.[1] The youngest brother, Mela, preferred however to make money as a private citizen, and he never left the equestrian rank. His only claim to fame is that he was Lucan's father (so Tac. *Ann.* 16.17). The whole family was very wealthy, and Juvenal can still speak some fifty or more years after Lucan's death of his marbled pleasure grounds (7.79f).

When he was seven months old Lucan was taken to Rome, where in due course he was given the now customary training in rhetoric. This education fitted a man for practice at the bar, and the law courts remained an avenue to wealth, fame, and a public career. It would seem that Lucan had some success as a pleader. It is worth noting that as a declamatory exercise he chose to compose a pair of speeches, one for and the other against Octavius Sagitta, who had committed a famous crime of passion in AD 58 (related by Tacitus at *Ann.* 13.44). Now it was usual for such pairs of contrasting speeches to be based upon a theme either imaginary or drawn from history, and in this book 262-455 is an instance of the latter. The fact that Lucan chose a theme of contemporary interest and of a sensational nature shows something

1

of the character of the man who took the civil war as his epic theme.

It is not clear when or how Lucan came to be noticed by Nero, who had ascended the throne in AD 54 at the age of 18. It is not unlikely that Seneca brought his gifted nephew forward in AD 59 when Nero showed a serious interest in the composition of poetry – up to that time he had concentrated his attention upon driving horses and the improvement of his singing (so Tac. *Ann.* 14.16). At any rate, in AD 60 at the first Neronian Games Lucan won the prize for poetry (Nero did not compete on this occasion, but he was awarded the prize for eloquence by acclamation; Tac. *Ann.* 14.21). Lucan's theme, *Laudes Neronis*, could not but succeed, and the poet was a born courtier. He now begins his public career. He was made a quaestor before the legal age of 25, perhaps in AD 60, giving him entry to the Senate; he was also made an augur. The life of the poet which is attributed to an unknown Vacca (a late work, but independent of that which is attributed to Suetonius) implies that Lucan almost immediately after his public success began his epic poem. It is his sole extant work – many others of which we know the names are lost – and it was unfinished at his death. He probably entitled the work *De Bello Ciuili*, but it has long been popularly known as *Pharsalia* (this may be due to a misunderstanding of 9.985 *Pharsalia nostra*, as much as to the success of the seventh book in which the battle is described[2]). Before discussing Lucan's own poem, however, it is necessary to give a brief sketch of the sort of literature that was being written in the Neronian age, and the spirit which animated it.

Neo-Augustanism

When Nero came to the throne he tacitly repudiated the policies of government implemented by some of his predecessors. This was his promise: 'ex Augusti praescripto imperaturum se professus' (Suet. *Nero* 10.1). Throughout his reign he clung to this principle of government, albeit in somewhat superficial forms. For example, he conspicuously honoured the statue of Augustus, he drove in his triumphal car, he gave the name Augusta to his wife Poppaea, and he formed a special troop of *Augustiani equites* (Suet. *Nero* 12.3, 25.1, Tac. *Ann.* 15.23.1 and 14.15.8). In a word, it seems that the notion of an 'Augustan Age' as a classic model was first formulated in the time of Nero, perhaps by Nero himself. However that may be, the emperor's official policy is clear, and it finds its reflection in contemporary literature. The poets are remarkable in that they return to the Augustan age (or to be more precise, to the poets deemed to be Augustan, though their works may have appeared before 27 BC) for their generic models. Calpurnius Siculus is the first poet we know of to revive the bucolic poetry of Virgil; the two fragmentary Einsiedeln Eclogues are also evidence of a fresh initiative in this department of literature. Columella, an agricultural writer, devoted his tenth book to a versified exposition of gardening, and in the preface frankly acknowledged his debt to the *Georgics*. It seems that after his

2

death Horace's poetry suffered eclipse. He is not, for example, mentioned by Velleius Paterculus as one of the glories of the age (2.36); the elder Seneca never speaks of him, nor are snatches of his verse to be found upon Pompeian walls. But in Nero's reign his poetry is taken up again. In Petronius's novel, *Satyricon*, the rhetor Eumolpus acknowledges with justness the *curiosa felicitas* of the poet (118.5).[3] More significantly, his lyric poetry found an imitator in Caesius Bassus, who also devoted much of a metrical treatise, dedicated to Nero, to expounding Horatian metres. Persius found his inspiration for satire in Horace, and his own poems are something of a cento of the earlier model. Persius's sixth satire is a letter to Caesius Bassus, and this may be claimed as a revival of Horace's *Epistulae*. Seneca too quotes the *Sermones* in his *Moral Letters to Lucilius*. Erotic elegy seems to have found a fresh champion in Petronius, if a handful of elegant poems that have come down to us are correctly attributed to him. The only Augustan poet who does not seem to have been openly challenged was Ovid, unless Lucan's own unfinished tragedy of *Medea* was modelled upon the now lost work of Ovid. (Perhaps the fact that Ovid offended Augustus deterred imitators; at any rate his influence upon later writers is all-pervasive.)

Apart from reviving the genres of the Augustan age, the Neronian poets were addicted to Trojan themes. Labeo translated the *Iliad*, and Baebius Italicus wrote an *Ilias Latina*, now generally accepted as Neronian, though it could have been composed under any of the Julio-Claudians. Lucan himself wrote an *Iliacon*, and Nero's *Troica* was his masterwork. In the *Satyricon* Petronius includes a brief account of the capture of Troy (89). In the *Pharsalia*, Lucan went so far as to invent for Caesar an unhistorical visit to Troy, 9.961-79. It must be assumed that all of this activity was inspired by the *Aeneid*, and by the claim of the Julian house to be descended from Aeneas. Such then is the background against which Lucan's choice of epic theme must be set.

Lucan's Poem

The theme of the *Pharsalia* is the civil war fought between Caesar and Pompey, which began in 49 BC and ended at Munda in 45 BC. It appears to have been a novel choice (so Statius implies at *Siluae* 2.7.48-53, but it must be noted that he is there contrasting the worn-out themes of mythology with the relevance of a *togatum carmen*). Was this theme likely to have seemed controversial in its day? The answer is by no means clear, but certain considerations will suggest that the theme was unexceptionable. It must be remembered that Julius Caesar had overthrown the Republic and had seemed to aim at kingship. For this reason he was something of a skeleton in the closet of the Julio-Claudian house. Augustan literature therefore largely avoids mentioning him, and its tone is overwhelmingly Pompeian. That is to say, it supports

3

Senatorial government and its supposed defender, Pompey, when it turns to political themes at all. About Caesar it tends to keep silence, but it is remarkable that Horace can joke about his assassination at *Serm.* 1.7.33-5 and Virgil manages to rebuke him guardedly in the person of Anchises at *Aen.* 6.834f.[4] In official life, Augustus did not always point to Caesar as his father, but on coins and inscriptions he tended to favour the vague title *diui filius.* But the emperors after Tiberius expelled Caesar the dictator from their official genealogies, which always began with Augustus instead. So when Lucan chose a theme that would entail praise of Pompey and Cato, he was not necessarily running a risk of being charged with political disaffection. For officially Caesar was nothing to Nero, and it was accepted that the principate, in the person of Nero, was a restored Republic (see 94n). Indeed the tone of Lucan's first book is so temperate, that it has been suggested that he could have gone on to conclude his epic with praise of the emperor as guardian of peace and liberty.[5] This suggestion gains in plausibility when we recall the general Augustan tone, as sketched above, of Neronian policy and literature.

It is hard to believe that Lucan did not at least commence his poem in a spirit consonant with the prevailing fashion; at any rate, nothing in the ancient accounts of the young courtier's life suggests an aloof and reflective independence. Yet it is common nowadays to speak of the *Pharsalia* as an anti-*Aeneid.* Such a description is not unfair to certain parts of the epic, but it implies a crude approach to Virgil's work. The poet of the *Aeneid* did not close his eyes to the fact that the establishment of the Roman people had cost the lifeblood of many attractive men and women, who were caught willy-nilly in Fate's toils; this did not, however, make Rome any less precious (if anything, it raised her value). Lucan, it may be suggested, tried to follow Virgil's tragic vision – 'non passibus aequis' – and to show in an historical, rather than a mythological, epic just how dearly bought was the Augustan settlement under which Romans were once again living, thanks to Nero. Certainly these words in praise of Nero support this interpretation:

> quod si non aliam uenturo fata Neroni
> inuenere uiam magnoque aeterna parantur
> regna deis . . .
> iam nihil, o superi, querimur; scelera ipsa nefasque
> hac mercede placent.   (1.33-38)

The assertion of these lines is so uncompromising that modern critics, who are in fact less crude than the poet himself, assume that they must be ironical. But Lucan's mind is not subtle, and he tends to say what he means bluntly. And if he chose to say that Nero was worth all the suffering of the civil war, what was the moral cost to him? His family had not been involved in the conflict,[6] and they had risen to

4

prosperity and prominence under the rule of the Julio-Claudian emperors. The notion is therefore worth entertaining that, at the outset while the poet still basked in Nero's favour, he intended, not an anti-*Aeneid*, but an historical poem complementary in theme to its earlier model, a new *Aeneid* for the new Augustan age. The emphasis was to be, as in the *Aeneid*, upon the suffering and death which issued in the present benign dispensation. That would hardly be criticism of the new regime. But as it happened, Lucan's attitude, and so the tone of his poem, changed with events.

Some Characters in the Poem

The view that Lucan was at first unwilling to step outside the circle described by the Augustan age is to some extent corroborated by his treatment of some individuals who act in the poem. Here we shall look briefly at Sextus Pompey, Brutus and Cicero.

In the early principate Sextus Pompey was regarded as a renegade because of the war he waged, with the disgraceful use of slaves, against Octavian in Sicily from 39-36 BC. He never received the slightest favourable notice in history or in literature. But Lucan could have made use of Sextus's undeniable loyalty to his father's memory.[7] In the *Pharsalia* however he is hardly more than a name, except in the sixth book where he consults the witch Erichtho about the outcome of the impending battle at Pharsalia. Lucan wanted an opportunity to rival the descent of Aeneas into Hell in the sixth *Aeneid*, but his historical theme precluded direct imitation of the model (he did write, as it happens, a *Catacthonion*). Necromancy however was feasible, but so disgusting that only a degraded individual could have recourse to it. The Sextus of propaganda and tradition was degraded enough, and so he is deputed by the poet to go to the Thessalian witch. (In fact Sextus was too young to be under arms yet, and was with his mother in Lesbos.) There is no motive behind the choice save opportunism, and Lucan's sketch of Sextus at 6.419-22 is in complete conformity with the propaganda of the earliest years of the principate.

The treatment of Brutus is instructive in a negative way. By assassinating Caesar, Brutus became the enemy of his adoptive son Octavian, and so his reputation was somewhat tarnished. At any rate, he was under a cloud. In the *Pharsalia* his role is surprisingly insubstantial, except for a walk-on part in the seventh book which will be discussed below. His only other appearance is in the second book where he seeks to discover what action Cato means to take. In a word, he is a cipher. Cicero too was not an Augustan favourite; perhaps the princeps had a guilty conscience about proscribing him. But Plutarch does tell a story in which Augustus praised the orator as a patriot; what is significant in the anecdote is this: Augustus's grandson was surprised whilst covertly reading Cicero, and the emperor spoke to allay the child's fear. So the child knew how his grandfather was reckoned to feel towards Cicero (Plut. *Cic.* 49).[8] Lucan's picture of the orator is unflattering. For Cicero, in his one (unhistorical) appearance in the poem, urges upon a reluctant Pompey the engagement at Pharsalia. He uses his great oratorical powers to disastrous effect. Thus it is arguable that in the details of the treatment of his epic theme Lucan keeps within bounds.

Civil War

That the theme itself was also unexceptionable in Nero's day is strongly indicated by a passage in the *Satyricon* (118 ff). In it the disreputable rhetorician Eumolpus discourses on the high attainments required of a poet, and most of what he says on this score is sound common sense. Out of the blue he remarks 'ecce, belli ciuilis ingens opus quisquis attigerit nisi plenus litteris sub onere labetur' (118.6). He goes on to lay down laws for the composition of historical epic, almost every one of which is *observed* by Lucan,[9] and he then offers a 295 line long specimen poem on the civil war. It is now allowed that Petronius was writing in the time of Nero, and so the remarks of Eumolpus (or the author) are seen to be a reflection, favourable or not, upon Lucan. Whatever view is taken about the attitude of 'Eumolpus' to Lucan, one fact is plain: he sees nothing dangerous in the theme of the civil war. It appears to be just one among many themes for an historical epic, of which there was a long tradition in Rome.[10] Neither Suetonius nor Tacitus says that the theme of civil war gave offence to anyone, and the passage in the *Satyricon* makes it highly unlikely that civil war was seen as necessarily a dangerous theme, at least in the age of Nero.

The Break with Nero

What did give offence to Nero? Tacitus says expressly that it was Lucan's fame. He published three books of his epic — and publication in those days meant recitation before an audience of connoisseurs — probably the first three. By AD 64 Nero came to envy Lucan, and so sought to wreck him by forbidding any form of publication (Tac. *Ann.* 15. 49, an important passage too often ignored nowadays). The Vaccan life confirms this story, and adds that Lucan was also forbidden to plead at the bar. None of the ancient evidence so much as hints that it was the subject matter of the poem which lead to the breach. Personal envy is the only motive. The ban on publication was savage; there was no reason to suppose that it would ever be lifted so long as Nero lived. For this reason, and apparently no other, Lucan joined the ramshackle conspiracy that centred around Calpurnius Piso. The purpose of the conspiracy, too often overlooked in some recent studies, was not the restoration of senatorial government through freely elected magistrates. (Indeed, Atticus

6

Vestinus, consul in 66, was kept out of the conspiracy just because it was feared that he might attempt some such restoration; so Tac. *Ann.* 15.52.) On the contrary, the Pisonian conspiracy was far from radical, and aimed only at replacing an arbitrary tyrant, Nero, with a new princeps who might prove more alive to the claims of the nobility – by now an old story in the relations between emperor and Senate.

The Aftermath

Because of the ban on publication there appears in the later books of the *Pharsalia* a clear animus against the Julio-Claudian house, which is now seen, contrary to its own propaganda, as the true line of Julius. At 4.823 it is the 'Caesareae domus series' and so linked with Sulla, Marius, and Cinna in its unrestrained power of life and death. It should however be borne in mind that, since these books were not published, the denunciations in them never saw the light of day, unless passages were recited to fellow conspirators. Moreover such passages are few – none, for example, in this book, against the Caesars as a family. The impression grows that Lucan added his denunciations to books already composed, and that these books were not revised to accommodate them. Lucan's treatment of L. Domitius Ahenobarbus, who was Nero's great-great-grandfather, provides a clue. In the second book, probably one of the three published, Domitius is depicted in a favourable light; quite untruly, he is made out to be the gallant defender of Corfinium and defier of Julius. Plainly the episode and its treatment are meant to flatter Nero. But the seventh book fell under the ban, and so it contains an excellent satire upon the deification of emperors (455-9); Domitius, nevertheless, is *still* depicted favourably as a brave fighter, though it would have been truer to history and perhaps gratifying to Lucan's wounded pride to show him as the coward he was, or to drop him altogether. But the episode has been neither rewritten nor suppressed, though the flattery which it was first designed to administer is no longer intended. This patchwork quality is further illustrated in the seventh book by the re-appearance of Brutus. It has already been pointed out that he is a cipher, used once and then dropped. But suddenly he pops up again, in a passage rich with unintended comedy (586-96). Lucan has just been describing the butchery of the noblest Romans, and line 597, 'hic patriae perit omne decus', plainly carries on that episode. The eleven lines in which Brutus appears do not suit this context, for he is not killed, nor even is he clearly endangered as he skulks about seeking to assassinate Caesar. Lucan, who is of course here treely inventing history, says this is premature and he urges Brutus to wait until Caesar has deserved such a fate by acting the tyrant. It seems most likely that this passage would not have been found in Lucan's first draft of the book. If the lines are omitted, the suture between 585 and 597 is invisible. It can therefore be maintained that they

7

were composed *after* the poet joined the conspiracy. He was then faced with a problem: where to put the eleven lines? For Brutus was hitherto a nonentity, with no clear role in this, or in any book after the second. But Brutus did fight at Pharsalia, and so it might be expected that he would there have been found among the noblest Romans. The section where the noblest Romans are described begins at 545 'uentum erat ad robur Magni mediasque cateruas'. It is a thrilling moment, energetically told: they are all patricians and all killed, except Brutus! That he is a later addition, somewhat badly assimilated to his context, seems plain. This passage comes from the hand of one who, Suetonius said, openly praised tyrannicides and offered Nero's head to all and sundry.

The over-ripe Pisonian conspiracy was detected, and Lucan, despite base attempts to exonerate himself, was told to commit suicide. On 30 April AD 65 his veins were opened, and he died, in his twenty-sixth year, reciting some of his own verses descriptive of a dying soldier (Tac. *Ann.* 15.70). The *Pharsalia* remained unfinished; the tenth book is clearly short, and in some books we seem to see doublets, that is, passages that duplicate each other, only one of which would have been left in the final draft (e.g., 6.187,207). How Lucan intended it to end is still debated, but to no purpose. For he does not seem to have had a fixed notion of what the poem was to contain. This is shown by the Nile excursus of the tenth book. It is now known that this section is chiefly indebted to a passage in the fourth book of Seneca's *Naturales Quaestiones* (1-2), a work that is not reckoned to have been begun until after his retirement in AD 62. If Lucan began his epic in AD 60 he cannot have intended at the outset to write at length on the rising of the Nile. He was an opportunist: he saw how he could use his uncle's researches and freely inserted them into his poem without much thought for their relevance. This decision can only have been made once the poem was well under way. It does not seem likely that this is the method of a careful artist who premeditates his every move.

The Sources

If Lucan really read and absorbed as many authors as he is claimed to have done (and Sallust has recently entered the ranks of source material), then he will have had very little time in his brief life for all the writing we know he published. For an excursus, such as that on the Nile or that describing the snakes of Libya in the ninth book, he will have turned to an appropriate authority. But for the narrative of the course of the war Livy was his main, and probably his only guide. In this matter, it is worth while to point to the practice of the somewhat later poet, Silius Italicus; his epic on the Punic wars is derived from Livy. This use of a single source stands to reason. For Lucan was not interested in historical narrative; as Eumolpus said, the historians do it better. What he wanted was to describe exemplary episodes, and to juxtapose contrasting events. What need then for a comparison of sources?[11] Lucan was moreover a rapid and copious writer. Unlike the scrupulous Virgil he left no half-lines in his unfinished work. A single source, over which the imagination is allowed to play, would better suit so deft and unreflective a talent. But he is not bound by his source. As we have seen, he is capable of inventing incidents. In this book the mission of Deiotarus is just such an invention, and the character of Cordus is wholly fictional. Livy was Lucan's mainstay, but for the rest his vigorous imagination, sleek upon its diet of Virgil and Ovid, was free to choose, dispose, and invent as it would.

The Fate of the Poem

We do not known when or how the unfinished poem was at length published. It is likely that after Nero's death in AD 68 Lucan's devoted wife, Polla Argentaria,[12] who long survived him, will have seen to this. The walls of Pompeii have yet to offer any quotes from the *Pharsalia*, but we can gauge the poem's success by the constant imitation of it to be found in the epics of Valerius Flaccus and Silius Italicus, who both took to composition not very long after Lucan's death (Valerius may have begun as early as AD 70). Martial, however, records adverse opinion (14.194). But less than a hundred years after its composition darkness settled upon the poem. The archaist movement was coming into full flood, and Lucan along with most of the too refined post-Augustan poets was ignored. It was not until the mid-fourth century that these writers were once again read with sympathy. About this time, and certainly no earlier, the poem was given a more or less learned commentary; some of the material from it can be found, overlaid with later accretions, in separate but related collections, called *Commenta Bernensia* and *Adnotationes super Lucanum*. (The late composition of the scholia must always be borne in mind, especially where the scholiast seems to be detecting a contemporary allusion on the part of the poet; the first scholiast to Lucan lived some three hundred years after the poet and had no traditional material to found his views upon.) From that time Lucan was once again a popular author. He was the constant study of Claudian and Corippus, and his text was frequently copied.

Text and Translation

Suetonius tells us at the end of his life of Lucan that careful copies of the poem were sold in his day (c. AD 100), but also inaccurate ones. From late antiquity we have a parchment fragment of some lines of the second book, as well as two fragmentary palimpsests of the sixth and seventh books. For the text of the eighth book we rely upon the witness of six mediaeval Mss. All attempts to widen the basis of the textual evidence have failed to show that any other Mss. are independent of these six,

9

or that they add to our knowledge of what Lucan actually wrote. A full account of the readings of these six Mss. is only to be found in Hosius. The interrelation of the independent witnesses to the text was elucidated by Lejay, by Housman, and by Fraenkel (2.267-308). The text for this edition of the eighth book is substantially that of Housman. There is no need to repeat here the arguments by which he defended his choice of reading. There is no apparatus criticus to the text; variant readings and conjectures are discussed in the body of the commentary. The translation is an adaptation of the one made by J.D. Duff in 1928 for the Loeb Classical Library, with some revisions in later printings. I am most grateful to the trustees of the Loeb Classical Library, especially to Professor G.P. Goold, for granting me permission to reprint the substance of Duff's careful work. Professor O.A.W. Dilke has also been so good as to discuss with me some passages; his own verse translation of the book is soon to appear.

II. STYLE

Ever since the elder Scaliger gave it as his opinion that Lucan seemed to bark rather than to sing, the poet's style has been faulted. Montaigne allowed that it did not attract him. The following sketch, therefore, of aspects of Lucan's style and composition is largely apologetic. It is far from thorough, and only offers observations upon salient and distinctive features of the poet's manner. In general, the traditional judgments and insights of Lucan's readers must recommend themselves to the modern critic. No surprises, therefore, are to be expected from what will be said below. But while the critics of the past are rarely wrong in noticing what is special about Lucan, they are inclined to condemn (the French are, despite Scaliger and Montaigne, exceptions). In the sections that follow some considerations are advanced which it is to be hoped may lead to a more favourable appreciation of Lucan's real, if misdirected, genius.

A. Metre
Lucan's metrical practice is rarely praised. Housman called it commonplace. But its regularity and strictness are really 'common' only in the Neronian age. More sympathetically, Butler observed that Lucan strikes out on a line of his own, but that the influence of the *Metamorphoses* prompts the smooth monotony of his verses (123); one characteristic, however, is ponderosity (Butler's word), and to this ponderosity will be devoted the bulk of the following sketch. But first the matter of smoothness must be addressed.

With felicitous irony Summers called Lucan's hexameters well-oiled (40). By using this metaphor he implies that the verse is efficient, and that like an efficient machine the lines do not draw attention to themselves as they go about their work. And what is this work? Moving the reader's or audience's emotions. E.P. Barker remarked upon the peculiar detonant vehemence of Lucan's verse ('The poet in the forcing-house', 19). But is so narrow a spectrum required to bring this about? Perhaps not. For one factor, which can also be pointed to in the case of diction, is that Lucan was composing fast, and fast composition, as the *Siluae* of Statius show, is the death of nicety. But above all the manner of presentation, or first publication, would tend to prompt an unobtrusive metrical technique. This view is shared by Nisard, 2. 337f. As a Frenchman writing in the age of Hugo, Nisard knew what true declamation was and the bad effect it could have on style, above all its power and monotony. While the Augustans composed for a hearing reader or at most a small audience of friends, Lucan wrote with his eye on public delivery, the *recitatio*, which was the curse of Silver Latin letters. Declaimed verse does not admit of the same delicate crafting that is found in the *Aeneid*; nor are the well-paced verses of the *Metamorphoses* designed for a full-throated delivery. Lucan's metric is a declaimer's vehicle. The restriction of elision, and its limitation to certain types, the unvaried use of caesurae [13], and the ponderosity all together serve the manner in which the poem was to be presented to its public. For the greatest Latin poets metre could be to some degree an end in itself. But Lucan, who has something urgent to say, cannot stop to refashion a pause or modulate his lines. Such delicate strokes furthermore would be lost on an audience. [14] Set beside the Augustans Lucan's technique is impoverished, but it is nevertheless a powerful tool.

The ponderosity of the verse gives it a majestic vigour. One means of achieving it is the frequent use of a self-contained spondee in the first foot (noticed by Müller, 241). For the sake of comparison it is worth looking at the practice of Virgil and of Ovid. Virgil may use this weighty opening about twenty times in a book of his epic, and we notice recurrent patterns of use for special emphasis. But Ovid preferred to sacrifice this expressive element in his metre, and the last book of the *Metamorphoses* has only one significant self-contained spondee in the first foot. [15] Lucan however restores its dignity to the first foot; he often sets there a spondaic disyllable, usually to emphasize the word, but sometimes simply to weight the whole line. From the eighth book may be cited the following lines: 84, 103, 238, 243, 246, 258, 317, 411, 564, 653, 660f., 700, 721, 744, 789, 843, 859: eighteen in all of note. One feature is common to a number of examples, and clearly shows that the placement is not fortuitous. Let us consider 653 'uita digna fui' Nothing prevented Lucan from writing 'digna fui uita', or, as Ovid might have done (cf. *Met*. 10. 633), 'uiuere digna fui'. But his choice is characteristic, and *uita* so placed is more striking and weighty.

Quite a number of the lines listed above are of this reversible sort, or at least they could easily have been rewritten so as to set a dactyl in the first foot. But Lucan avoids the lighter measure, and reading aloud justifies his practice.

Butler reckoned that this ponderosity was all Lucan's own, but his view needs widening. As was mentioned above, Petronius has left us a long specimen of epic verse. Within its 295 lines there are no fewer than twenty-four such openings, far more in smaller compass than Lucan or Virgil ever allow. This excess is no parody of Lucan's moderation, but the similarity of opening points to the practice of the Neronian age (and one of the emperor's own verses is of the reversible sort, FPL 131 Morel[16]). Not only does the Petronian specimen show that Lucan conforms, albeit not monotonously, to the metrical practice of his day, but it also firmly ties this style of composition to recitation. For Eumolpus had described how the poet's *liber spiritus* must be rushed headlong through its material. He calls his own poem an *impetus*, and after he has recited it, the narrator describes his *ingens uolubilitas* (124), a word more appropriate to an orator than to a poet. This all looks to the contemporary manner of presentation, so graphically mocked by Persius in his first satire, especially 'grande aliquid quod pulmo animae praelargus anhelat' (14). Lucan and Petronius were writing with this manner in mind, and their powerful but grace-less hexameters are contrived to serve the needs of delivery. But fulness of expression and force are lost.

Thus when Summers asks (41) if there is in all of Lucan a really tuneful line, he has loaded the dice against the poet, assuming that tunefulness was something that Lucan might have aimed at, or that his audience might have appreciated. A similar unfairness is found when Summers goes on to wonder if Lucan ever has a beautiful scene. In a poem treating of the collapse of the Roman world, an epitaph on an age, both beautiful scenes and tuneful lines may be held to be irrelevant. [17]

B. Diction

In turning from metre to diction we are not surpised to find a similar state of affairs. Just as the infrequent use of a rare rhythm or a careful variety of pauses would have been lost upon the audience at a recitation, so too would choice language have been wasted. How could an archaism, for example, used only once to flavour a line, or to recall an out of the way poet, retain its effect in the full flood of declamation? Virgil and Horace could reasonably strive to charge each lonely word with all the charm of all the Muses, but such art would not tell from the declaimer's platform. Lucan's 'epitaph' gives a realistic judgement: 'fulminis in morem quae sunt miranda citentur:/ haec uere sapiet dictio quae feriet' (Hosius p. 338).

Lucan refined his diction, like his metre, to a hard brightness, and his working vocabulary is not large. An unwelcome result of this narrowing process is his habit

12

of repeating the same word within a few lines, and to modern taste this is apt to be objectionable. Housman treats of the textual aspect of this matter in his preface, p. xxxiii, but here repetition will be dealt with as a literary problem. At 2.209-20, for example, Lucan describes the choking of the Tiber's course by corpses as follows:

> congesta recepit
> 210 omnia Tyrrhenus Sullana cadauera gurges.
> in fluuium primi cecidere, in corpora summi.
> praecipites haesere rates, et strage cruenta
> interruptus aquae fluxit prior amnis in aequor,
> ad molem stetit unda sequens. iam sanguinis alti
> 215 uis sibi fecit iter campumque effusa per omnem
> praecipitique ruens Tiberina in flumina riuo
> haerentis adiuuit aquas; nec iam alueus amnem
> nec retinent ripae, redditque cadauera campo.
> tandem Tyrrhenas uix eluctatus in undas
> 220 sanguine caeruleum torrenti diuidit aequor.

In this passage it is clear that Lucan tries to avoid repetition by using every available synonym for blood, body, water; such words as recur are so colourless that they remain unobtrusive. The basic flaw in the passage is that the poet is trying to say too much with excessive detail, and his luxuriant imagination is drawing upon an already diminished stock of words. In this example 'praecipites haesere rates' at 212 is a fair conceit, although hardly necessary to enhance the horror of the scene. But when further on we read *praecipiti* (216) and *haerentis* (217) we inevitably reject the pointless redundancy of expression. These more offensive repetitions might have been avoided if Lucan had simply pruned his lines and refrained from squeezing as much as possible out of an incident.

Apart from over-exuberant writing — an endearing fault — there is a general lack of care, and the more casual repetitions have been noted in the commentary. But why have they occurred at all in the work of one who was 'iterum quae digna legi sint scripturus'? It may be that Lucan was insensitive in an unusual degree to repetition; but it seems more likely that it was haste of composition in a refined medium that led to unwelcome echoes. Let Statius serve as an example. He boasts that he took two days to compose an epithalamium for Stella at *Siluae* 1. 2. Towards the close of the poem, where he prays for beauty in the hoped-for child and in its mother, unintentional repetition is common: *decoris* 272, 275; *uultus* 272, 277; *forma* 273, 277. The body of the poem too offers examples: *dextera* 65, 67; *dura* 200, 202; *coepit* 199, 202; *nitidae* 203, 212; *dulcia* 207, 211. Perhaps these will be judged unexceptionable, but they are still due to haste. Now Lucan was a master of the extempore, of which his lost *Orpheus* was an example (Statius mentions the

13

poem at *Siluae* 2. 7. 59). There can be little doubt that most of the *Pharsalia* was written in haste. For if he had any sense, Lucan must have seen that the Pisonian conspiracy might fail, and that he, almost its standard-bearer, must build his monument rapidly in case of detection and exposure. This is of course conjecture, but there are in the poem clear signs of altered technique. Golden lines, for example, decline in frequency after the early books, as do instances of bracketing or encompassing word order (cf. Caspari 83ff). Diction too offers a token of less artistic, and so perhaps more hasty writing. Compound adjectives, especially ones formed upon the suffixes *-fer* or *-ger*, are common throughout the poem, but coinages are found chiefly at the outset, e.g., *flammiger, criniger, taurifer, ensifer* in the first book, and *monstrifer* in the second. [18]

Lucan is with justice not regarded as a lord of language; words, like metre, are just a tool for him, powerful undeniably, but not a secondary end in themselves. His message is too urgent and stark for adornment, and haste forestalls selection. One even has a sense that he is consciously avoiding elevated language; *pubes*, for example, might have appeared more than once in a work describing young soldiers. But his usage of two words, *gladius* and *cadauer*, calls for special attention. Details of their usage in other poets will be found in the notes to 385-6 and 438 respectively. Lucan is uncommonly fond of the words. Why did he return to them so often? Admittedly his diction betrays occasional and so perhaps inadvertent prosy turns, e.g., *palam est* 6. 416, *cladis eo . . . ne* 7. 406, *meum est* 7. 739, *ad hoc aeui* 10. 195, but the high frequency of *gladius* and *cadauer* should be deliberate. This perhaps is the *uilitas uerborum* deplored by Eumolpus in the *Satyricon* 118. 4 (doubted however by P.A. George in *CQ* 24. 1974. 122, n. 2). The reason for this frequency is, perhaps, to be sought in the words themselves. Epic poets are inclined to speak of the corpses of men as *corpora*, a colourless word; *enses* is as remote from 'swords' as is our own 'brands'. Lucan disdains this. He wants us to see and feel Rome's death throes, and so he calls corpses and swords by their common names, without poetic distancing. He has deliberately elevated *cadauer* (Virgil had used it of the monster Cacus), and increases the frequency of *gladius* as against *ensis* with a view to making his description vivid and realistic (cf. Pichon, *Histoire* 562 and especially 578). He snatches away the veil of fine writing; this is the 'dictio quae feriet'.

C. Rhetoric

The subject of Lucan's rhetorical technique is inexhaustible, so the following remarks will be limited to only a couple of points, especially the structuring of episodes and sentences in the poem.

In his introduction to the first book (xliv-lxvi) Getty well illustrated Lucan's use of tropes and figures, and what is here offered is only by way of refinement. It might be argued that the avoidance of a figure is as significant as its use. Syllepsis, for example, is very close to Ovid's heart; the figure is discussed and illustrated (but not named) by Leo (197-200), who observed Ovid's fondness for the turn even in his epic, e.g., *Met.* 9. 409 'exul mentisque domusque' (where *exul* is only used metaphorically with *mentis*). Leo says that epic poets after Ovid freely use the figure, but this misrepresents at least Lucan, who seems to have only two instances, at 5. 63f 'regnumque sorori/ ereptum est soceroque nefas' and at 9.365 'abstulit arboribus pretium (i.e., the golden apples) nemorique laborem': both unremarkable. The small number of instances and their unobtrusiveness is instructive. It is possible that Lucan felt the figure too flippant, and modern readers concur. For the sheer verbal dexterity of 'et pariter uultusque deo plectrumque colorque excidit' at *Met.* 2. 601f destroys any inherent pathos in the situation so described. Even in the restrained narrative of Ceyx and Alcyone (*Met.* 11) Ovid must intrude a phrase like 'lacrimas mouet atque lacertos' (674). No-one denies that Lucan has the resource for such cleverness in him, but he avoided this chance of display. Unconsciously or of set purpose he rejected a device which he may have regarded as improper to a work so saturated with the poet's personal involvement in his theme (a common fault of epic poets, according to Aristotle at *Poetica* 1460 a 5-11; Summers quipped that Lucan is the hero of his own poem, 41). Verbal play can defuse pathos, and too clearly separates the writer from his subject. Lucan will have none of it.

Conversely, a figure he overworks is apostrophe, for apostrophe, along with exclamation (cf. 604n), and closely followed by ἐρώτημα (cf. 31-2n), is the most striking weapon in the arsenal of pathos. Homer had used apostrophe with practised skill, as has been demonstrated by A. Parry in *HSCP* 76. 1972. 9-21. Homer's scholiasts knew that the device was evidence of the poet's sympathy (cf. on *Il.* 4. 127). In Latin apostrophe enters poetry at the beginning with Livius Andronicus' *Oduṣsia* (it is remarkable that in one instance he uses it independently of Homer: 'neque tamen te oblitus sum Lartie noster', fr. 4B). Thereafter it is part of the poets standard equipment. In Lucan apostrophe is found once in every fifty-six lines. [19] By any standard this is too high an average, even excepting such examples as 3.161 'quidquid parcorum mores seruastis auorum', in which the address to *mores* is just a matter of metrical convenience. [20] But the high average of use can be explained as well as deplored. Lucan, it is obvious, did not see that over-use of such an emotional device was 'counter-productive' and leads to frigidity. But he constantly employs it just because it is in his nature as a man to indulge himself in the luxury of passionate outburst (cf. G. Williams, *Change and Decline* (1978), 237). So fired is he by his theme that he can apostrophize *luxuries* at 4.374, among other abstractions (cf. below 454, 547, and 542-60n). This is not sober writing, but simply to

15

regard it as a failure of technique is to miss a personal characteristic of the poet in his poem. Surely it was this very fault which led Quintilian to describe Lucan as 'ardens et concitatus' (*I.O.* 10.1.90)?

Lucan's use of alliteration, if noticed at all, has been underestimated, though Wight Duff has been appreciative (262). Heitland has hard words for the poet (xcviii-xcix), and says that alliteration is used timidly and seldom well; the criteria for its use are unstated. One suspects that Heitland, who deserved well of Lucan, never read the verse aloud. The proem to the *Pharsalia* lacks this aural emphasis in only one line, the sixth. Writing of George Herbert in *Scrutiny* 12. 1944. 175, L.C. Knights observed that he uses alliteration in the 'native Elizabethan way, not, that is, as a poetic or musical device, but as a means of controlling emphasis and movement so as to obtain the maximum immediacy' (which seems poetic, if not musical). This can be said of Lucan with equal justice; for him alliteration is not musical, but it is above all emphatic, and so it is most often found at the end of a line (cf. 21n), as is only to be expected once it is recalled that the poem was meant for declamation. It goes without saying that Lucan is not as restrained as Virgil in his use of this, or indeed of any other, device, but gentle Ovid had to some degree avoided the Latin vigour of alliteration, and Lucan, who declared he was writing a Roman poem at 1. 66, restores a quality native to the language.

Let us turn now to a consideration of those rhetorical practices which cover the entire process of arranging and presenting material. The passages under discussion will be 1. 584-695, 6. 333-412, 7. 139-50 and 617-30; they are too long to quote, but their drift, which is here the chief concern, will be clear from what follows. All of these passages have been faulted, but not for the right reasons. Butler (116) and Summers (30f) object to the close of the first book on the ground that it is too long for what is actually said. But they fail to observe that each instance of divination gives clearer disclosures than its predecessor (cf. R. Faust, *De Lucani Orationibus*, diss. Königsberg 1908, 33). Arruns sees in the entrails that something terrible will occur, and he refuses to be more specific (584-638). But Figulus is more specific; he makes it clear that years of war lie ahead, that the war will end in tyranny (no-one is specified by *dominus* in 670), and that the war will be civil, a point revealed only in the very last line (639-72). Lucan saves his most spectacular prophet for last; a Roman matron under direct possession sees that the whole world will be drawn into the conflict, and that all will have to be gone through again (673-94, with a closing alliteration). The pace is leisurely, but each portion is materially different, and Lucan has carefully structured the passage so that it becomes both clearer in import and more impassioned as we read along.

In the sixth book Thessaly is described from lines 333 to 412, a section faulted by Heitland (lxxiv-lxxv), Butler (116, n. 4), and Summers (32) as long and unnecessary.

16

Long it may be, but Lucan is clearly answering in advance the question at 7. 301f, 'quone poli motu, quo caeli sidere uerso/ Thessalicae tantum, superi, permittitis orae?' (cf. Ribbeck 117f). Furthermore almost every detail of his description is chosen to show how apt Thessaly was to be a stage for the last scene of Roman liberty. At 349 Lucan remarks that the country would have done better to stay submerged (its drainage was, like bridge building or sailing, contrary to natural law in the first place). Protesilaus, the first man killed at Troy, came from there, and it was in Thessaly that Agave sought refuge. Even the excursus on rivers is rhetorically structured, for Titaressos, which closes the catalogue, is said to flow from hellish Styx. Thessaly was the home of the warlike Centaurs, and even Chiron, Pindar's 'divine beast', is depicted as a soldier. At 395-412 Lucan characteristically breaks out into direct abuse of the land (cf. 'noxia . . . tellus Aegyptia' 823), and ends his tirade by recalling that it was in Thessaly that the Giants fought the gods.

That myth leads to a consideration of 7. 139-50, which Heitland said is meant to be graphic and is miserable (lxxiii). Pompey's troops are readying their gear for battle: they sharpen swords, repoint spears, fill quivers, and look to their saddlery. At 144 the enumeration ends, and hesitantly Lucan compares these human activities to the preparations made by the gods before their battle with the Giants. Apart from the hint that Caesar and his men are like the rebellious sons of Earth, the comparison is rhetorically engineered to magnify the purely human conflict and set it alongside mythical engagements. Elsewhere too (cf. 551n) Lucan has recourse to this same myth just because, so far as he was concerned, civil war was a disaster unexampled in all human history, let alone in Roman annals (cf. 7. 408-11). The only struggle of comparable significance and magnitude was the war against heaven. Granting then that the passage is of a piece with Lucan's vision of Pharsalia, is there also a principle of order at work here? Lucan had named three weapons, sword, spear, and bow and arrows. When he turns to divine arms he names in the same order the sword of Mars, Neptune's spear, and Apollo's arrows, an exact correspondence. But in the last two lines emphasis shifts, and we see weapons peculiarly divine, the Gorgon shield of Pallas, and, last and greatest, Jove's thunderbolts. This is the high point, we can go no further. So the poet must return to narrative. Rhetorically considered, these lines are faultless. Only their composition is gauche: seven end-stopped lines which are syntactically unintegrated.

The final passage to be considered is also from the seventh book, 617-30. With great boldness Lucan refuses to follow the usual epic path by recounting individual encounters on the battle field (such encounters cannot have been too common in contemporary warfare, so Lucan is asserting his modernity). The way

17

he goes about this is by employing the common device of *omissio*, whereby the speaker tells us precisely what he is *not* going to talk about. By this means he is nevertheless able to produce a long list of possible forms of death and wounding. Gagliardi, the most recent commentator on the seventh book, says that the list is decidedly too long, a fair criticism. But the rhetorical structure and climax of the list pass unnoticed. At 625f the jet of blood is probably the most vivid piece of description so far. But then Lucan goes on to describe the killing and beheading of a brother (626-8), and he closes the section with the worst crime of all, parricide (628-30). This must recall what was earlier said at 550 in the first shock of battle: 'ille locus fratres habuit, locus ille parentis'. The list is long, but it rises by well defined levels to a climax of criminality in civil war, the killing of one's own father.

D. *Sentence Structure*

Particular discussion of the variety of sentence structure will be found in the notes to lines 1-5, 303-5, 335-9, 390-4, 422-4, 484-95, 506, 617, 729-35, 815. Here therefore some passages from other books will be dealt with. Occasionally Lucan's sentences are periodic, though as his 'epitaph' justly observed 'plus mihi comma placet'. Of course the extended tricolon structure found in Virgil (cf. Norden 376f) or in Horace (cf. L.P. Wilkinson, *Golden Latin Artistry* (1966), 207f) is hardly to be expected in a poem so hastily composed. Yet Lucan does use isolated swelling periods to achieve rhetorical climax. 7. 195-6 is noteworthy:

'uenit summa dies, geritur res maxima' dixit
'inpia concurrunt Pompei et Caesaris arma . . . '

In this tricolon crescendo, the first limb is stolen from *Aen.* 2. 324, but *summa* is here more charged with pathos, for it is Rome's last day. In a way the second limb is padding, though the superlative *maxima* keeps up the uncompromising tone. The last line is neatly bracketed (cf. 39n), and the names of the protagonists, rarely so juxtaposed, form the climax by explaining what was left unclear. Equally impressive is 7. 760-3:

capit inpia plebes
caespite patricio somnos, stratumque cubile
regibus infandus miles premit, inque parentum
inque toris fratrum posuerunt membra nocentes.

The crescendo is not one of mechanical length, but of shock. The first clause sets up the opposition between plebeian and patrician, and morally judges the former. The second limb is grander and more comprehensive, setting ranker, again morally judged, against king. But the last, longest, and most impressive limb stresses that the war is civil; social distinction is now less remarkable than the crime of civil war, and *nocentes* could not be more emphatically placed. The tricolon structure gives weight and swing to the denunciation. In fact such isolated tricola are not that uncommon,

18

but they seem to be casual rather than a guiding principle of composition. Thus the effect of a number of tricola is diffused because they are simply a part of more rambling structures; as such they tend to pass unnoticed.

One most striking feature of Lucan's sentences is the diminished role of the verb (cf. 335-9n), and a consequent reliance upon participles or vaguely circumstantial ablatives. This is what makes Lucan one of the hardest writers to construe; it can only be supposed that his audience, though deaf to the niceties of metre and diction, would be flattered by an appeal to their wits. An example is 1.266f: 'expulit ancipiti discordes urbe tribunos/ uicto iure minax iactatis curia Gracchis' (The senate flouted the laws; it menacingly boasted of the Gracchi and drove the seditious tribunes from the anxious city). The thought is compressed and non-verbal. *Victo iure* defines the action, *expulit*, while *minax* is clarified by *iactatis Gracchis*. No word fails to pull its weight, and the lapidary tone of the lines is due to the preponderance of nouns. If one troubles to count the number of finite verbs in any hundred lines of Virgil or of Ovid, it will readily appear how much more liveliness there is in their sentences, thanks to the high number of verbs. But let us look at the first seven lines of the *Pharsalia*; the numerous objects all revolve about a single verb. Lucan's reliance upon participles also deserves notice. Heitland faulted his practice of using them to replace relative clauses (cvi), but the practice was common enough in the Golden age; he is right however to see the participle as overworked. The first sentence of this book is a fair example. The subject, *Magnus*, is qualified by two, *petens* and *agens*, both of which have objects. The object of *agens*, *cornipedem*, is qualified by participles. The main verb, *turbat*, has for its object *uias*, which also is qualified by a participle. Lucan is merciless. In the next sentence *nemorum* is qualified by *motorum*, and a participle serves as object of the verb. This approach to sentence structure allows Lucan to tack on phrases seemingly without end. Editors are therefore sometimes unsure whether a clause ends one sentence or begins another (in this book 225, 517-9 and 549f have caused trouble, and Housman's notes should be consulted). Even in antiquity Fronto, the tutor of Marcus Aurelius, and a leading light of the archaist movement, criticised this cumulative tendency in Lucan; he wittily if wrong-headedly showed that the proem to the *Pharsalia* could be increased *ad libitum* (*Epist. ad Antonin. Imp. de Orationibus*, p. 151 van den Hout). Though Fronto rather misses the point, he is right about accumulation of detail. It was for that reason that 7. 144-50, discussed above, was faulted.

E. Compression

Lucan's sentences ramble. But they are afflicted as well with a *diuersa lues* (to use his own phrase). For within the shapeless structures there are phrases or clauses which are concise to the point of obscurity. An example from the fifth book will illustrate this. The spokesman of Caesar's mutinous troops presents a seven line list of non-negotiable demands. One of them is to be allowed 'coniugis illabi lacrimis' (281). Cortius long ago observed that it would have made sense to write *manibus* (arms) instead of *lacrimis*. He is on the right lines, for the sense of the phrase must be 'to sink into the arms of a weeping wife' (Duff). This would seem to be the notion with which Lucan at least started, but he felt that, as such, it lacked punch. In Duff's translation the phrase contains four ideas: sinking, arms, tears, wife. One, arms, carries no load of pathos. It seems then that Lucan chose to omit it altogether and to set in its place the notion that describes the wife, tears. The syntax however is unaltered, and so *lacrimis* is the indirect object of *illabi*. The poet has produced a vigorous three word phrase, each part of which is significant if pathos is the touchstone. But as Latin it is nearly incomprehensible, and even once the true sense is ferreted out, we are presented with no vivid picture. The failure to see what he describes and to give that picture to the reader is serious. For words become counters to be juggled, and a new kind of verbal dexterity stands between the reader and the scene which should move him. The rhetoric of pathos has become self-destructive.

Another instance of compression, and of Lucan's writing at its best, must be introduced with a line from Ovid, *Her.* 4. 153f, in which Phaedra says to Hippolytus 'genibusque tuis regalia tendo bracchia'. Some emphasis here falls on *regalia*, for we are meant to feel the pathos of a queen who must beg for attention, a point to which I shall return. In Lucan this scene is mirrored when Cleopatra meets Caesar in the tenth book. After greeting him she says 'complector regina pedes' (89). Once again Lucan has dispensed with a part of the picture, the woman's arms, perhaps as being merely sensual, as at Catull. 66. 10 'leuia protendens bracchia'. But the picture is nonetheless vivid. It is not the knees that are touched, but the feet that are embraced — a deeper abasement, a more passionate gesture. And above all the speaker's status is given its full due; it is not, as in the Ovidian passage, glanced at by an adjective, but has the dignity and emphasis of a noun in apposition to the unexpressed subject, *ego*. [21] The final touch is that *regina* and *pedes* are juxtaposed to heighten the contrast, and these words, moreover, end the sentence too. At this sort of writing Lucan has no rivals: concise, pointed, and vivid.

F. Pathos and Magniloquence

A queen on her knees is a striking picture, and the scene ought to move us. But much that Lucan reckoned would affect his audience will leave cold a modern reader, who is used to middle-class novels and the plain style. Does Lucan fail in 'human intelligibility', or, to put it another way, do his men and women speak conformably to human experience? On the whole it would seem that they do not, if the general neglect of the poem, except by enthusiasts, is a representative judgment. The purpose of this section is to help a modern reader to see in Lucan a reliable reflector of the sensibility of his age. It is assumed that the way in which the men and women of his age faced experience is no more nor less interesting – or valid – than the way we do now.

A simple illustration of the gap which divides the sensibility of the modern reader from his counterpart in the first century is the scene in which the personified Roma appears at night to Caesar as he stands on the banks of the Rubicon (1. 185-203). It is probable that nowadays we assume that this is no more than a literary device, and that such an apparition was more a part of poetic furniture than of every-day life. If so, we should be wrong. It stands on record that Drusus, the father of the emperor Claudius, was forced to break off his conquest of Germany at the bidding of a superhuman female figure, who was probably regarded as being Germania herself (Suet. *D.C.* 1.2). Pliny was sceptical about visions and ghosts, but his conversion is related at *Ep.* 7.27; a young official, Curtius Rufus, stationed in Africa, was walking one afternoon in a portico when a vast female form, claiming to be the genius of Africa, appeared to him and foretold his future (the story is also in Tac. *Ann.* 11.21). As E.R. Curtius has said, such ideal figures formed part of the world of experience of these transitional centuries (*European Literature and the Latin Middle Ages* [Eng. trans. 1953], 102). The appearance of Roma is a literary device, but it is one securely founded upon the experience of the day. To the first century audience it would not have lacked human intelligibility.

Let us consider for a moment, not Lucan, but a work of his uncle, Seneca. Near the end of his tragedy of *Oedipus* (a work of uncertain date but assigned to his exile during the 40's), when all has been revealed, Jocasta contemplates suicide and runs over, in a manner reminiscent of Dorothy Parker, the means to hand. At last she has it: 'hunc, dextra, hunc pete/ uterum capacem qui uirum et natum tulit' (1038f). The picture is so horrible that we should be glad to dismiss it as rhetorical conceit (and *capacem* is a conceit). But we would be hasty. At *Ann.* 14. 8, Tacitus describes the death of Agrippina in AD 59. Alone in her bedroom she is confronted by thugs. One strikes her down with a blow to the head, and as the other draws his sword, the emperor's mother has the wit to say 'uentrem feri'. That these were her last words is also attested by Dio (who spoils the epigram by having her explain it, 61. 13. 5), and by the post-Neronian tragedy of *Octavia*, 369ff. This is not just another example of what Wilde called literature's constant anticipation of life; rather it shows, in a small way, that a real woman, faced with murder, spoke and thought like a cardboard character from a Senecan play. But no-one would suggest that an Agrippina was ever anything less than flesh and blood.

We now return to Lucan. In this book Cornelia resolves to die when she sees

21

Pompey cut down (653). Finally she asks someone on the ship to stab her. As a whole the scene cannot seem convincing to a modern reader. But once again contemporary history shows us how close Cornelia is to the attitude of the age. In AD 65 Seneca, implicated, perhaps unjustly, in the Pisonian conspiracy, had to commit suicide. Tacitus sympathetically describes the scene (*Ann.* 15.63). Secretaries are there to catch the last words. Seneca encourages and consoles his gathered friends (how public a thing was death). Then he turns to his wife and urges her to pass her widowhood in the contemplation of his virtuous life. But she refuses to live longer: 'manum percussoris exposcit'. Now a *percussor* is an assassin or an executioner, or even someone who aids a suicide (cf. *Ann.* 2. 31), but it seems extravagant applied to the physician who was to cut the veins. Seneca's wife is making a public gesture of loyalty, and her husband sees its value and purpose when he says 'nec inuidebo exemplo'. But in so doing her language becomes overheated. We may be sure that the wives of Seneca and of Pompey would have understood one another, for they are eager not just to die with their husbands, but to be seen to want to die. Setting an example is what matters to them, and to set an example you need an audience.[22]

The death of Pompey as described in this book is similar. The interior monologue at 622-35 has not lacked critics; and yet its sentiments are not likely to be so different from what we may imagine Seneca said to his friends with the secretaries in attendance. Pompey and Seneca were men of note and conscious that their lives were lived before the public gaze; they were therefore eager to deserve the attention of their contemporaries and of posterity. In life, but perhaps more tellingly in death, a man could be a paradigm of behaviour, hence Seneca's advice to his wife. Thus Lucan's Pompey asserts that future ages will fix their gaze upon the small boat in which he dies (an example of that grandiloquence which will soon be illustrated). Pompey must not disappoint his audience, and their amazement will serve as affection (635). The exemplary and public nature of death is explicitly stated at 4.496f where Vulteius promises his doomed shipmates that by their mutual murder they will achieve a 'magnum et memorabile exemplum'. When Lucan himself faced 'the distinguished thing' and committed suicide, he recited some of his own verses (cf. Tac. *Ann.* 15. 70). This was proud and exemplary defiance, for Nero had forbidden him to publish his verse. But since death was so public an act, Lucan could 'publish' his verse in his last moments, and, like Pompey, prove that in death he was *sui iuris*.

A heavy price is paid by constantly aiming at the exemplary. The unique qualities of individual character are ignored. Thus any attempt to see characterization in Lucan founders. (On the whole ancient biography is little different; Plutarch and Suetonius have not Boswell's desire to draw a complete, veristic picture.) So, in Lucan, Caesar is always vigorous, Pompey is hesitant out of fear for his reputation, Cornelia is duty personified, and Cato is stern. Beyond that Lucan does not trouble

22

to go. Nor would his readers have expected him to do so. This strikes us as under-nourished, but it is the common way of Latin letters. Achilles in Homer is a whole man with many moods, but Horace would have but one side of his nature displayed: 'inpiger, iracundus, inexorabilis, acer' (*A.P.* 121). [23] The whole of the *Aeneid* leaves us with but one successful character, Dido. Thus when Lucan declines to characterize, and aims instead at the general and exemplary, he is treading the broad highway of classical Latin literature.

Lucan's instinct, however, is unclassical and approaches what we should now-adays call baroque sensibility. As a descriptive term, baroque has been transferred, not without imprecision, from the visual to the verbal arts. But for a working definition we may turn to Leo Spitzer, who reckoned that what tends to characterize and unite examples of that violent sensibility is a love of any striking juxtaposition of contrasted or unexpected images and notions. The reader is to be moved by what is abnormal or at least unusual. As luck would have it, the model line that he cites from a play of Grillparzer is 'Seht wie ein König kniet!', 'Lo, a king on his knees!'. Spitzer feels that wherever a similar notion is found, a baroque sensibility is at work (cf. *Linguistics and literary history* [1948], 120). As we have seen above, Lucan offers us this very scene, in which Cleopatra, a queen, embraced Caesar's feet and drew particular attention to her rank. She furthermore stressed that though she was a princess descended of so many royal kings, she was also an exile. That is the sort of contrast that Lucan cannot resist (cf. 207-9 n). And we have seen also how he is able to heighten the pathos by juxtaposing *regina* and *pedes*. Something more should now be said about the syntax of *regina*. As a nominative it is in apposition to the un-derstood subject, 'I'. Cleopatra is here identifying herself with her rank (and the importance of high rank to Lucan, also a baroque preoccupation, is discussed on 70-85 n). The rhetorical device was called in antiquity 'emphasis' (cf. 80 n), and its commonest form occurs when an individual speaks of himself in the third person. It is not a figure found upon the lips of the humble or unselfconscious. Not surprisingly it is common in Lucan. This rarer form, in which the person identifies himself with his rank, allows the sort of pathetic juxtaposition that Lucan approves. For example, in the fifth book when Caesar is about to be overwhelmed by a storm at sea he says 'quamuis plenus honorum/ et dictator eam Stygias et consul ad undas.' (666f). Here Caesar speaks of himself as dictator and consul, and these high magistracies are set among the waters of hell: glory in the grave. This too reveals Lucan's sensibility.

Love of contrast runs like a crimson thread through the poet's thought and expression. When, for example, he describes Pompey's departure from Thessaly at the beginning of this book he goes about it by stressing that Pompey is still master of a fleet off Corcyra and in the bay of Leucas, that he is lord of Cilicia, whose pirates he conquered, and of Liburnia, and that he is sneaking into a tiny skiff (37-9).

23

Just so at the end of the second book as he goes into exile from Italy he is called 'adhuc ingens populis comitantibus exul' (730). The sentiments are in both cases paradoxical and pathetic, notably so in the second, because *exul*, a dreadful word to a Roman, is the last word of a sentence addressed to Pompey by the poet. The example from the eighth book shows another facet of baroque art, the accumulation of proper names to give an impression of vast spatial sweep. (We are most used to this in Milton, and it may be that 'Ganges and Hydaspes, Indian streams' is owed to line 227.) The love of contrast, which is meant to be stirring, is found in Pompey's last speech, where he says 'speculatur ab omni/ orbe ratem' (623f). Here the words for 'world' and 'skiff' are juxtaposed to force us to see the scene. Lucan can use this device to achieve grand effects that set him apart from even the best poets of antiquity. His writing can fuse into pure imagination. For example, in the seventh book at the close, the poet's mind plays over the corpse-strewn battlefield. His sympathy for the dead rises to identification at 803, *petimus . . .* , 'we do not ask for individual pyres'. Then begins a meditation of great nobility upon death and decay, a passage to which Sir Thomas Browne recurred in *Urne-Buriall*. In it the poet reckons that burning and burial are after all of scant importance; Nature gathers all to her bosom, and in corpses is found their own dissolution. Final conflagration will serve as their pyre: 'communis mundo superest rogus ossibus astra/ mixturus' (814f). 'To mingle stars with bones': the image is violent but concrete, and we would look in vain for anything to match it. It is at such times that Lucan speaks with his own distinct voice.

One final example of Lucan's grand manner, instructive because it shows him reworking a commonplace. Demosthenes, in his speech *On the Crown* (18. 205) said that the Athenians of former days reckoned they were born, not just for the sake of their parents (to look after them in their old age), but for the State too. The sentiment may have been echoed by Plato, for Cicero says that he told Archytas that he was 'non sibi . . . soli natum . . . , sed patriae, sed suis' (*De Fin.* 2. 46). The treatise *Ad Herennium* has the wise man reflect thus: 'non mihi soli sed etiam atque adeo multo potius natus sum patriae' (4.55). Despite differences the pattern is clear. But when Lucan comes to describe Cato at 2. 382f he writes 'patriaeque impendere uitam/ nec sibi sed toti genitum se credere mundo'. Here rhetorical climax is at work. His native land has already been mentioned, so Lucan must go one better, and he endows Cato with nothing short of cosmic status. Perhaps this seems excessive; but we should remember that as masters of the world the Romans could fairly claim worldwide interests.[24] Still, that the lines stick in the mind and have a modern fitness for all the vastness of their scope is shown by the fact that Arnold chose them, among others from this passage, to close his essay entitled 'Porro unum est necessarium'. The grand manner is Lucan's own province.

24

The foregoing sections represent, as was said at the outset, an attempt to pick out the distinctive elements, good and bad, of Lucan's style. As a whole it can be described as follows:

'It is the least simple style, probably, that ever was written; it bristles, it cracks, it swells and swaggers; but it is a perfect expression of the man's genius. Like his genius it contains a certain quantity of everything, from immaculate gold to flagrant dross. He was a very bad writer, and yet unquestionably he was a very great writer . . . He had the aid of an immense force of conviction. His imagination warmed to its work so intensely that there was nothing his volition could not impose upon it . . . This accounts for . . . his heroic attempts to furnish specimens of things of which he was profoundly ignorant . . . He has against him that he lacks that slight but needful thing – charm . . . But our last word about him is that he had incomparable power.' (Henry James on Balzac in *French Poets and Novelists* [1878] , 149f).

III. MSS SIGLA

M = Montepessulanus H 113
V = Vossianus XIX f.51
P = Parisinus bibl. publ. lat. 7502
Z = Parisinus bibl. publ. lat. 10314
U = Vossianus XIX f.63
G = Bruxellensis 5330 bibliothecae Burgundicae
N = fragmenta Vindobonensia et Neapolitana
Ω = the agreement of all or the majority of the above MSS.

NOTES TO INTRODUCTION

1. In AD 56 for the younger Seneca; the arguments for this date are set out by M. Griffin in *Seneca, A Philosopher in Politics* (1976), p. 73, n. 6.
2. It is noteworthy that one of the earliest translations of the poem, the Irish *In Cath Catharda*, breaks off after the grand battle, plainly out of lack of interest in the sequel.
3. This an important but overlooked point. Eumolpus in praising Horace is not mouthing the cant of the schools. On the contrary he is showing a modern interest in a neglected author. This leads one to suspect that Eumolpus is here only a mouthpiece for Petronius.
4. This trend is discussed by R. Syme in *The Roman Revolution* (1939), 317f, and in *Tacitus* (1958), 432ff.
5. So A. Momigliano, *Secondo Contributo alla Storia degli Studi Classici* (1960), 459 = *CQ* 38.1944.99.
6. An Acilius, who may be related to Lucan in his mother's line, is a Caesarian; see Caes. *BC* 3.15,16,39,40.
7. For Sextus see Syme, *Rom. Rev.*, 157 and 228, and esp. Plin. *NH* 7.178-9.
8. For Brutus and Cicero see Syme, *Papers* 1.434-6 = *HSCP* 64.1959.60f.
9. The only exception is in the matter of divine machinery, *deorum ministeria*. Lucan dispensed with this, rightly in the view of modern critics. But it should be noted that he may not have been the first to do so in an historical epic. Ennius seems not to have introduced the gods into the action of the later and so more contemporary books of his *Annales*. It does not seem likely however that Lucan would have read Ennius, and so we may credit him with a rediscovery of a correct approach to his theme.
10. Historical epic in Rome tended to identify itself with panegyric. Lucan is unique in having composed a work which does not focus upon an individual and his praise. But annalistic epic must also have shared out among a number of characters its eulogies.
11. Comparison of sources in the ancient book roll was an irksome business; the effect of this is well brought out by C.B.R. Pelling in *JHS* 99.1979.92f in the case of Plutarch.
12. Polla becomes more of a creature of flesh and blood thanks to R.G.M. Nisbet in *JRS* 68. 1978.1-11.
13. Lucan's commonest pattern of caesurae is 2s, 3s, 4s, as one might expect. But he also shows a penchant for 2s, 3w, 4s (and in this he follows a growing fashion), often with a slight sense-pause at 4s (see Winbolt 82f).
14. Juvenal, however, was able to combine metrical refinement with declamatory power. But, unlike Lucan, he does not appear to have composed in haste, and also unlike Lucan, it is not clear that he was a success in his own day.
15. By 'significant' is meant that the line opens with a word other than a conjunction, particles, or pronouns.
16. 'reddit quaesitas iam non quaerentibus undas', a neat allusion to the underground course of Tigris, for which see *CQ* 28.1978.241f.
17. So too C.A. Martindale in *BICS* 23.1976.47.
18. There is a second flowering of new compounds in the Cato episode of the ninth book, but the instance is too isolated to affect the overall pattern.
19. The result is cited from E. Hampel *De Apostrophae apud Romanos Poetas Usu*, diss. Jena, 1908 by R.D. Williams on Statius *Th.* 10.498.
20. Macaulay said of Robert Montgomery that he belonged to that class of poets which believed personification was a simple matter of capital letters. Ovid and his imitators are little different, and regard apostrophe in some cases as a simple matter of the use of the

second person of the verb. This is too often the line of least resistance.

21. Either apposition or a secondary predicate, which is 'often employed to denote the character in which . . . a person . . . acts' (Roby 1017c); see also KS 1.246f.

22. The first century had something of a literature of death. Titinius Capito wrote *Exitus Illustrium Virorum* (Plin. *Ep.* 8.12.4), and Fannius started a work on those who had been killed or exiled by Nero (*ibid.* 5.5.3). This taste reflects current events and attitudes; see Curtius, *European Lit.*, p.138.

23. To do Horace justice, he is describing how Achilles should appear in a play, where there might not be much scope for a rounded portrayal.

24. And of course Stoic cosmopolitanism informs this description of Cato.

LUCAN VIII

TEXT AND TRANSLATION

LIBER OCTAVUS

iam super Herculeas fauces nemorosaque Tempe
Haemoniae deserta petens dispendia siluae
cornipedem exhaustum cursu stimulisque negantem
Magnus agens incerta fugae uestigia turbat
5   inplicitasque errore uias. pauet ille fragorem
motorum uentis nemorum, comitumque suorum
qui post terga redit trepidum laterique timentem
exanimat. quamuis summo de culmine lapsus
nondum uile sui facinus scit sanguinis esse,
10   seque, memor fati, tantae mercedis habere
credit adhuc iugulum, quantam pro Caesaris ipse
auolsa ceruice daret. deserta sequentem
non patitur tutis fatum celare latebris
clara uiri facies. multi, Pharsalica castra
15   cum peterent nondum fama prodente ruinas,
occursu stupuere ducis uertigine rerum
attoniti, cladisque suae uix ipse fidelis
auctor erat. grauis est Magno, quicumque malorum
testis adest. cunctis ignotus gentibus esse
20   mallet et obscuro tutus transire per urbes
nomine; sed poenas longi Fortuna fauoris
exigit a misero, quae tanto pondere famae
res premit aduersas fatisque prioribus urguet.
nunc festinatos nimium sibi sentit honores
25   actaque lauriferae damnat Sullana iuuentae,
nunc et Corycias classes et Pontica signa
deiectum meminisse piget. sic longius aeuum
destruit ingentes animos et uita superstes
imperio. nisi summa dies cum fine bonorum

BOOK VIII

Now beyond wooded Tempe, the Gorge of Hercules, Magnus made by circuitous paths for the lonely forests of Thessaly; as he urged on his horse which was worn out by rapid flight and deaf to the spur, he confused the traces of his retreat and made a labyrinth of his tracks. He dreads the sound of the trees in the wind; and any of his comrades who falls back to join him causes him terror in his agitation and fear of ambush. Though fallen from his lofty eminence, he knows that his murder is not yet a cheap act; and, mindful of fate's power, he believes that his death can still earn as great a reward as he himself would give for the severed head of Caesar. Though he seeks solitude, his known features do not allow him to hide his disaster in safe concealment. Many who were on their way to the camp at Pharsalia, before rumour had published his defeat abroad, were startled to meet their leader and astounded by the sudden change of fortune; and he was scarcely believed when he reported his own defeat. The presence of any witness of his woes was grievous to him. He would choose to be unknown to all nations, and to pass safely through the cities with a name unknown to fame; but Fortune, who long had favoured him, now demands from her victim the penalty of that favour; she throws all the weight of his renown into the scale of adversity and crushes him beneath his former successes. Now he feels to his cost the honours that came too quick upon him; and he curses the exploits of his triumphant youth in Sulla's day; now he hates in his fall to remember the fleets of Cilicia and the armies of Pontus. Thus length of days and life surviving power humble the proudest heart. Unless the end of life comes together with the end of happiness, and anticipates

31

30   adfuit et celeri praeuertit tristia leto,
       dedecori est fortuna prior. quisquamne secundis
       tradere se fatis audet nisi morte parata?
          litora contigerat, per quae Peneius amnis
       Emathia iam clade rubens exibat in aequor.
35   inde ratis trepidum uentis ac fluctibus inpar,
       flumineis uix tuta uadis, euexit in altum.
       cuius adhuc remis quatitur Corcyra sinusque
       Leucadii, Cilicum dominus terraeque Liburnae
       exiguam uector pauidus correpsit in alnum.
40   conscia curarum secretae in litora Lesbi
       flectere uela iubet, qua tunc tellure latebas
       maestior, in mediis quam si, Cornelia, campis
       Emathiae stares. tristes praesagia curas
       exagitant, trepida quatitur formidine somnus,
45   Thessaliam nox omnis habet; tenebrisque remotis
       rupis in abruptae scopulos extremaque curris
       litora; prospiciens fluctus nutantia longe
       semper prima uides uenientis uela carinae,
       quaerere nec quidquam de fato coniugis audes.
50   en ratis, ad uestros quae tendit carbasa portus!
       quid ferat, ignoras; et nunc tibi summa pauoris
       nuntius armorum tristis rumorque sinister.
       uictus adest coniunx. quid perdis tempora luctus?
       cum possis iam flere, times. tum puppe propinqua
55   prosiluit crimenque deum crudele notauit,
       deformem pallore ducem uoltusque prementem
       canitiem atque atro squalentes puluere uestes.
       obuia nox miserae caelum lucemque tenebris
       abstulit, atque animam clausit dolor; omnia neruis
60   membra relicta labant, riguerunt corda, diuque
       spe mortis decepta iacet. iam fune ligato
       litoribus lustrat uacuas Pompeius harenas.
       quem postquam propius famulae uidere fideles,
       non ultra gemitus tacitos incessere fatum
65   permisere sibi, frustraque attollere terra

sorrow by speedy death, past greatness is a mockery. Does any dare to trust prosperity, unless he has the means of death at hand?

He had reached the shore where the river Peneus, already red with the slaughter of Pharsalia, passed out into the sea. From there a boat, no match for winds and waves and scarcely safe in the shallow river, bore him out trembling over the deep. He whose oars still churn the waters of Corcyra and the bays of Leucas, he, the lord of the Cilicians and the Liburnian land, slinks as a frightened passenger into a little boat. He bids them bend the sail towards the secluded shore of Lesbos – the shore that shares his loving anxieties; in that land Cornelia was hidden, but she was sadder than if she had stood in the centre of Pharsalia's field. For her sorrow is intensified by forebodings, and her sleep broken by anxious fears. Every night brings Pharsalia before her; and, when darkness disappears, she hastens to the peak of a steep cliff or to the shore's edge and looks out over the waves; she is always the first to see the sails of an approaching vessel dipping in the distance, but she dare ask no question concerning her husband's fate. But see! a ship spreading her sail towards the harbours of Lesbos! What it brings, she knows not; even now her worst fear is only evil news of the war and ominous report; but the messenger is her husband, and his message, defeat. Why waste the time when you might mourn? Though you might weep already, you only fear. Then, as the ship came close, she sprang up and marked the guilt and cruelty of Heaven, the shameful pallor of the general, the white hair that hid his face, and the black dust that defiled his garments. Darkness closed upon her grief and robbed her of the light of heaven; sorrow stopped her breath; betrayed by the muscles, all her limbs relaxed, her heart ceased to beat, and long she lay deceived by the hope that this was death. Now the cable was made fast to the shore, and Pompey trod the solitary strand. When her faithful handmaids saw him close at hand, they dared not rail at destiny except with stifled groans, and tried in vain

semianimem conantur eram; quam pectore Magnus
ambit et astrictos refouet conp'exibus artus.
coeperat in summum reuocato sanguine corpus
Pompei sentire manus maestamque mariti
70   posse pati faciem: prohibet succumbere fatis
Magnus et inmodicos castigat uoce dolores:
"nobile cur robur fortunae uolnere primo,
femina tantorum titulis insignis auorum,
frangis? habes aditum mansurae in saecula famae.
75   laudis in hoc sexu non legum cura nec arma,
unica materia est coniunx miser. erige mentem,
et tua cum fatis pietas decertet, et ipsum,
quod sum uictus, ama. nunc sum tibi gloria maior,
a me quod fasces et quod pia turba senatus
80   tantaque discessit regum manus: incipe Magnum
sola sequi. deformis adhuc uiuente marito
summus et augeri uetitus dolor: ultima debet
esse fides lugere uirum. tu nulla tulisti
bello damna meo: uiuit post proelia Magnus
85   sed fortuna perit. quod defles, illud amasti."
    uocibus his correpta uiri uix aegra leuauit
membra solo tales gemitu rumpente querellas:
"O utinam in thalamos inuisi Caesaris issem
infelix coniunx et nulli laeta marito!
90   bis nocui mundo: me pronuba ducit Erinys
Crassorumque umbrae, deuotaque manibus illis
Assyrios in castra tuli ciuilia casus,
praecipitesque dedi populos cunctosque fugaui
a causa meliore deos. o maxime coniunx,
95   o thalamis indigne meis, hoc iuris habebat
in tantum fortuna caput? cur inpia nupsi,
si miserum factura fui? nunc accipe poenas,
sed quas sponte luam: quo sit tibi mollius aequor,
certa fides regum totusque paratior orbis,
100   sparge mari comitem. mallem felicibus armis
dependisse caput: nunc clades denique lustra,

34

to lift their fainting mistress from the ground; but Pompey folded her in his arms and brings back life to the rigid limbs by his embrace. Back came the blood to the surface of the body; she began to be aware of Pompey's touch, and to be able to endure the sorrowful face of her husband. Magnus forbids her to be conquered by destiny and thus reproves her excessive sorrow: "Adorned as you are by the fame of such mighty ancestors, why do you suffer the first stroke of Fortune to break down the courage of your noble race? Here is your opportunity for undying fame. To your sex neither peaceful government nor war is a field for glory: a husband's sorrow alone can win it. Lift up your heart, let your devotion wrestle with destiny, and let the very fact that I have been conquered be dear to you. For I bring you greater distinction now, when the magistrates and devoted ranks of the Senate and all my retinue of kings have parted from me: from this time be the sole companion of Magnus. The depth of woe, woe that admits of no increase, is unbecoming while your husband still lives; to mourn him dead should be your last proof of fidelity. My warfare has brought no loss to you; for Magnus survives the battle, though his greatness has gone; that which you weep for is what you really loved."

Thus rebuked by her husband, slowly she raised her ailing limbs from the ground, and her wailing broke out into complaints like these: "Would that I had been wedded to hated Caesar; for disaster was my dower and I have brought happiness to no husband. Twice have I brought a curse on mankind; the Fury and the ghosts of the Crassi gave me in marriage; and I, devoted to those dead, have brought the disaster of Carrhae to the camp of civil war, and hurled nations to their doom, and driven all Heaven away from the better side. O mighty husband, too good for such a wife, had my luck such power over one so great? Why was I guilty of marrying you, if I was to bring you sorrow? Now accept the penalty — a penalty which I will gladly pay: that the sea may be smoother for you, the kings steadfast in their loyalty, and the whole world more ready to serve you, fling your companion into the deep. I had rather have laid down my life to buy you victory; as it is, at least expiate your defeat by my death. Let

Magne, tuas. ubicumque iaces ciuilibus armis
nostros ulta toros, ades huc atque exige poenas,
Iulia crudelis, placataque paelice caesa
105 Magno parce tuo." sic fata iterumque refusa
coniugis in gremium cunctorum lumina soluit
in lacrimas. duri flectuntur pectora Magni,
siccaque Thessaliae confudit lumina Lesbos.
      tunc Mytilenaeum pleno iam litore uolgus
110 adfatur Magnum: "Si maxima gloria nobis
semper erit tanti pignus seruasse mariti,
tu quoque deuotos sacro tibi foedere muros
oramus sociosque lares dignere uel una
nocte tua: fac, Magne, locum, quem cuncta reuisant
115 saecula, quem ueniens hospes Romanus adoret.
nulla tibi subeunda magis sunt moenia uicto:
omnia uictoris possunt sperare fauorem,
haec iam crimen habent. quid, quod iacet insula ponto,
Caesar eget ratibus? procerum pars magna coibit
120 certa loci, noto reparandum est litore fatum.
accipe templorum cultus aurumque deorum.
accipe, si terris, si puppibus ista iuuentus
aptior est; tota, quantum ualet, utere Lesbo.
[accipe: ne Caesar rapiat, tu uictus habeto.]
125 hoc solum crimen meritae bene detrahe terrae,
ne nostram uideare fidem felixque secutus
et damnasse miser." tali pietate uirorum
laetus in aduersis et mundi nomine gaudens
esse fidem "nullum toto mihi" dixit "in orbe
130 gratius esse solum non paruo pignore uobis
ostendi: tenuit nostros hac obside Lesbos
adfectus; hic sacra domus carique penates,
hic mihi Roma fuit. non ulla in litora puppem
ante dedi fugiens, saeui cum Caesaris iram
135 iam scirem meritam seruata coniuge Lesbon,
non ueritus tantam ueniae committere uobis
materiam. sed iam satis est fecisse nocentes:
fata mihi totum mea sunt agitanda per orbem.

36

relentless Julia, wherever she is, come here and exact the penalty; she has punished our marriage by civil strife; let her be appeased by the death of her rival and spare her own Magnus." With these words she fell back into her husband's arms, and the eyes of all were melted to tears. The stern heart of Magnus was moved, and Lesbos made wet the eyes that were dry at Pharsalia.

Next the people of Mytilene, who had now flocked to the shore, addressed Magnus thus: "Since it will ever be our chief boast to have guarded the treasure of so great a husband, do you also, we beg, honour the city bound to you by sacred ties, and deem our friendly dwellings worthy to shelter you for one night at least. Make this, Magnus, a place of pilgrimage for all ages, a place where strangers may come from Rome and worship. No city is more fit for you to enter after defeat: though all others may hope for the clemency of the conqueror, ours is already guilty. Besides, Lesbos is an island, and Caesar has no fleet. Most of the senators, knowing where to find you, will gather here; you must restore your destiny on this known shore. Take the ornaments of our temples and the treasure of our gods; take our manhood's strength, to use on land or at sea, wherever it is most serviceable; make use of all Lesbos to the utmost of her power. [Accept our gifts; though conquered, take them that Caesar may not rob us of them.] Only of this charge acquit a land that has served you well: let it not appear that in adversity you doubted our protection which you secured in your good fortune." Cheered in his hour of defeat to find such devotion among men, and glad, for the sake of humanity, that loyalty truly existed, Pompey replied: "By no small pledge I have proved to you that no land on earth is more acceptable to me: Lesbos held my heart, while Cornelia was your hostage; here was my hearth and home, all that was dear and sacred; here was Rome for me. To no other shore did I first direct my vessel in my flight; and, though I knew that Lesbos had already earned Caesar's anger by keeping safe my wife, I did not fear to put in your hands so mighty a means of gaining his forgiveness. But here I must call a halt and make you guilty no more. My own destiny I must follow up over all the world.

heu nimium felix aeterno nomine Lesbos,
140 siue doces populos regesque admittere Magnum,
seu praestas mihi sola fidem. nam quaerere certum est,
fas quibus in terris, ubi sit scelus. accipe, numen
si quod adhuc mecum es, uotorum extrema meorum:
da similes Lesbo populos, qui Marte subactum
145 non intrare suos infesto Caesare portus,
non exire uetent." dixit maestamque carinae
inposuit comitem. cunctos mutare putares
tellurem patriaeque solum: sic litore toto
plangitur, infestae tenduntur in aethera dextrae.
150 Pompeiumque minus, cuius fortuna dolorem
mouerat, ast illam, quam toto tempore belli
ut ciuem uidere suam, discedere cernens
ingemuit populus; quam uix, si castra mariti
uictoris peteret, siccis dimittere matres
155 iam poterant oculis: tanto deuinxit amore
hos pudor, hos probitas castique modestia uoltus,
quod summissa animi, nulli grauis hospita turbae,
stantis adhuc fati uixit quasi coniuge uicto.
iam pelago medios Titan demissus ad ignes
160 nec quibus abscondit, nec si quibus exerit orbem,
totus erat. uigiles Pompei pectore curae
nunc socias adeunt Romani foederis urbes
et uarias regum mentes, nunc inuia mundi
arua super nimios soles Austrumque iacentis.
165 saepe labor maestus curarum odiumque futuri
proiecit fessos incerti pectoris aestus,
rectoremque ratis de cunctis consulit astris,
unde notet terras, quae sit mensura secandi
aequoris in caelo, Syriam quo sidere seruet,
170 aut quotus in Plaustro Libyam bene derigat ignis.
doctus ad haec fatur taciti seruator Olympi:
"signifero quaecumque fluunt labentia caelo
numquam stante polo miseros fallentia nautas,
sidera non sequimur; sed, qui non mergitur undis

38

Ah, too happy Lesbos, and famous for ever, whether she teaches other nations and kings to harbour me or alone proves faithful to me. For I am resolved to search the world and find out where goodness is, and where crime. Hear my last prayer, ye gods, if any god is still upon my side: may I find nations like to Lesbos, who will suffer a defeated man, pursued by Caesar, to enter their ports and also suffer him to sail out again." Thus he spoke and set his sorrowing companion on board. One might have thought that all the people were leaving their native soil for a foreign land; such wailing rose from all the shore; and menacing hands were stretched towards heaven. Pompey's departure they felt less – his ill-fortune only had stirred their grief; but when they saw Cornelia leaving them, Cornelia whom throughout the war they looked on as a fellow-citizen, then the people groaned aloud; if she were seeking the camp of a victorious husband, scarce could the matrons now have parted from her without tears; with such love had she attached some by her gentle-ness, others by her goodness and her pure and modest looks, because, humble of heart and a burdensome guest to none of the people, she lived, while her fortune stood firm, as if her husband had been conquered already

By now the sun had sunk half his ball of fire in the sea, and his disc was not wholly seen either by those from whom he withdrew it, or by those, if such there be, to whom he revealed it. The cares that kept watch in Pompey's breast turned at one time to the allied cities in league with Rome and to the wavering allegiance of the kings, at another time to the pathless lands of the region that lies beyond the burning suns of the south. So sad and troubling were his thoughts, such his loathing of the morrow, that often he threw off the wearisome disquiet of his conflicting purposes, and questioned the steersman concerning all the stars; in what region does he mark the land? what rule and measure for cleaving the sea does the sky afford? by what star does he keep a course to Syria? or which of the seven stars in the Wain is a sure guide to Libya? The skilled watcher of the silent sky replied to him thus: "All those lights which move and glide through the starry heavens mislead the hapless seaman, because the sky is ever shifting; to them we pay no heed; but that pole, which never sets or

39

175 axis inocciduus gemina clarissimus Arcto,
ille regit puppes. hic cum mihi semper in altum
surget et instabit summis minor Ursa ceruchis,
Bosporon et Scythiae curuantem litora Pontum
spectamus. quidquid descendet ab arbore summa
180 Arctophylax propiorque mari Cynosura feretur,
in Syriae portus tendit ratis. inde Canopos
excipit, australi caelo contenta uagari
stella timens Borean: illa quoque perge sinistra
trans Pharon, in medio tanget ratis aequore Syrtim.
185 sed quo uela dari, quo nunc pede carbasa tendi
nostra iubes?" dubio contra cui pectore Magnus
"hoc solum toto" respondit "in aequore serua,
ut sit ab Emathiis semper tua longius oris
puppis, et Hesperiam pelago caeloque relinquas:
190 cetera da uentis. comitem pignusque recepi
depositum; tum certus eram, quae litora uellem,
nunc portum fortuna dabit." sic fatur; at ille
iusto uela modo pendentia cornibus aequis
torsit et in laeuum puppim dedit, utque secaret
195 quas Asinae cautes et quas Chios asperat undas
hos dedit in proram, tenet hos in puppe rudentes.
aequora senserunt motus aliterque secante
iam pelagus rostro nec idem spectante carina
mutauere sonum. non sic moderator equorum,
200 dexteriore rota laeuum cum circumit axem,
cogit inoffensae currus accedere metae.
  ostendit terras Titan et sidera texit.
sparsus ab Emathia fugit quicumque procella,
adsequitur Magnum; primusque a litore Lesbi
205 occurrit natus, procerum mox turba fidelis.
nam neque deiecto fatis acieque fugato
abstulerat Magno reges fortuna ministros:
terrarum dominos et sceptra Eoa tenentes
exul habet comites. iubet ire in deuia mundi

sinks beneath the waves, brightest with the two Bears, it guides our ships. When I see the Little Bear mount ever towards the zenith, and when she stands on the highest point of the lifts, then we face towards the Bosporus and the Black Sea that hollows the Scythian shore. But whenever Bootes sinks from the topmast and the Little Bear moves nearer the horizon, the ship is making for the ports of Syria. Next after that comes Canopus, a star that dreads the North and limits its movements to the southern sky; if you keep it also on the left and sail on past Pharos, your vessel will strike the Syrtis in mid-ocean. But whither do you bid me shape our course, and with which sheet shall the canvas be stretched?" With unsettled purpose, Magnus answered him thus: "Wherever we sail, be this your only care, to turn your bark ever further from the shore of Thessaly, and to leave the West behind in sailing and steering; all else trust to the winds. I have taken on board my companion, the pledge I left for safety; then I had no doubt what shore to make for, but now chance must provide a harbour." Thus he spoke; immediately the steersman tugged at the sails that hung in equal lengths from the squared yard-arms, and turned the vessel to the left; and, that she might cleave the waves made rough by Chios and the rocks of Asina, he slackened the ropes toward the bow and made taut those toward the stern. The sea was conscious of the movement and gave a different sound, when the beak cut the water in a new direction and the ship's course was altered. With less skill the charioteer makes the right wheel spin round the left end of the axle and forces his car close to the turning-post without striking it.

The sun revealed the earth and veiled the stars. All who had fled far and wide from the fatal field of Pharsalia rallied round Magnus; first to meet him, after quitting the shore of Lesbos, was his son, and next came his loyal band of eminent companions; for even when cast down by destiny and routed in battle, he was not deprived by Fortune of kings to serve him: the exile was escorted by the lords of earth and the monarchs

210   Deiotarum, qui sparsa ducis uestigia legit.
      "quando" ait "Emathiis amissus cladibus orbis,
      qua Romanus erat, superest, fidissime regum,
      Eoam temptare fidem populosque bibentes
      Euphraten et adhuc securum a Caesare Tigrim.
215   ne pigeat Magno quaerentem fata remotas
      Medorum penetrare domos Scythicosque recessus
      et totum mutare diem, uocesque superbo
      Arsacidae perferre meas: 'si foedera nobis
      prisca manent mihi per Latium iurata Tonantem,
220   per uestros astricta magos, inplete pharetras
      Armeniosque arcus Geticis intendite neruis,
      si uos, o Parthi, peterem cum Caspia claustra
      et sequerer duros aeterni Martis Alanos,
      passus Achaemeniis late decurrere campis
225   in tutam trepidos numquam Babylona coegi.
      arua super Cyri Chaldaeique ultima regni
      qua rapidus Ganges et qua Nysaeus Hydaspes
      accedunt pelago, Phoebi surgentis ab igne
      iam propior quam Persis eram: tamen omnia uincens
230   sustinui nostris uos tantum desse triumphis,
      solusque e numero regum telluris Eoae
      ex aequo me Parthus adit. nec munere Magni
      stant semel Arsacidae; quis enim post uolnera cladis
      Assyriae iustas Latii conpescuit iras?
235   tot meritis obstricta meis nunc Parthia ruptis
      excedat claustris uetitam per saecula ripam
      Zeugmaque Pellaeum. Pompeio uincite, Parthi,
      uinci Roma uolet'." regem parere iubenti
      ardua non piguit, positisque insignibus aulae
240   egreditur famulo raptos indutus amictus.
      in dubiis tutum est inopem simulare tyranno;
      quanto igitur mundi dominis securius aeuum
      uerus pauper agit! dimisso in litore rege
      ipse per Icariae scopulos, Ephesonque relinquens
245   et placidi Colophona maris, spumantia paruae

42

of the East. Deiotarus, who had tracked his leader through his wanderings, he bade repair to the ends of the earth. "Since," said he, "the world, so far as it was Roman, has been lost by the disaster of Pharsalia, it remains, O most loyal of my kings, to test the allegiance of the East, of the nations who drink the Euphrates and the Tigris, rivers as yet unmolested by Caesar. Seeking success for me, refuse not to explore the distant home-land of the Medes and remote Scythia; be willing to change your clime completely, and bear to the proud scion of Arsaces this message from me: 'If our ancient treaty holds good – the treaty which I swore to observe in the name of the Roman Thunderer, and which was made fast by your Wise Men – then fill full your quivers, and stretch the bows of Armenia with the strings of the Getae; for, when I marched towards the Caspian Gates and pursued the hardy Alani, ever at war, I suffered the Parthians to ride at will over the Persian plains and never forced them to take hasty refuge in Babylon. I passed the realm of Cyrus and the uttermost parts of the Chaldean kingdom, where the impetuous Ganges and Nysaean Hydaspes join the sea; and I was nearer to the flame of the rising sun than Persia is; though I was everywhere victorious, I forbore to add the Parth-ians, and them alone, to the list of my triumphs; and, alone among the kings of the East, the Parthian approached me on equal terms. And a second time, thanks to me, the sons of Arsaces were saved. For who else curbed the righteous anger of Rome that followed the blow of the defeat in Assyria? Now let Parthia, bound by so many benefits from me, burst her bounds, to cross the bank forbidden for many centuries and pass the Bridge of Alexander. If the Parthians conquer for Pompey's sake, Rome will welcome her conqueror.' " Hard was the task enjoined, but the king did not refuse; he laid aside the badges of royalty and left the ship, wear-ing garments taken in haste from a menial. In danger a king finds safety in the disguise of a beggar; how much safer then is the lot of the really poor man than that of the lords of earth! The king was dispatched upon the shore; and Pompey himself sailed past the rocks of Icaria, and skirted the foaming cliffs of little Samos, shunning Ephesus and Colophon with their calm waters; the breeze blew fresh from the shore of Cos; next

radit saxa Sami; spirat de litore Coo
aura fluens; Cnidon inde fugit claramque relinquit
sole Rhodon magnosque sinus Telmessidos undae
conpensat medio pelagi.   Pamphylia puppi
250   occurrit tellus, nec se committere muris
ausus adhuc ullis, te primum, parua Phaseli,
Magnus adit; nam te metui uetat incola rarus
exhaustaeque domus populis, maiorque carinae
quam tua turba fuit.   tendens hinc carbasa rursus
255   iam Taurum Tauroque uidet Dipsunta cadentem.
        crederet hoc Magnus, pacem cum praestitit undis,
et sibi consultum? Cilicum per litora tutus
parua puppe fugit.   sequitur pars magna senatus
ad profugum collecta ducem; paruisque Syhedris,
260   quo portu mittitque rates recipitque Selinus,
in procerum coetu tandem maesta ora resoluit
uocibus his Magnus: "comites bellique fugaeque
atque instar patriae, quamuis in litore nudo,
in Cilicum terra, nullis circumdatus armis
265   consultem rebusque nouis exordia quaeram,
ingentes praestate animos.   non omnis in aruis
Emathiis cecidi, nec sic mea fata premuntur,
ut nequeam releuare caput cladesque receptas
excutere.   an Libycae Marium potuere ruinae
270   erigere in fasces et plenis reddere fastis,
me pulsum leuiore manu fortuna tenebit?
mille meae Graio uoluuntur in aequore puppes,
mille duces; sparsit potius Pharsalia nostras
quam subuertit opes.   sed me uel sola tueri
275   fama potest rerum, toto quas gessimus orbe,
et nomen, quod mundus amat.   uos pendite regna
uiribus atque fide Libyam Parthosque Pharonque,
quemnam Romanis deceat succurrere rebus.
ast ego curarum uobis arcana mearum
280   expromam mentisque meae quo pondera uergant.

he avoided Cnidos and Rhodes, famous island of the sun, and shortened the long circuit of the bay of Telmessus by keeping the open sea. The land of Pamphylia now confronted his vessel; so far he had not dared to trust himself to any city, but now he entered the walls of little Phaselis; for she was robbed of her terrors by her scanty population, and her houses were drained of their inhabitants; there were more men on board the ship than in all the town. From hence he set sail again, and soon came in view of Mount Taurus and Dipsus falling down the mountain-side.

Could Magnus have believed, when he gave peace to the sea, that he would profit by it himself as well? He flees unharmed along the coast of the Cilician pirates in his little vessel. He was followed by a number of senators who rallied round their fugitive leader; and at little Syhedra — the harbour which sends forth and receives again the ships for Selinus — Magnus at last opened his sorrowful lips at a meeting of the nobles, and spoke thus: "Comrades in battle and in flight, you who represent our country, though I, who ask your counsel and seek to set a new enterprise on foot, stand here on an unprotected shore in the land of Cilicia, and have no armies round me, still display your courage. I did not fall for ever on the field of Pharsalia; nor has my destiny sunk so low that I can never again raise my head and shake off the defeat I have suffered. If the Libyan ruins of Carthage could raise Marius to office and replace him in the Calendar, full already of his name, shall Fortune keep me down, whom she has smitten with a lighter blow? Mine are a thousand ships that toss on Grecian waters, and mine a thousand leaders; Pharsalia scattered my resources but did not overthrow them. If it had, I could find safety merely in the fame of the mighty deeds I wrought over all the earth, and in that name which the whole world loves. It is for you to weigh well the kingdoms in point of strength and loyalty — Libya, Parthia, and Egypt — and to decide who may with honour retrieve the fortunes of Rome. But I will unveil to you my own secret thoughts and the purpose to which the balance of my mind inclines. I mistrust the youth of

45

aetas Niliaci nobis suspecta tyranni est,
ardua quippe fides robustos exigit annos.
hinc anceps dubii terret sollertia Mauri;
namque memor generis Carthaginis inpia proles
285   inminet Hesperiae, multusque in pectore uano est
Hannibal, obliquo maculat qui sanguine regnum
et Numidas contingit auos. iam supplice Varo
intumuit uiditque loco Romana secundo.
quare agite Eoum, comites, properemus in orbem.
290   diuidit Euphrates ingentem gurgite mundum,
Caspiaque inmensos seducunt claustra recessus,
et polus Assyrias alter noctesque diesque
uertit, et abruptum est nostro mare discolor unda
Oceanusque suus. pugnandi sola uoluptas.
295   celsior in campo sonipes et fortior arcus,
nec puer aut senior letales tendere neruos
segnis, et a nulla mors est incerta sagitta.
primi Pellaeas arcu fregere sarisas
Bactraque, Medorum sedem, murisque superbam
300   Assyrias Babylona domos. nec pila timentur
nostra nimis Parthis, audentque in bella uenire
experti Scythicas Crasso pereunte pharetras.
spicula nec solo spargunt fidentia ferro,
stridula sed multo saturantur tela ueneno;
305   uolnera parua nocent, fatumque in sanguine summo est.
o utinam non tanta mihi fiducia saeuis
esset in Arsacidis! fatis nimis aemula nostris
fata mouent Medos, multumque in gente deorum est.
effundam populos alia tellure reuolsos
310   excitosque suis inmittam sedibus ortus.
quod si nos Eoa fides et barbara fallent
foedera, uolgati supra commercia mundi
naufragium fortuna ferat: non regna precabor,
quae feci. sat magna feram solacia mortis
315   orbe iacens alio, nihil haec in membra cruente,

the Egyptian king; for difficult loyalty requires the years of manhood. Next, I fear the two-faced cunning of the fickle Moor; for that impious son of Carthage, mindful of his pedigree, threatens Italy, and his empty head is full of Hannibal — Hannibal, who by collateral descent disgraces the dynasty and is related to his Numidian ancestors. Already, when Varus begged his aid, Juba swelled with pride to see Rome take the second place. Therefore, my companions, let us be up and hasten to the Eastern clime. The waters of the Euphrates shut off from us a mighty world, and the Caspian Gates hide boundless solitudes; in Assyria a different hemisphere makes the changes of night and day; they have an ocean of their own, and a sea severed from ours and unlike in the colour of its water. Their one passion is for war. Tall is their warhorse on the plain, and strong their bow; youth and age are quick to stretch the deadly string, and death follows sure from every shaft. Their archers were the first to break the Macedonian phalanx, and they took Bactra, the seat of the Medes, and Babylon, the city of Assyria, with her proud walls. Nor is the Roman javelin much dreaded by the Parthians; but they come boldly to battle, having proved their Scythian quivers on the day when Crassus fell. And the shafts which they shower do not depend on steel alone, but their hurtling missiles are thoroughly steeped in poison. Even a slight wound is fatal, and death is in a mere scratch. (Would that I had not to place so much reliance upon the cruel sons of Arsaces! The destiny which controls the Medes rivals too closely that of Rome, and their nation is greatly blessed of Heaven.) I shall pour forth nations uprooted from another land; I shall summon all the East from its habitations and hurl it against my foe. But if the loyalty of the East and my treaty with the barbarians shall fail me, then let chance bear my shattered fortunes beyond the trodden highways of the world. I will not sue to the kings I made. If I fall at the end of the earth, this will be sufficient consolation for my death, that Caesar has been guilty of no outrage against my corpse, and guilty of no respect. But when I

nil socerum fecisse pie. sed cuncta reuoluens
uitae fata meae, semper uenerabilis illa
orbis parte fui, quantus Maeotida supra,
quantus apud Tanain toto conspectus in ortu!
320   quas magis in terras nostrum felicibus actis
nomen abit, aut unde redit maiore triumpho?
Roma, faue coeptis; quid enim tibi laetius umquam
praestiterint superi, quam, si ciuilia Partho
milite bella geras, tantam consumere gentem
325   et nostris miscere malis? cum Caesaris arma
concurrent Medis, aut me fortuna necesse est
uindicet aut Crassos." sic fatus murmure sensit
consilium damnasse uiros; quos Lentulus omnes
uirtutis stimulis et nobilitate dolendi
330   praecessit dignasque tulit modo consule uoces:
"sicine Thessalicae mentem fregere ruinae?
una dies mundi damnauit fata? secundum
Emathiam lis tanta datur? iacet omne cruenti
uolneris auxilium? solos tibi, Magne, reliquit
335   Parthorum fortuna pedes? quid transfuga mundi,
terrarum totos tractus caelumque perosus,
auersosque polos alienaque sidera quaeris,
Chaldaeos culture focos et barbara sacra,
Parthorum famulus? quid causa obtenditur armis
340   libertatis amor? miserum quid decipis orbem,
si seruire potes? te, quem Romana regentem
horruit auditu, quem captos ducere reges
uidit ab Hyrcanis, Indoque a litore, siluis,
deiectum fatis, humilem fractumque uidebit
345   extolletque animos Latium uaesanus in orbem,
se simul et Romam Pompeio supplice mensus?
nil animis fatisque tuis effabere dignum:
exiget ignorans Latiae commercia linguae,
ut lacrimis se, Magne, roges. patimurne pudoris
350   hoc uolnus, clades ut Parthia uindicet ante
Hesperias, quam Roma suas? ciuilibus armis

review the whole story of my life, I was ever worshipful in that Eastern world: how great was I beyond the Maeotian Mere and by the Tanais, the cynosure of all the East! Into no lands did my name go forth with more glorious exploits, and from none did it return more triumphant. Rome, smile on my enterprise! For no greater boon can Heaven confer on you than that you should use Parthians to fight your civil wars, and so destroy that great nation and make them share our calamities. When Caesar's armies clash with the Medes, the issue must avenge either me or the Crassi." Thus he spoke; but he perceived by their muttering that the meeting had condemned his plan. Lentulus was superior to them all in keen sense of honour and generous indignation; and thus he spoke in terms befitting one who had just been consul: "Has the defeat of Pharsalia so utterly destroyed your judgement? Has a single day fixed the world's destiny? Is the mighty issue to be decided by the result of Pharsalia? Is all cure for our bleeding wound impossible? Has Fortune left you no course, Magnus, save to fall at the Parthians' feet? Why do you fly from our world, and shun whole regions of earth and sky? Why seek a heaven turned from ours and foreign stars, in order to worship Chaldaean fires with savage rites, and to serve Parthians? Why was the love of freedom put forward as the pretext of war? Why thus deceive a suffering world, if you can stoop to be a slave to any? The Parthian heard your name and trembled when you were ruler of Rome, and saw you lead kings captive from the Hyrcanian forests and Indian shores; shall he now see you cast down by destiny, a beaten, broken man, and raise his mad ambition against the Roman world, measuring himself and Rome together by the prayers of Pompey? You will utter nothing worthy of your pride and destiny; unskilled to communicate in the Latin tongue, he will require you, Magnus, to appeal to him by your tears. Must we endure this stain upon our honour, that Parthia shall forestall Rome in avenging Rome's own disaster in the West? Rome chose you surely as a leader for civil

elegit te nempe ducem: quid uolnera nostra
in Scythicos spargis populos cladesque latentes?
quid Parthos transire doces? solacia tanti
355   perdit Roma mali, nullos admittere reges
sed ciui seruire suo? iuuat ire per orbem
ducentem saeuas Romana in moenia gentes
signaque ab Euphrate cum Crassis capta sequentem?
qui solus regum fato celante fauorem
360   defuit Emathiae, nunc tantas ille lacesset
auditi uictoris opes aut iungere fata
tecum, Magne, uolet? non haec fiducia genti est.
omnis in Arctois populus quicumque pruinis
nascitur, indomitus bellis et mortis amator:
365   quidquid ad Eoos tractus mundique teporem
ibitur, emollit gentes clementia caeli.
illic et laxas uestes et fluxa uirorum
uelamenta uides. Parthus per Medica rura,
Sarmaticos inter campos effusaque plano
370   Tigridis arua solo, nulli superabilis hosti est
libertate fugae; sed non, ubi terra tumebit,
aspera conscendet montis iuga, nec per opacas
bella geret tenebras incerto debilis arcu,
nec franget nando uiolenti uorticis amnem,
375   nec totum in pugna perfusus sanguine membra
exiget aestiuum calido sub puluere solem.
non aries illis, non ulla est machina belli,
aut fossas inplere ualent, Parthoque sequenti
murus erit quodcumque potest obstare sagittae.
380   pugna leuis bellumque fugax turmaeque uagantes,
et melior cessisse loco quam pellere miles;
inlita tela dolis, nec Martem comminus usquam
ausa pati uirtus, sed longe tendere neruos
et quo ferre uelint permittere uolnera uentis.
385   ensis habet uires, et gens quaecumque uirorum
bella gerit gladiis. nam Medos proelia prima
exarmant uacuaque iubent remeare pharetra.

war only: why do you publish among the Scythian nations our mutual sufferings and disasters, of which they were ignorant? Why do you teach the Parthians to cross the Euphrates? Is Rome to lose the one mitigation of her great suffering — that she submits to no foreign ruler but owns a son of her own as master? Does it please you to march across the world against the walls of Rome, with savage nations at your back, and preceded by the standards taken together with the Crassi at the Euphrates? One king alone was absent from Pharsalia, while Fortune still concealed her preference; and will he now challenge the mighty strength of the one who he has heard defeated you? Will he now be willing to make common cause with you? Such self-reliance does not belong to that people. Every native of the Northern snows is vehement in war and courts death; but every step you go towards the East and the torrid zone, the people grow softer as the sky grows kinder. There one sees loose garments and flowing robes worn even by men. In the land of Media, amid the plains of Sarmatia and in the level lands that extend by the Tigris, the Parthian cannot be conquered by any foe, because he has room for flight; but, where earth rises in hills, he will never climb the rough mountain ridges, nor fight on through thick darkness when crippled by the failure of his bow, nor stem a river in fierce eddy by swimming; nor, when his limbs are drenched in blood of battle, will he endure a long summer day beneath the stifling dust. They have no battering-rams and no war-engines of any kind, and no strength to level ditches; but any defence that can keep out an arrow will be a wall against pursuing Parthians. Their battle is a skirmish, their tactics flight, their squadrons rove at large. Their soldiers are more swift to yield their own ground than to dislodge the foe from his. Their missiles are smeared with guile; their valour nowhere dares to face the enemy at close quarters, but only to draw the bow at a distance and suffer the winds to carry their wounding weapons whither they will. Strength belongs to the sword, and every manly race uses cold steel to fight with. Moreover the first hour of battle disarms the Parthians and bids them retreat with emptied quivers. All their reliance is on poison, and none on the strong

51

nulla manus illis, fiducia tota ueneni est.
credis, Magne, uiros, quos in discrimina belli
390 cum ferro misisse parum est? temptare pudendum
auxilium tanti est, toto diuisus ut orbe
a terra moriare tua, tibi barbara tellus
incumbat, te parua tegant ac uilia busta,
inuidiosa tamen Crasso quaerente sepulchrum?
395 sed tua sors leuior, quoniam mors ultima poena est
nec metuenda uiris. at non Cornelia letum
infando sub rege timet. num barbara nobis
est ignota Venus, quae ritu caeca ferarum
polluit innumeris leges et foedera taedae
400 coniugibus, thalamique patent secreta nefandi
inter mille nurus? epulis uaesana meroque
regia non ullis exceptos legibus audet
concubitus: tot femineis conplexibus unum
non lassat nox tota marem. iacuere sorores
405 in regum thalamis sacrataque pignora matres.
damnat apud gentes sceleris non sponte peracti
Oedipodionias infelix fabula Thebas:
Parthorum dominus quotiens sic sanguine mixto
nascitur Arsacides! cui fas inplere parentem,
410 quid rear esse nefas? proles tam clara Metelli
stabit barbarico coniunx millesima lecto,
quamquam non ulli plus regia, Magne, uacabit
saeuitia stimulata Venus titulisque uirorum;
nam, quo plura iuuent Parthum portenta, fuisse
415 hanc sciet et Crassi; ceu pridem debita fatis
Assyriis trahitur cladis captiua uetustae.
haereat Eoae uolnus miserabile sortis,
non solum auxilium funesto ab rege petisse
sed gessisse prius bellum ciuile pudebit.
420 nam quod apud populos crimen socerique tuumque
maius erit, quam quod uobis miscentibus arma
Crassorum uindicta perit? incurrere cuncti
debuerant in Bactra duces et, ne qua uacarent

hand. Do you count those as men, Magnus, who are not content to face the risk of battle with the steel alone? Is it worth your while to seek a shameful alliance, in order that you may die parted by the whole world from your country, that foreign earth may rest upon your bones, that a tomb may cover you, poor indeed and petty, but yet shameful while Crassus seeks burial in vain? But your lot is easier, since death, the utmost penalty, is not terrible to the brave. But death is not what Cornelia has to fear in the power of that infamous king. Are we ignorant of that barbarous lust, which in the blind fashion of beasts defiles the binding sanctities of marriage with a myriad wives, and in which the secrets of the infamous bridal-chamber are displayed in the presence of a thousand women? Royalty, maddened with feasting and wine, ventures on unions that no laws have ever specified; a single male is not exhausted by a whole night spent in the arms of so many concubines. Their own sisters lie on the couches of the kings, and, for all the sanctity of the relation, their own mothers. Thebes, the city of Oedipus, is condemned in the eyes of mankind by the gloomy legend of the crime which he committed unwittingly: how often an Arsaces is born from such a union to rule the Parthians! What can I consider unpermitted to one who permits himself to impregnate his mother? The noble daughter of Metellus will wait by the bed of the barbarian, one among a thousand wives, though, Magnus, the king's lust will be devoted to her more than to any other, for it will be heated by cruelty and by the fame of her husbands. For the Parthian will know that she was once the wife of Crassus also, further gratifying omens; as if long due to the doom of Carrhae, she is being carried off as a captive taken in the defeat of long ago. If the pitiful disaster which we suffered in the East rankles in your heart, you will blush, not only to beg help from the death-dealing king, but also to have made war on Romans before Parthians. For what greater reproach will the Roman world bring against you and Caesar than this — that, when you two meet in conflict, vengeance for the Crassi has been forgotten? All our leaders should have made haste to Bactra; and, that every sword might be

arma, uel Arctoum Dacis Rhenique cateruis
425 imperii nudare latus, dum perfida Susa
in tumulos prolapsa ducum Babylonque iaceret.
Assyriae paci finem, Fortuna, precamur;
et, si Thessalia bellum ciuile peractum est,
ad Parthos, qui uicit, eat. gens unica mundi est,
430 de qua Caesareis possim gaudere triumphis.
non tibi, cum primum gelidum transibis Araxen,
umbra senis maesti Scythicis confixa sagittis
ingeret has uoces? 'tu, quem post funera nostra
ultorem cinerum nudae sperauimus umbrae,
435 ad foedus pacemque uenis?' tum plurima cladis
occurrent monimenta tibi: quae moenia trunci
lustrarunt ceruice duces, ubi nomina tanta
obruit Euphrates et nostra cadauera Tigris
detulit in terras ac reddidit. ire per ista
440 si potes, in media socerum quoque, Magne, sedentem
Thessalia placare potes. quin respicis orbem
Romanum? si regna times proiecta sub Austro
infidumque Iubam, petimus Pharon aruaque Lagi.
Syrtibus hinc Libycis tuta est Aegyptos; at inde
445 gurgite septeno rapidus mare summouet amnis.
terra suis contenta bonis, non indiga mercis
aut Iouis; in solo tanta est fiducia Nilo.
sceptra puer Ptolemaeus habet tibi debita, Magne,
tutelae commissa tuae. quis nominis umbram
450 horreat? innocua est aetas. ne iura fidemque
respectumque deum ueteri speraueris aula:
nil pudet adsuetos sceptris; mitissima sors est
regnorum sub rege nouo." non plura locutus
inpulit huc animos. quantum, spes ultima rerum,
455 libertatis habes! uicta est sententia Magni.
        tum Cilicum liquere solum Cyproque citatas
inmisere rates, nullas cui praetulit aras
undae diua memor Paphiae — si numina nasci

engaged, they should have left even the northern frontier of the empire
exposed to the Dacians and the hordes of the Rhine, until treacherous
Susa and Babylon were laid in ruins so as to be the tombs over the Crassi.
We pray to Fortune that peace with Assyria may end; and if the civil
war was settled by Pharsalia, let it be the conqueror who goes to Parthia.
They are the one nation on earth whom I could rejoice to see Caesar
triumph over. As soon as you cross the cold Araxes, will not the ghost
of that sorrowing old man, riddled with Scythian arrows, hurl this reproach
upon you? 'We unburied ghosts hoped that you would come after our
death to avenge our ashes: do you come to make a treaty and a peace?'
Next, memorials of the defeat will crowd upon your sight — the walls,
round which the headless bodies of our generals were dragged; the place
where the Euphrates closed over such famous men, and the Tigris carried
the Roman dead underground and then restored them to sight again. If
you can pass through these scenes, Magnus, you can also sue to Caesar
enthroned on the field of Pharsalia. Why not turn your eyes to the
Roman world? If you fear faithless Juba and his realm that stretches
far to the South, then Pharos and the land of Lagus is our goal. On the
West Egypt is protected by the Libyan Syrtes; and on the North the
rapid river with its seven channels drives back the sea; rich in its native
wealth, the land has no need of foreign wares or of Heaven's rain, so
great is her reliance upon the Nile alone. The sceptre which the boy
Ptolemy holds, he owes to you, Magnus; it was entrusted to your guard-
ianship. Who would dread a mere empty name? His is the age of innoc-
ence; look not for justice or loyalty or fear of the gods in a court where
the king has long reigned; use of power robs kings of all shame; the
subjects' yoke is lightest where their king is new." Lentulus said no
more, but he turned all minds to his view. How free are desperate men
to speak their minds! The policy of Magnus was outvoted.

Then they left Cilician soil and steered their vessels in haste for
Cyprus — Cyprus which the goddess, mindful of the Paphian waves, prefers to any of her shrines (if we believe that deities have birth, or if it is

credimus aut quemquam fas est coepisse deorum.
460 haec ubi deseruit Pompeius litora, totos
emensus Cypri scopulos, quibus exit in Austrum,
inde maris uasti transuerso uertitur aestu;
nec tenuit gratum nocturno lumine montem,
infimaque Aegypti pugnaci litora uelo
465 uix tetigit, qua diuidui pars maxima Nili
in uada decurrit Pelusia septimus amnis.
tempus erat, quo Libra pares examinat horas,
non uno plus aequa die, noctique rependit
lux minor hibernae uerni solacia damni.
470 conperit ut regem Casio se monte tenere,
flectit iter; nec Phoebus adhuc nec carbasa languent.
    iam rapido speculator eques per litora cursu
hospitis aduentu pauidam conpleuerat aulam.
consilii uix tempus erat; tamen omnia monstra
475 Pellaeae coiere domus, quos inter Acoreus
iam placidus senio fractisque modestior annis
— hunc genuit custos Nili crescentis in arua
Memphis uana sacris; illo cultore deorum
lustra suae Phoebes non unus uixerat Apis —
480 consilii uox prima fuit, meritumque fidemque
sacraque defuncti iactauit pignora patris.
sed melior suadere malis et nosse tyrannos
ausus Pompeium leto damnare Pothinus
"ius et fas multos faciunt, Ptolemaee, nocentes;
485 dat poenas laudata fides, cum sustinet," inquit
"quos fortuna premit. fatis accede deisque,
et cole felices, miseros fuge. sidera terra
ut distant et flamma mari, sic utile recto.
sceptrorum uis tota perit, si pendere iusta
490 incipit, euertitque arces respectus honesti.
libertas scelerum est, quae regna inuisa tuetur,
sublatusque modus gladiis. facere omnia saeue
non inpune licet, nisi cum facis. exeat aula,
qui uolt esse pius. uirtus et summa potestas

lawful to hold that any of the gods had a beginning). When Pompey had left that shore, having sailed past the long line of cliffs with which Cyprus projects to the South, from there he sailed a fresh course along the cross-current of the open sea. Unable to make the tower whose light the seaman blesses in darkness, with difficulty he reached the furthest shore of Egypt with battling sail, where the largest branch of the divided Nile, one of seven rivers, runs out to the shoals of Pelusium. It was the season when Libra balances the hours of day and night in equal scales, and stays level for one day only; for the shortening day makes compensation to the winter nights for their loss in spring. When he learnt that the king was encamped on Mount Casius, Pompey bent his course thither; the sun was not yet setting, nor the sails flagging.

By now a mounted watchman, after galloping along the shore, had filled with the news of the guest's arrival the frightened court. There was scarce time to deliberate; yet all the portentous figures of the Macedonian household assembled. Among them was Acoreus, made mild by feeble age and taught moderation by decrepitude. Idolatrous Memphis give him birth – Memphis which measures the Nile when it rises to flood the fields; and during his priesthood more than one Apis had lived through the term assigned him by the Moon, his mistress. He spoke first at the council, dwelling on benefits received and loyalty and the sacred promises of the dead monarch's will. But there was one, more fit to counsel wicked kings and know their heart, and a Pothinus dared to sign the death-warrant of a Pompey. He said: "Ptolemy, keeping the laws of God and man makes many guilty: we praise loyalty, but it pays the price when it supports those whom Fortune crushes. Take the side of destiny and Heaven, and court the prosperous, shun the afflicted. Expediency is as far from the right as the stars from earth or fire from water. The power of kings is utterly destroyed, once they begin to weigh considerations of justice; and regard for virtue levels the strongholds of tyrants. It is boundless wickedness and unlimited slaughter that protect an unpopular sovereign. If all your deeds are cruel, you will suffer for it the moment you cease from cruelty. If a man would be righteous, let him depart from a court. Virtue is incompatible with absolute power. He who is

495   non coeunt; semper metuet, quem saeua pudebunt.
non inpune tuos Magnus contempserit annos,
qui te nec uictos arcere a litore nostro
posse putat. neu nos sceptris priuauerit hospes,
pignora sunt propiora tibi: Nilumque Pharonque,
500   si regnare piget, damnatae redde sorori.
Aegypton certe Latiis tueamur ab armis.
quidquid non fuerit Magni, dum bella geruntur,
nec uictoris erit. toto iam pulsus ab orbe,
postquam nulla manet rerum fiducia, quaerit
505   cum qua gente cadat. rapitur ciuilibus umbris.
nec soceri tantum arma fugit: fugit ora senatus,
cuius Thessalicas saturat pars magna uolucres,
et metuit gentes, quas uno in sanguine mixtas
deseruit, regesque timet, quorum omnia mersit,
510   Thessaliaeque reus nulla tellure receptus
sollicitat nostrum, quem nondum perdidit, orbem.
iustior in Magnum nobis, Ptolemaee, querellae
causa data est. quid sepositam semperque quietam
crimine bellorum maculas Pharon aruaque nostra
515   uictori suspecta facis? cur sola cadenti
haec placuit tellus, in quam Pharsalica fata
conferres poenasque tuas? iam crimen habemus
purgandum gladio. quod nobis sceptra senatus
te suadente dedit, uotis tua fouimus arma.
520   hoc ferrum, quod fata iubent proferre, paraui
non tibi, sed uicto; feriam tua uiscera, Magne,
malueram soceri: rapimur, quo cuncta feruntur.
tene mihi dubitas an sit uiolare necesse,
cum liceat? quae te nostri fiducia regni
525   huc agit, infelix? populum non cernis inermem
aruaque uix refugo fodientem mollia Nilo?
metiri sua regna decet uiresque fateri.
tu, Ptolemaee, potes Magni fulcire ruinam,
sub qua Roma iacet? bustum cineresque mouere
530   Thessalicos audes bellumque in regna uocare?

ashamed to commit cruelty must always be apprehensive. Let Magnus
suffer for having despised your youth; he thinks you cannot repel even
a beaten man from our coast. And, that it may not be a stranger who
robs us of the throne, remember that you have others nearer of kin; if
your crown is uneasy, restore the Nile and Pharos to the sister you have
condemned. Let us in any case protect Egypt from the arms of Rome.
Whatever did not belong to Pompey during the war will not belong to
Caesar either. Driven from all the world, with no reliance left upon his
fortunes, he seeks a people to share his fall. He is dragged down by the
ghosts of those who fell in civil war. It is not merely Caesar's sword
that he flies from: he flies also from the face of the senators, of whom
so many are now glutting the vultures of Thessaly; and he fears the
foreign nations, whom he forsook and left weltering in one slaughtered
heap together; and he dreads the kings, whose all he destroyed; and
guilty of Pharsalia, rejected by every country, he tries to draw in our
part of the world, which he has not yet destroyed. But we, Ptolemy, can
complain more justly of Pompey than he of us: why does he stain secluded and peace-loving Pharos with the guilt of war and bring down
victorious Caesar's displeasure on our land? Why when falling did he
choose this country of all others to bring to it the curse of Pharsalia and
the punishment which he alone should pay? Even now we have incurred
guilt, which we cannot purge away except by using the sword. On his
motion the Senate granted us the sovereignty of Egypt, and therefore we
prayed for his victory. The sword, which destiny bids me bring forth, I
did not intend for Pompey but for the loser, whichever he might be.
Yours will be the heart I pierce with it, Magnus; I had rather have slain
Caesar; but we are borne by the current that carries the whole world
away. Do you doubt whether I must do you violence? I must, because
I may. What reliance upon our kingdom brings him hither, ill-fated man?
Does he not see our unwarlike population, scarce able to till the fields
softened by the falling Nile? We must take the measure of our kingdom
and confess our weakness. Are you, Ptolemy, strong enough to prop the
fall of Pompey – that fall beneath which Rome is crushed? Dare you
disturb the pyre and ashes of Pharsalia, and summon war to your own

ante aciem Emathiam nullis accessimus armis:
Pompei nunc castra placent, quae deserit orbis?
nunc uictoris opes et cognita fata lacessis?
aduersis non desse decet, sed laeta secutos:
535   nulla fides umquam miseros elegit amicos."
       adsensere omnes sceleri. laetatur honore
rex puer insueto, quod iam sibi tanta iubere
permittant famuli. sceleri delectus Achillas,
perfida qua tellus Casiis excurrit harenis
540   et uada testantur iunctas Aegyptia Syrtes,
exiguam sociis monstri gladiisque carinam
instruit. o superi, Nilusne et barbara Memphis
et Pelusiaci tam mollis turba Canopi
hos animos? sic fata premunt ciuilia mundum?
545   sic Romana iacent? ullusne in cladibus istis
est locus Aegypto Phariusque admittitur ensis?
hanc certe seruate fidem, ciuilia bella;
cognatas praestate manus externaque monstra
pellite, si meruit tam claro nomine Magnus
550   Caesaris esse nefas. tanti, Ptolemaee, ruinam
nominis haud metuis caeloque tonante profanas
inseruisse manus, inpure ac semiuir, audes?
non domitor mundi nec ter Capitolia curru
inuectus regumque potens uindexque senatus
555   uictorisque gener, Phario satis esse tyranno
quod poterat, Romanus erat: quid uiscera nostra
scrutaris gladio? nescis, puer inprobe, nescis,
quo tua sit fortuna loco: iam iure sine ullo
Nili sceptra tenes; cecidit ciuilibus armis
560   qui tibi regna dedit. iam uento uela negarat
Magnus et auxilio remorum infanda petebat
litora; quem contra non longa uecta biremi
appulerat scelerata manus, Magnoque patere
fingens regna Phari, celsae de puppe carinae
565   in paruam iubet ire ratem, litusque malignum
incusat bimaremque uadis frangentibus aestum,

realms? Before the battle of Pharsalia we took neither side: do we now adopt Pompey's cause when all the world is forsaking it? Do you now challenge the might and proved success of Caesar? To support the loser in adversity is right, but right only for those who have shared in his prosperity; no loyalty ever picked out the wretched as friends."

All gave their voices for the crime. The boy-king was pleased by a deference seldom shown him, when his servants allowed him to give such important orders. Achillas was chosen to execute the crime, and manned a small boat with armed accomplices for the horrid deed, where the land of traitors juts out into the sands of Mount Casius, and the Egyptian shoals tell of the neighbouring Syrtes. Ye gods! Do the Nile and barbarous Memphis, and the effeminate people of Egyptian Canopus, aspire so high as this? Does the curse of the civil war weigh thus on all the world? Has Rome fallen so low? What room is there for Egypt in our tragedy, and what part for the sword of Egypt? Thus far at least civil war should keep faith: it should provide Roman hands to fall by and keep foreign fiends far away, since the famous name of Magnus entitled him to be Caesar's guilt. Do you, Ptolemy, not dread the crash of that great name? Do you, foul mockery of a man, dare to thrust in your sacrilegious hands when heaven is thundering? If Pompey were not a world-conqueror, not one who had thrice driven in triumph to the Capitol; if he were not the ruler of kings, the champion of the Senate, and the son-in-law of Caesar, he was at least a Roman, and that might have been enough for a king of Egypt; why do you probe a Roman heart with your sword? Presumptuous boy, you do not realise your own position: already you wear the crown of Egypt with no right to it, because he who gave it to you has been overthrown by civil warfare. Now Magnus had robbed the wind of his sails and was using oars to bring him to the accursed coast, when the murderous band came alongside to meet him in a little two-banked boat. Pretending that he was welcome to the kingdom of Egypt, they invited him to step into their little craft from the stern of his tall vessel, blaming the scanty anchorage, and the surf of two seas that broke upon

qui uetet externas terris adpellere classes.
quod nisi fatorum leges intentaque iussu
ordinis aeterni miserae uicinia mortis
570 damnatum leto traherent ad litora Magnum,
non ulli comitum sceleris praesagia derant:
quippe, fides si pura foret, si regia Magno,
sceptrorum auctori, uera pietate pateret,
uenturum tota Pharium cum classe tyrannum.
575 sed cedit fatis classemque relinquere iussus
obsequitur, letumque iuuat praeferre timori.
ibat in hostilem praeceps Cornelia puppem,
hoc magis inpatiens egresso desse marito,
quod metuit clades. "remane, temeraria coniunx,
580 et tu, nate, precor, longeque a litore casus
expectate meos et in hac ceruice tyranni
explorate fidem" dixit. sed surda uetanti
tendebat geminas amens Cornelia palmas:
"quo sine me crudelis abis? iterumne relinquor
585 Thessalicis summota malis? numquam omine laeto
distrahimur miseri. poteras non flectere puppem,
cum fugeres alto, latebrisque relinquere Lesbi,
omnibus a terris si nos arcere parabas.
an tantum in fluctus placeo comes?" haec ubi frustra
590 effudit, prima pendet tamen anxia puppe,
attonitoque metu nec quoquam auertere uisus
nec Magnum spectare potest. stetit anxia classis
ad ducis euentum, metuens non arma nefasque
sed ne summissis precibus Pompeius adoret
595 sceptra sua donata manu. transire parantem
Romanus Pharia miles de puppe salutat
Septimius, qui, pro superum pudor, arma satelles
regia gestabat posito deformia pilo,
inmanis, uiolentus, atrox nullaque ferarum
600 mitior in caedes. quis non, Fortuna, putasset
parcere te populis, quod bello haec dextra uacaret,
Thessaliaque procul tam noxia tela fugasses?

the shallows and hindered foreign ships from access to the land. But for the law of destiny, and but for the approach of a tragic end inflicted by decree of the eternal order, which were drawing Magnus to the shore under sentence of death, there was no lack of hints of the crime for any of his companions to see; for, if there were genuine loyalty, if the palace were thrown open with true devotion to Magnus who conferred the royal power upon it, then the Egyptian monarch would have come with all his fleet. But Pompey yielded to destiny and obeyed when asked to leave his ships, and chose to die rather than betray fear. Cornelia hastened to enter the hostile craft, the less willing to be left behind by her husband when he disembarked because she feared disaster. But he said: "Stay behind, rash wife, and you, my son, I pray; watch from afar what befalls me on shore, and use my head to test the loyalty of the king." But Cornelia, deaf to his refusal, wildly stretched out both her hands: "Whither are you departing and cruelly leaving me behind? Am I deserted a second time, I who was kept away from the horrors of Pharsalia? Ill-omened ever are our partings. You might, when you fled across the sea, have sailed straight on and left me in my hiding-place at Lesbos, if you intended to exclude me from every shore. Is my company displeasing to you except at sea?" When she had poured forth this remonstrance in vain, yet in her agony she hung over the end of the ship, and panic fear prevented her either from turning her eyes away or from looking steadily at Magnus. The ships lay there at anchor, uneasy for the fortunes of their leader; they feared not murderous weapons, but that Pompey might bow with humble petitions before the sceptre his own hand had bestowed. As he prepared to step across, a Roman soldier hailed him from the Egyptian boat. This was Septimius, who – shame on the gods! – had laid down the pilum and carried the unworthy weapons of the king whose minion he was: a savage, wild, and cruel man, and no gentler than a wild beast to its slaughtered prey. Who would not have thought that Fortune showed mercy to mankind when she banished a sword so guilty far from Pharsalia, and when his hand took no part in the battle? No:

disponis gladios, ne quo non fiat in orbe,
heu, facinus ciuile tibi. uictoribus ipsis
605 dedecus et numquam superum caritura pudore
fabula: Romanus regi sic paruit ensis,
Pellaeusque puer gladio tibi colla recidit,
Magne, tuo. qua posteritas in saecula mittet
Septimium fama? scelus hoc quo nomine dicent,
610 qui Bruti dixere nefas? iam uenerat horae
terminus extremae, Phariamque ablatus in alnum
perdiderat iam iura sui. tum stringere ferrum
regia monstra parant. ut uidit comminus ensis,
inuoluit uoltus atque, indignatus apertum
615 fortunae praebere, caput; tum lumina pressit
continuitque animam, ne quas effundere uoces
uellet et aeternam fletu corrumpere famam.
sed postquam mucrone latus funestus Achillas
perfodit, nullo gemitu consensit ad ictum
620 respexitque nefas, seruatque inmobile corpus,
seque probat moriens atque haec in pectore uoluit:
"saecula Romanos numquam tacitura labores
attendunt, aeuumque sequens speculatur ab omni
orbe ratem Phariamque fidem: nunc consule famae.
625 fata tibi longae fluxerunt prospera uitae;
ignorant populi, si non in morte probaris,
an scieris aduersa pati. ne cede pudori
auctoremque dole fati: quacumque feriris,
crede manum soceri. spargant lacerentque licebit,
630 sum tamen, o superi, felix, nullique potestas
hoc auferre deo. mutantur prospera uita:
non fit morte miser. uidet hanc Cornelia caedem
Pompeiusque meus: tanto patientius, oro,
clude, dolor, gemitus; natus coniunxque peremptum,
635 si mirantur, amant." talis custodia Magno
mentis erat, ius hoc animi morientis habebat.
    at non tam patiens Cornelia cernere saeuum,

she scatters her assassins, that murder of Roman by Roman may be wrought in every part of earth to please her. A disgrace even to the victorious party, a tale that will always bring reproach on Heaven — a Roman sword obeyed such a behest of a king, and the head of Magnus was cut off with his own sword by the Macedonian boy. With what reputation will posterity hand the name of Septimius down to future ages? What name will those who called the crime of Brutus an abomination apply to this man's crime? — Now the limit of his last hour had come; he was borne off into the Egyptian boat and had already lost the power of free action. Next, the king's creatures begin to bare the steel. When Pompey saw the blades come close, he covered his face and head, disdaining to expose them bare to the stroke of doom; then he closed tight his eyes and held his breath, that he might have no power of utterance and might not mar his immortal glory by tears. But when murderous Achillas had driven the point through his side, he did not acknowledge the blow by any groan or take heed of the horror, but remained motionless, and tested his strength in the hour of death; and these thoughts passed through his mind: "Future ages, that will never forget the tragedy of Rome, are watching now, and from every quarter of the world time coming gazes at this boat and the treachery of Egypt; think now of fame. Through a long life the tide of your success never slackened; men cannot know, unless you prove it by your death, whether you were able to endure adversity. Sink not beneath the shame, nor resent the instrument of doom: whatever the hand that slays you, believe it to be the hand of your kinsman. Though men scatter and mutilate my limbs, nevertheless, ye gods, I am a fortunate man, and of this no god can deprive me. For life brings change to prosperity, but death can make no man wretched. Cornelia and my son see this murder done; therefore I call on my resentment to stifle its complaints all the more steadfastly; my wife and son do indeed love me dead, if my death win their admiration." Such control had Magnus over his thoughts, such mastery over his mind, when he was dying.

But Cornelia, less patient to behold a cruel outrage than to endure

quam perferre, nefas miserandis aethera conplet
uocibus: "o coniunx, ego te scelerata peremi:
640 letiferae tibi causa morae fuit auia Lesbos,
et prior in Nili peruenit litora Caesar;
nam cui ius alii sceleris? sed, quisquis, in istud
a superis inmisse caput uel Caesaris irae
uel tibi prospiciens, nescis, crudelis, ubi ipsa
645 uiscera sint Magni; properas atque ingeris ictus,
qua uotum est uicto. poenas non morte minores
pendat et ante meum uideat caput. haud ego culpa
libera bellorum, quae matrum sola per undas
et per castra comes nullis absterrita fatis
650 uictum, quod reges etiam timuere, recepi.
hoc merui, coniunx, in tuta puppe relinqui?
perfide, parcebas? te fata extrema petente
uita digna fui? moriar, nec munere regis.
aut mihi praecipitem, nautae, permittite saltum,
655 aut laqueum collo tortosque aptare rudentes,
aut aliquis Magno dignus comes exigat ensem;
Pompeio praestare potest, quod Caesaris armis
inputet. o saeui, properantem in fata tenetis?
uiuis adhuc, coniunx, et iam Cornelia non est
660 iuris, Magne, sui: prohibent accersere mortem;
seruor uictori." sic fata interque suorum
lapsa manus rapitur trepida fugiente carina.
     at Magni cum terga sonent et pectora ferro,
permansisse decus sacrae uenerabile formae
665 iratamque deis faciem, nil ultima mortis
ex habitu uoltuque uiri mutasse fatentur,
qui lacerum uidere caput. nam saeuus in ipso
Septimius sceleris maius scelus inuenit actu,
ac retegit sacros scisso uelamine uoltus
670 semianimis Magni spirantiaque occupat ora
collaque in obliquo ponit languentia transtro.
tunc neruos uenasque secat nodosaque frangit
ossa diu; nondum artis erat caput ense rotare.

66

it herself, filled the air with pitiful cries: "Dear husband, I am guilty of your death: your fatal delay was caused by the remoteness of Lesbos, and Caesar has reached the banks of the Nile before you. Who else could have power to command this crime? But whoever you are who have been sent by Heaven against that life, whether serving the anger of Caesar or your own advantage, you know not, ruthless man, where the very heart of Magnus lies; in haste you shower your blows where he, in his defeat, welcomes them. Let him pay a penalty not less than death by seeing my head fall first. I am not blameless in respect of the war; for I was the only matron who followed him on sea and in camp; I was deterred by no disasters, but harboured him in defeat, which even kings were afraid to do. And is this my reward from my husband, to be left behind in the safety of the ship? Were you, after all, trying to spare me, faithless husband? Did I deserve to live when you went to your death? I shall die, nor owe it to King Ptolemy. Suffer me, ye sailors, either to leap headlong, or to fit a noose of twisted rope round my neck; or let some friend of Pompey prove worthy of Pompey by driving home his sword in my body. He may discharge an obligation to Pompey and yet lay the blame on Caesar's arms. Cruel men, do you check my haste to die? Though you my husband, are still alive, Cornelia has already ceased to be free; they forbid me to summon death, and I am kept alive for Caesar." Thus she spoke, and was carried away, swooning, in friendly arms, while the ship made haste to fly.

But those who saw the severed head of Magnus admit that, when the steel clashed on his back and breast, the majestic beauty of those sacred features, and the face that frowned at Heaven, suffered no change; and that the last moments of death made no alteration in the bearing and countenance of the hero. The head was severed; for savage Septimius, in the very doing of his crime, devised a crime still worse. He slit the covering and unveiled the sacred features of the dying man; he seized the still breathing head and laid the drooping neck across a thwart. Next, he severed the muscles and veins and hacked long at the knotted bones: it was not yet a profession to send a head spinning with a sword-cut. But

at postquam trunco ceruix abscisa recessit,
675   uindicat hoc Pharius, dextra gestare, satelles.
degener atque operae miles Romane secundae,
Pompei diro sacrum caput ense recidis,
ut non ipse feras? o summi fata pudoris!
inpius ut Magnum nosset puer, illa uerenda
680   regibus hirta coma et generosa fronte decora
caesaries conprensa manu est, Pharioque ueruto,
dum uiuunt uoltus atque os in murmura pulsant
singultus animae, dum lumina nuda rigescunt,
suffixum caput est, quo numquam bella iubente
685   pax fuit; hoc leges Campumque et rostra mouebat,
hac facie, Fortuna, tibi, Romana, placebas.
nec satis infando fuit hoc uidisse tyranno:
uolt sceleris superesse fidem. tunc arte nefanda
summota est capiti tabes, raptoque cerebro
690   adsiccata cutis, putrisque effluxit ab alto
umor, et infuso facies solidata ueneno est.
    ultima Lageae stirpis peritura que proles,
degener, incestae sceptris cessure sorori,
cum tibi sacrato Macedon seruetur in antro
695   et regum cineres extructo monte quiescant,
cum Ptolemaeorum manes seriemque pudendam
pyramides claudant indignaque Mausolea,
litora Pompeium feriunt, truncusque uadosis
huc illuc iactatur aquis. adeone molesta
700   totum cura fuit socero seruare cadauer?
hac Fortuna fide Magni tam prospera fata
pertulit, hac illum summo de culmine rerum
morte petit cladesque omnes exegit in uno
saeua die, quibus inmunes tot praestitit annos,
705   Pompeiusque fuit, qui numquam mixta uideret
laeta malis, felix nullo turbante deorum
et nullo parcente miser; semel inpulit illum
dilata Fortuna manu. pulsatur harenis,

when the neck was severed and parted from the body, the Egyptian minion claims this privilege – to carry it in his right hand. A Roman soldier sinks so low as to take a second part: he cuts off the sacred head of Pompey with his cursed sword in order that another may carry it! What a depth of ignominy was his! That the sacrilegious boy might recognise Magnus, those manly locks that kings revered and the hair that graced his noble brow were gripped by the hand; and while the features still showed life and the sobbing breath drove sound through the lips, and the stark eyes stiffened, the head was stuck on an Egyptian pike – that head, whose call to war ever banished peace; the head, which swayed the Senate, the Campus, and the Rostrum; that was the face which the Fortune of Rome was proud to wear. The sight of it was not enough for the infamous king: he wished proof of his guilt to remain. Thereupon, by their hideous art the blood was drained from the head, the brain torn out, and the skin dried; the corrupting moisture was drawn out from the inmost parts, and the features were hardened by the infusion of drugs.

Last scion of the line of Lagus, doomed and degenerate king, who must surrender your crown to your incestuous sister, though you preserve the Macedonian in consecrated vault and the ashes of the Pharaohs rest beneath a mountain of masonry, though the dead Ptolemies and their unworthy dynasty are covered by pyramids and mausoleums too good for them, the shore batters Pompey, and his headless body is tossed hither and thither in the shallows. Was it so troublesome a task to keep the whole body for his kinsman to see? So true to her bargain, did Fortune continue to the end the prosperity of Magnus; so true to her bargain, she summoned him only at his death from his pinnacle of glory, and ruthlessly made him pay in a single day for all the disasters from which she protected him for many years; and Pompey was the only man who never experienced good and evil together: his prosperity no god disturbed, and on his misery no god had mercy. Fortune held her hand for long and then overthrew him with one blow. He is tossed on the sands

carpitur in scopulis hausto per uolnera fluctu,
710 ludibrium pelagi, nullaque manente figura
una nota est Magno capitis iactura reuolsi.
　　　ante tamen Pharias uictor quam tangat harenas,
Pompeio raptim tumulum fortuna parauit,
ne iaceat nullo uel ne meliore sepulchro:
715 e latebris pauidus decurrit ad aequora Cordus.
quaestor ab Icario Cinyreae litore Cypri
infaustus Magni fuerat comes. ille per umbras
ausus ferre gradum uictum pietate timorem
conpulit, ut mediis quaesitum corpus in undis
720 duceret ad terram traheretque in litora Magnum.
lucis maesta parum per densas Cynthia nubes
praebebat; cano sed discolor aequore truncus
conspicitur. tenet ille ducem conplexibus artis
eripiente mari; tunc uictus pondere tanto
725 expectat fluctus pelagoque iuuante cadauer
inpellit. postquam sicco iam litore sedit,
incubuit Magno lacrimasque effudit in omne
uolnus, et ad superos obscuraque sidera fatur:
"non pretiosa petit cumulato ture sepulchra
730 Pompeius, Fortuna, tuus, non pinguis ad astra
ut ferat e membris Eoos fumus odores,
ut Romana suum gestent pia colla parentem,
praeferat ut ueteres feralis pompa triumphos,
ut resonent tristi cantu fora, totus ut ignes
735 proiectis maerens exercitus ambiat armis.
da uilem Magno plebei funeris arcam,
quae lacerum corpus siccos effundat in ignes;
robora non desint misero nec sordidus ustor.
sit satis, o superi, quod non Cornelia fuso
740 crine iacet subicique facem conplexa maritum
imperat, extremo sed abest a munere busti
infelix coniunx nec adhuc a litore longe est."
sic fatus paruos iuuenis procul aspicit ignes
corpus uile suis nullo custode cremantes.

70

and mangled on the rocks, while his wounds drink in the wave; he is the plaything of the sea, and, when all shape is lost, the one mark to identify Magnus is the absence of the severed head.

But before Caesar could reach the sands of Egypt, Fortune devised a hasty burial for Pompey, that he might not lack a tomb, or that he might not have a better. In fear and haste Cordus came down from his hiding-place to the sea; as quaestor he had made the ill-starred voyage with Magnus from the Icarian shore of Cyprus, where Cinyras once reigned. Under cover of darkness he dared to come, and forced his fear, mastered by duty, to seek the body amid the waves, and draw it to land and drag Magnus to the shore. A sad moon shed but scanty light through thick clouds; but the headless body was visible by its different colour in the foaming waves. He grasped his leader tight against the snatching of the sea; then, unequal to that mighty burden, he waited for a wave and then pushed on the body with the sea to help him. When it came to rest above the water-line, he cast himself upon Magnus, pouring tears into every wound; and thus he addressed Heaven and the dim stars: "No costly pyre with heaped-up incense does your favourite, Pompey, ask of you, Fortune; he does not ask that the rich smoke should carry to the stars Eastern perfumes from his limbs; that devoted Romans should bear on their shoulders the dear father of his country; that the funeral procession should display tokens of his past triumphs; that the Forums should be filled with mournful music; or that a whole army, with arms cast down, should march mourning around the burning pile. But grant to Magnus the paltry coffin of a pauper's burial, to spill out the mutilated body on the unfed fires; let not the hapless corpse lack wood or a mean hand to kindle it. Be content with this, ye gods, that Cornelia does not lie prostrate with dishevelled hair — does not embrace her husband and bid the torch be applied; that his unhappy wife, though still not far distant from the shore, is not here to pay her last tribute to the dead." When the youth had spoken thus, he saw at a distance a feeble fire that was burning a corpse uncared for and unguarded. Thence he took fire in

745   inde rapit flammas semustaque robora membris
          subducit. "quaecumque es," ait "neglecta nec ulli
          cara tuo sed Pompeio felicior umbra,
          quod iam conpositum uiolat manus hospita bustum,
          da ueniam; si quid sensus post fata relictum,
750   cedis et ipsa rogo paterisque haec damna sepulchri,
          teque pudet sparsis Pompei manibus uri."
          sic fatus plenusque sinus ardente fauilla
          peruolat ad truncum, qui fluctu paene relatus
          litore pendebat. summas dimouit harenas
755   et collecta procul lacerae fragmenta carinae
          exigua trepidus posuit scrobe. nobile corpus
          robora nulla premit, nulla strue membra recumbunt:
          admotus Magnum, non subditus, accipit ignis.
          ille sedens iuxta flammas "o maxime" dixit
760   "ductor et Hesperii maiestas nominis una,
          si tibi iactatu pelagi, si funere nudo
          tristior iste rogus, manes animamque potentem
          officiis auerte meis: iniuria fati
          hoc fas esse iubet; ne ponti belua quidquam,
765   ne fera, ne uolucres, ne saeui Caesaris ira
          audeat, exiguam, quantum potes, accipe flammam,
          Romana succense manu. Fortuna recursus
          si det in Hesperiam, non hac in sede quiescent
          tam sacri cineres, sed te Cornelia, Magne,
770   accipiet nostraque manu transfundet in urnam.
          interea paruo signemus litora saxo,
          ut nota sit busti; si quis placare peremptum
          forte uolet plenos et reddere mortis honores,
          inueniat trunci cineres et norit harenas,
775   ad quas, Magne, tuum referat caput." haec ubi fatus,
          excitat inualidas admoto fomite flammas.
          carpitur et lentum Magnus destillat in ignem,
          tabe fouens bustum. sed iam percusserat astra
          Aurorae praemissa dies: ille ordine rupto

haste and drew the charred logs from beneath the body. "Whoever you are," he said, "uncared for and unloved by any of your kin, but yet more fortunate after death than Pompey, pardon the stranger hand that robs your pyre once laid. If aught of feeling survives death, you willingly resign your pyre and permit this robbery of your grave; and you are ashamed, when the body of Pompey is divided, to find cremation yourself." Thus he spoke, and having filled his cloak with the burning embers he flew back to the body, which, as it hung upon the shore, had nearly been carried back by a wave. He scraped away the surface of the sand, and hastily laid in a narrow trench the pieces of a broken boat which he had gathered at a distance. That famous corpse rests upon no logs, on no pile are the limbs laid; the fire that receives Magnus is not laid beneath him but beside him. Sitting near the fire, Cordus said: "Mighty captain and unequalled glory of the Roman people, if this pyre is more distressful to you than to be tossed by the sea, or to be an unburied corpse, then turn away your spirit and your mighty ghost from the service I render; the wrong of Fate makes this right; that no sea monster or beast or bird or wrath of cruel Caesar may venture anything, accept, so far as you can, this scanty flame; a Roman hand has kindled your corpse. If Fortune grant us a return to Italy, not here will these sacred ashes rest; but Cornelia will recover you, Magnus, and will transfer you from my hand to an urn. Meanwhile, let me mark the place on the shore with a small stone to be a token of your grave; if any man haply desires to make atonement to your spirit and give you your due of funeral honours, let him find the ashes of the body, and recognise the strand to which he must restore your head." Having spoken thus, he brightens the feeble flame with a fresh supply of fuel. Magnus is consumed and melts into the slow fire, feeding the pyre with the dissolving flesh. But by now the daylight which precedes the dawn had smitten the stars; and he broke

780　funeris, attonitus latebras in litore quaerit.
　　quam metuis, demens, isto pro crimine poenam,
　　quo te fama loquax omnes accepit in annos?
　　condita laudabit Magni socer inpius ossa:
　　i modo securus ueniae fassusque sepulchrum
785　posce caput. cogit pietas inponere finem
　　officio. semusta rapit resolutaque nondum
　　ossa satis neruis et inustis plena medullis
　　aequorea restinguit aqua congestaque in unum
　　parua clausit humo. tunc, ne leuis aura retectos
790　auferret cineres, saxo conpressit harenam,
　　nautaque ne bustum religato fune moueret,
　　inscripsit sacrum semusto stipite nomen:
　　"hic situs est Magnus." placet hoc, Fortuna, sepulchrum
　　dicere Pompei, quo condi maluit illum
795　quam terra caruisse socer? temeraria dextra,
　　cur obicis Magno tumulum manesque uagantes
　　includis? situs est, qua terra extrema refuso
　　pendet in Oceano; Romanum nomen et omne
　　imperium Magno tumuli est modus; obrue saxa
800　crimine plena deum. si tota est Herculis Oete
　　et iuga tota vacant Bromio Nyseia, quare
　　unus in Aegypto Magni lapis? omnia Lagi
　　arua tenere potest, si nullo caespite nomen
　　haeserit. erremus populi cinerumque tuorum,
805　Magne, metu nullas Nili calcemus harenas.
　　quod si tam sacro dignaris nomine saxum,
　　adde actus tantos monimentaque maxima rerum,
　　adde trucis Lepidi motus Alpinaque bella
　　armaque Sertori reuocato consule uicta
810　et currus, quos egit eques, commercia tuta
　　gentibus et pauidos Cilicas maris; adde subactam
　　barbariem gentesque uagas et quidquid in Euro
　　regnorum Boreaque iacet. dic semper ab armis
　　ciuilem repetisse togam, ter curribus actis
815　contentum multos patriae donasse triumphos.

off the rites and sought in terror his hiding-place upon the shore. What punishment do you dread, poor fool, for your crime, because of which vocal Fame has made you welcome for all time to come? His unnatural kinsman will approve the burial of Pompey's bones. Nay go, secure of pardon, confess that you buried him, and demand the head. – Duty compels him to complete his service. He snatched the charred bones not yet entirely parted from the muscles, and quenched them, full of the scorched marrow, with sea water; then he piled them together and hid them beneath a handful of earth. Next, lest a light breeze should bare and scatter the ashes, he pressed down the sand under a stone; and that no sailor might disturb the tomb by tying his rope there, he used a charred stick to write the sacred name upon it: "Here Magnus lies." Is it the will of Fortune to call this the grave of Pompey – this grave which Caesar preferred for his son-in-law to no burial at all? Rash hand, why do you thrust a tomb on Magnus, and imprison the spirit that roams free? His burial-place extends as far as the most distant land that floats on the circling stream of Ocean; the Roman name and all the Roman empire are the limit of Pompey's grave. Away with that stone, eloquent in re- proach of Heaven! If all Oeta belongs to Hercules, and the hills of Nysa own no lord but Bacchus alone, why is there but a single stone in Egypt for Magnus? He can possess all the kingdom of Lagus, if his name were fixed upon no grave. Then we Romans would be in doubt, and, from fear to tread on the ashes of Magnus, we should avoid altogether the sands of Nile. But, if you think the stone worthy of that sacred name, then add his great achievements and the records of his mighty deeds; add the rising of fierce Lepidus and the Alpine war; the victory over Sertorius, when the consul was recalled, and the triumph which he celebrated while yet a knight; write of commerce made safe for all nations, and of the Cilicians scared from the sea. Tell how he subdued the barbarian world, and nomad peoples, and all the empires of East and North. Say that ever after war he donned again the citizen's gown, and that, content with three triumphal pageants, he excused his country many triumphs. What

quis capit haec tumulus? surgit miserabile bustum
non ullis plenum titulis, non ordine tanto
fastorum; solitumque legi super alta deorum
culmina et extructos spoliis hostilibus arcus
820   haud procul est ima Pompei nomen harena
depressum tumulo, quod non legat aduena rectus,
quod nisi monstratum Romanus transeat hospes.
     noxia ciuili tellus Aegyptia fato,
haud equidem inmerito Cumanae carmine uatis
825   cautum, ne Nili Pelusia tangeret ora
Hesperius miles ripasque aestate tumentes.
quid tibi, saeua, precer pro tanto crimine, tellus?
uertat aquas Nilus quo nascitur orbe retentus,
et steriles egeant hibernis imbribus agri,
830   totaque in Aethiopum putres soluaris harenas.
nos in templa tuam Romana recepimus Isim
semideosque canes et sistra iubentia luctus
et, quem tu plangens hominem testaris, Osirim:
tu nostros, Aegypte, tenes in puluere manes.
835   tu quoque, cum saeuo dederis iam templa tyranno,
nondum Pompei cineres, o Roma, petisti;
exul adhuc iacet umbra ducis. si saecula prima
uictoris timuere minas, nunc excipe saltem
ossa tui Magni, si nondum subruta fluctu
840   inuisa tellure sedent. quis busta timebit,
quis sacris dignam mouisse uerebitur umbram?
imperet hoc nobis utinam scelus et uelit uti
nostro Roma sinu: satis o nimiumque beatus,
si mihi contingat manes transferre reuolsos
845   Ausoniam, si tale ducis uiolare sepulchrum.
forsitan, aut sulco sterili cum poscere finem
a superis aut Roma uolet feralibus Austris
ignibus aut nimiis aut terrae tecta mouenti,
consilio iussuque deum transibis in urbem,
850   Magne, tuam, summusque feret tua busta sacerdos.
nam quis ad exustam Cancro torrente Syenen

tomb has room for all this? There rises a pitiful gravestone, rich with no
records or long roll of offices; and the name of Pompey, which men were
wont to read upon lofty temples of the gods and upon arches reared with
spoils of our foes, — that name is little raised above the lowly sand, and
set so low upon the grave that a stranger must stoop to read it, and a
visitor from Rome would pass it by if it were not pointed out.

O land of Egypt, guilty of the destinies of civil war, with good reason did the Sibyl of Cumae warn us in her verse, that no Roman soldier
should visit the mouths of the Nile in Egypt, and those banks which the
summer floods. What curse can I invoke upon that ruthless land in reward for so great a crime? May Nile reverse his waters and be stayed in
the region where he rises; may the fields be barren and crave winter
rains; and may all the soil break up into the crumbling sands of Ethiopia.
Though we have admitted to Roman temples your Isis and your dogs
half divine, the rattle which bids the worshipper wail, and the Osiris
whom you prove to be mortal by mourning for him, yet you, Egypt, keep
our dead in your dust. Rome too, though she has already given a temple
to the cruel tyrant, has not yet claimed the ashes of Pompey, and his
ghost still lies in exile. If the first generation dreaded Caesar's threats,
now at least let her welcome the bones of her beloved Magnus, if they
still remain in that hated land and are not yet washed away by the sea.
Who will fear the tomb, and dread to remove the dead so worthy of worship? Oh, that Rome would bid me do this wrong, and deign to make
use of my arms! Happy, too happy, should I be, if it were mine to un-
earth the remains and convey them to Italy, and to violate a tomb so
unworthy of a general. Perhaps, when Rome shall want to pray to Heaven
for a cure for barren fields or pestilential winds or excessive heats or
earthquake, then, at the advice and bidding of the gods, you will pass,
Magnus, to your loved city, and the chief Pontiff will bear your ashes.
What man is there, who travels to Syene, parched by flaming Cancer,

ibit et imbrifera siccas sub Pliade Thebas
spectator Nili, quis rubri stagna profundi
aut Arabum portus mercis mutator Eoae,
855 Magne, petet, quem non tumuli uenerabile saxum
et cinis in summis forsan turbatus harenis
auertet manesque tuos placare iubebit
et Casio praeferre Iovi? nil ista nocebunt
famae busta tuae: templis auroque sepultus
860 uilior umbra fores. nunc est pro numine summo
hoc tumulo Fortuna iacens: augustius aris
uictoris Libyco pulsatur in aequore saxum.
Tarpeis qui saepe deis sua tura negarunt,
inclusum Tusco uenerantur caespite fulmen.
865 proderit hoc olim, quod non mansura futuris
ardua marmoreo surrexit pondere moles.
pulueris exigui sparget non longa uetustas
congeriem, bustumque cadet, mortisque peribunt
argumenta tuae. ueniet felicior aetas,
870 qua sit nulla fides saxum monstrantibus illud;
atque erit Aegyptos populis fortasse nepotum
tam mendax Magni tumulo quam Creta Tonantis.

and to Thebes, unwetted even when the rain-bearing Pleiads set, in order
to behold the Nile; what man, who seeks the waters of the Red Sea or
the ports of Arabia to traffic in Eastern wares, whom that gravestone, and
those ashes, perhaps disturbed and lying on the surface of the sand, will
not call aside to worship,and bid him appease the spirit of Magnus, and
give it the preference over Casian Jupiter? That grave will never mar his
fame; the dead would be less precious if buried in temples and gold.
Fortune, lying in this tomb, is now at last a supreme deity; prouder than
all Caesar's altars is the sea-beaten stone on the shore of Africa. Many,
who deny to the deities of the Tarpeian Capitol the incense which is
their due, worship the thunderbolt fenced in by the augur's turf. One
day it will prove a gain that no lofty pile of massive marble was raised
here to last for ever. For a short space of time will scatter the little heap
of dust; and the grave will fall in; and all proof of Pompey's death will
be lost. A happier age will come, when those who point out that stone
will be disbelieved, and perhaps our numerous descendants will consider
Egypt as false in her tale of Pompey's tomb as Crete when she claims the
tomb of Jupiter.

COMMENTARY

INTRODUCTION TO LINES 1-108

The eighth book of Lucan's *Pharsalia* opens with beaten Pompey in full flight from the battlefield; terrified and disgraced he seeks his wife, Cornelia, who is safe but equally apprehensive in Lesbos. To discover how Lucan builds up his scenes so as to make an emotional impact, a comparison with Plutarch's account of the same period in Pompey's career is illuminating. For Plutarch too dwells upon the romantic and tragic aspects of the lives he records, but drama is not on the whole his concern. His discursive biographies are founded upon the anecdote, moral and exemplary. His account of Pompey's flight begins at section 73 of the biography. Some friends accompany Pompey, with whom he discusses Fortune's blows; from Tempe they set sail in a river craft. Met by one Peticius, whose premonitory dream is described, Pompey and his companions sail on to Lesbos in a larger boat; Plutarch tells a story about Favorinus's devotion to his fallen commander. Of particular interest is the account of the meeting of husband and wife at 74: a messenger rushes up to Cornelia, and she faints at his tearful report. She pulls herself together, runs down to the beach, and immediately addresses her husband with self-reproaches. To cheer her, Pompey reflects upon mutability in human affairs (75). Plutarch's prose is unimpassioned, taking its tone from the first words of the account: 'Pompey departed calmly, in conversation'.

Lucan's approach is markedly different. Though he had allowed Pompey a stoic unconcern at the close of the seventh book (647-97), the eighth opens with his sense of personal danger ('lateri timentem' 7); Guyetus, a seventeenth century French scholar, noted this inconsistency and suggested that it was due to a reminiscence of the close of the second book of the *Aeneid*, in which the fears of Aeneas as he flees Troy are described. This is very likely, and Lucan's hasty composition must also be taken into account. But it is more important that there should be unity of emotional tone at the beginning of a single book: though apart, Pompey and Cornelia are alike terrified. This emotional sympathy between husband and wife is more important to Lucan than consistency between books. Moreover Lucan, like all rhetorical poets,

81

was interested in pathetic states, not in characterisation, as has already been noticed. He seeks a rhetorical propriety, and that is his peculiar excellence: he sustains it wonderfully. His account is uncluttered compared to Plutarch's: no Peticius, no Favorinus, no messenger, no mention even of Pompey's son, Sextus, as being on Lesbos. The focus is narrowed to two, husband and wife.

Such a technique of isolation is found in the work of another, and greater, baroque poet, Racine. The following appreciation of his method is from E. Auerbach's *Mimesis* (330): 'The tragic personage is always in sublime posture, in the foreground, surrounded by utensils, retinue, people, landscape, universe, as by so many trophies of victory which serve it or are at its disposal. In this posture the tragic personage abandons itself to its princely passions. And the most impressive stylistic effects of this sort are those in which whole countries, continents, or the universe appear as spectator, witness, background, or echo of the princely emotion.' That Lucan strives for just this sort of exalted isolation is clear from such passages as the mustering of Pompey's troops at 3.169f: 'interea *totum* Magni fortuna per *orbem*/secum casuras in proelia mouerat urbes.', or this from 2.632f: 'mundi iubeo temptare recessus:/ Euphraten Nilumque moue.', or in epigrams like 'felix qui potuit mundi nutante ruina/ quo iaceat iam scire loco.' at 4.393f. This impulse towards the magnificent, which was touched upon in the Introduction, prompts, for example, Rome's address to Caesar in the first book (186-92) or even Lucan's eulogy of Nero at 1.33-66.

The use of minor characters as mere props for the great is constant throughout ancient poetry, but Lucan tends to dispense even with these props, so intense is his concentration on the main figures. In this section, for example, there are unnamed companions (6), and unspecified *multi* (14), who are no more than excuses for elaborating Pompey's fears and for impressing upon us the shock of his defeat. There are also some functional maidservants at 63, whose grief is but an echo of Cornelia's. Finally at 106 an audience is implied by *cunctorum* that goes beyond Cornelia and her women, but it is not identified (unless it is prospective of what follows). Even more isolating is Lucan's use of what amounts to interior monologue at 19-27. He has designed a method of focussing not only upon the protagonist, but even upon unuttered reflection.

To return to the course of the narrative. Since Lucan's concern is with the depiction of emotional states, narration of events is less to his purpose. This is most noticeable in the seventh book, in which surprisingly little time is spent describing the battle of Pharsalia; the focus is rather on the feelings of the troops and of their leaders, and upon the emotional trauma of civil war. So in this book, Pompey's emotions are described, and his flight is woven into that description; thus the poet's moral reflection at 27-32 is hardly an interruption of a non-existent narrative flow.

Narrative is more or less found at 33-42, but even there the main interest is on the paradoxical notion that a leader whose fleets still ride the sea must slip into an unsafe dingy. Lucan ignores Pompey's voyage, but, at the mention of Lesbos, he turns to address Cornelia in her fearful watching. It is a brilliant stroke to have refrained from describing Pompey's appearance until the very moment when his wife sees him; so the reader sees him with his wife's eyes. Cornelia's faint is now more dramatic than in Plutarch, and it is her own husband who revives her and steels her to patience.

1-5   The articulation of the opening sentence deserves scrutiny. (Its heavy reliance upon participles was noticed in the Introduction, p. 19). The first line is an adverbial phrase in which the nouns and their epithets form the pattern a A b B. The second line however offers the 'golden' pattern a b B A; it is a participial phrase dependent upon the as yet unexpressed subject. The third line gives us the object, *cornipedem,* of a participle, *agens,* which occurs in the fourth line; *cornipedem* is itself defined by two nouns and participles chiastically disposed. Only in the fourth line do the subject and main verb appear; *turbat* has two objects, *uestigia* and *uias,* each of which is qualified. Such rambling construction of the first sentence will also be found in books 1, 3, 7, and 10. It is not haphazard, but it looks flaccid, though each line is carefully ordered.

1   **nemorosa** is no mere ornament, for a wood confuses pursuit (cf. 2.468 'qua siluae . . . fugit'). Though the fabled attraction of Tempe is in contrast to Pompey's condition, the wood has its sinister side (cf. 5f).
que is not really additive but points to a sort of hendiadys, as Housman observed in his note to 9.6; cf. below 541, 593, 655.

2   **dispendia**: the word is uncommon; it is the antonym of *compendium* 'short cut'.

3   **cornipedem**: after Seneca, the word is commonly found as a noun; it is typical of the high style. For such 'kennings' see Hollis on Ov. *Met.* 8.376, and 872 below.
negantem 'resists', looks like a reminiscence of Hor. *Serm.* 2.7.94 'subiectat lasso stimulos uersatque negantem'. The sense of the word is common in Statius, who owes it to Lucan (cf. Vollmer on *Siluae* 3.1.123).

4   **incerta** and **inplicitas** are predicates. Tacitus borrowed 'incerta fugae uestigia' at *Agr.* 38.3; he owes numerous phrases to Lucan, who is given honourable mention by Aper at *Dial.* 20.5, where he is ranked with Horace and Virgil as a source for the orator of 'poeticus decor'. Cf. A.W. Lintott in *CQ* 21. 1971. 504.

6   For fears exaggerated by wind-blown bushes see Nisbet-Hubbard on Hor. *Carm.* 1.23.4. *Nemora* means 'trees', as at 5.551, on the analogy of *siluae* (cf. 1.142, 3.409 and Baehrens on Catull. 4.10).

7   **post terga redit** seems to be an idiom meaning 'to be in flight', and so it should

apply to those who abandoned the field after Pompey and later joined him; but some see an allusion to scouts, sent on ahead, who return from behind. Lucan himself probably had no clear picture. (See Langen on V. Fl. 3.478 and Heitland in *CR* 11.1897.206f.)

8   **exanimat** is well positioned at the end of its sentence, but at the beginning of a line, to increase its force. The sentence as a whole is ringed by verbs, Pompey being the subject of the first and object of the second.

    summo de culmine: the image, as at 5.250f, is of a statue on a column, the sort of thing a Roman saw daily in the Forum. But the usage, as 702 below shows, was by this time wholly metaphorical.

9   **facinus** PU, **pretium** VG: Housman demonstrated that *facinus* satisfied the sense of the line, and to his examples may be added Livy 2.30.15 and Ov. *Her.* 14.82 (cf. Heinsius 132). *Facinus*, which was the preferred reading of Bentley, is choicer than *pretium,* since it is less easy to understand at a glance; the more obvious word may also be due to a scribe's recollection of Ov. *Her.* 18.163 'pretium non uile'.

10   **memor fati** has been variously translated so as to refer to Pompey's own fate. But its meaning is more general, 'mindful of Fate's power', e.g., to throw a man down and then raise him up again. Caesar can only be sure that fate does not mean to restore Pompey, if he is dead. And Pompey regards Pharsalia as no more than a setback (cf. 266f).

11   **iugulum** 'slaughter', a sense due to Lucan (*OLD* s.v. 3).

12   **ceruice:** at the very beginning of the book, the theme of decapitation is set before the reader. Lucan uses indifferently *ceruix, colla* or *ora* to mean 'head', doubtless for metrical facility; so too Greek poets (cf. Dodds on Eur. *Ba.* 241). **deserta,** here used as a noun, echoes the adjective in 2 and so marks the resumption of the narrative.

    sequentem: the meaning 'make for' is common; cf. Munro on Lucr. 1. 156, Palmer on Ov. *Her.* 7.10, Langen on V. Fl. 1.3, and Housman on Manil. 4.880; but failure to see this led Nutting to misunderstand 1.328 in U. Cal. Publ. Class. Phil. 11. 1934. 305-7, and Nisard to fault 9.4.

13   **tutis** is a constant epithet of *latebris* (v. Leo 2, n. 6). **fatum** 'disaster'; in Lucan's hands the word has a wide range of nuance, which is well discussed by Heitland, cii-ciii.

14   **uiri** is little more than a means of avoiding the pronoun *is,* which Lucan allows only five times; *dux* is another such stopgap. See Mackail on *Aen.* 1.91 and Lejay on Hor. *Serm.* 2.3.279.

    facies is kept for a position of prominence in its sentence. Pompey's face and head become a matter for the poet's passionate reflection at 684-91, and his emphasis on it now prepares the reader for the book's climax.

multi may refer to gradually arriving reinforcements. But they may have been local deputations or even sightseers, such as picnicked at Bull Run; Lucan does not care to be specific, for these folk are mere witnesses of Pompey's fall.

Pharsalica castra: for a general discussion of the supposed inelegance of the repeated syllable *ca* see 844n. The present instance is an example of cacemphaton, regularly faulted by the ancient grammarians, removed by editors (Bentley here), and ignored by pure-minded poets (v. *Aen.* 2.27 and Prop. 4.6.34; see Ritter in *RM* 3. 1835. 576).

15 **nondum fama prodente ruinas**: cf. Tac. *Hist.* 2.46 'maesta primum fama, dein profugi a proelio perditas res patefaciunt'.

16 **occursu Ω, occursum V**: *stupeo* is found at 6.760, but without an object; its use as a transitive verb is not impossible (v. Austin on *Aen.* 2.31 and add V. Fl. 4.549). Editors however favour the majority reading which is supported by Claud. *Bel. Got.* 373 'ducis adspectu cuncti stupuere'.

20 **urbes Ω, orbem PU**: the difference in number shows that these are true variants, and not casual errors as at 2.61 or Manil. 4.512. *Urbes* is, on the face of it, unattractive, just because Pompey is now at pains to avoid the beaten track, though he did pass through Larissa (7.712). *Orbem* would be unexceptionable, and characteristic of Lucan's magniloquence (cf. 138). But *urbes* is not only used to mean built-up towns, but can stand for peoples or countries, as Housman demonstrated in his note to Manil. 4.734; so in Greek, Hesychius glosses χώραν as πόλιν. Housman's view is supported by Hor. *Carm.* 2.20.5 (*urbis* 'the civilized habitations of men', Nisbet-Hubbard) and Ov. *Met.* 1.749f; at 3.170 above Rowe and Duff translate the word as 'nations'. In the present context this sense is also recommended by the parallel structure of the sentence: *ignotus* is picked up by *obscuro nomine*, and *gentibus* will be answered by *urbes*.

21 **longi . . fauoris** is a descriptive genitive; its use with proper names is rare before Nepos, Livy, Valerius Maximus and Pliny (LHS 69f). But Ovid set the seal of his authority upon the usage in poetry at *Am.* 1.15.19 'animosi Accius oris', and, in a higher genre, at *Met.* 11.351 'trepidi Trachinius oris'; cf. 7.541 'extremi orbis Hiberi' (there is no need to take *extremi* as nominative) and in this book 158, 223, 245, and 676n. Fortune's constant favour towards Pompey is a theme picked up from 7.705 'longo fatorum . . . fauori', and it will be developed at 701f below.

The line ends alliteratively: nothing could be more Latin in tone, as the following fragments of Cicero's poetry show. Fr. 2 'dulcia dicens', fr. 11.18 'lumine luna', and 24 'lumina liquit', fr. 23 'uestigia uitans', fr. 26 'laeta locabit'. It is one of Lucan's favourite devices, and it gives his verse its peculiar power.

24 **festinatos nimium . . . honores** refers both to the consulship of 70 B.C., which Pompey, at 36 years of age, was not yet entitled to hold (cf. Manil. 1.794 'ante diem princeps'), and to his triumph over the Marians (the year is doubtful, v. E. Badian, *Hermes* 83. 1955. 107ff).
sentit often has the sense 'feel to one's cost' (Page on Hor. *Carm.* 2.7.10), so there is no need to regard *festinatos* as predicate.

24-7 The sentence 'nunc . . . piget' forms a tricolon crescendo. Each line is neatly constructed but the whole has not gelled. There is a failure to use enjambement, and 25, which breaks the anaphora of *nunc*, is not integrated into its context.

25 **Sullana** defines both the time and the character of the *acta*, hence its effectiveness. Adjectives formed from proper nouns often have a sense other than possessive; they can be temporal, or locatival, or passive. For example, at 1.106 'Parthica damna' are 'losses inflicted by Parthia', at 1.581 'Sullani manes' are 'those slain by Sulla' (not, as Duff takes it, 'the ghost of Sulla'), at 5.703f 'Hesperii duces' are 'the generals in Italy', at 7.304 'Caesareae cruces' are 'crosses meant for Caesar and his followers', and at 92 below 'Assyrios casus' is 'the Roman disaster at Carrhae'. Lucan is free in his use of these adjectives but he is not alone; in Pindar *Pyth.* 4.9f τὸ ἔπος Θήραιον means 'the prophecy uttered at Thera', at *Aen.* 1.665 'tela Typhoea' are 'the weapons that slew Typhoeus', and in Caesar *B.G.* 7.47.7 'Auaricensibus praemiis' are 'the rewards promised at Avaricum'.

26 **Corycias classes** refers to Pompey's ridding the seas of pirates in about three months (a success that endured until late antiquity), and **Pontica signa** alludes to the defeat of Mithridates on land; these together made up Pompey's third triumph of 61 BC. Lucan combines a land victory with a sea victory to form what is sometimes called 'polar expression', in which a comprehensive term, e.g. 'everywhere', is analysed into two complementary but exclusive terms, e.g. 'on land and on sea'. It is however more exact to call this 'universalising doublet' — a term coined by E.L. Bundy in U. Cal. Publ. Class. Phil. 18.1962. 24, n. 56 — because all-inclusiveness is essential to the notion.

27 **longius aeuum** 'too long a life'; Livy recognised this: 'Cyrum . . . quid nisi longa uita sicut Magnum modo Pompeium uertenti praebuit fortunae?' (9.17. 6), and Juvenal in his tenth satire placed Pompey among those who should deter us from praying for length of days (10.283-6).

28 **ingentes animos**, a Virgilian phrase, is here used generally, but at 7.679 of Pompey himself. As Getty observed on 1.186 *ingens* has a pathetic sense of 'great in adversity'; so it is used of the senators at 266 below.

28-9 **uita superstes imperio** is a sentiment found also in Livy, 'superstes gloriae suae' (2.7.8); the conceit passes on to Pliny, *Ep.* 2.1.2, 'gloriae suae superuixit' and then to Florus 2.13.51 'superstes dignitatis suae' (said of Pompey), and down to Gibbon, who says that Gratian survived his reputation.

29 **fine bonorum** also described Pompey's condition at 7.19.

30 **adfuit** is a gnomic perfect; the development of the use of this tense is set out by Madvig in his *Opuscula Academica* (1887), 491f. The sentiment is found in Curtius applied to Alexander: 'uitae quoque finem eundem illi quem gloriae statuit (Fortuna)', 10.5.36. These lines were once among the best known from Lucan and they are often quoted by Jeremy Taylor in *Holy Dying.*

31 **dedecori** is a predicative dative.

fortuna prior was used of Pompey at 1.134f.

31-2 Lucan closes the opening section with a rhetorical question, just as at 5.12f. The device is meant to give directness and vigour to speech; both Quintilian and Longinus use the figure to begin their discussion of it (cf. *I.O.* 9.2.6-16 and *De Subl.* 18).

It should be observed how little action has been described in these thirty-odd lines. Lucan's interest is not Pompey's journey to the sea, so much as his state of mind, his fears, hopes and gnawing sense of shame. Mingled with this are the poet's own moralising reflections upon the unreliability of Fortune; the comm. Bern. rightly compared Ov. *Met.* 3.135-7.

33 **Peneius amnis:** the epithet is not possessive, but appositive, as Housman called it in his note to Manil. 5.557, where he compared Ov. *Pont.* 4.10.53 'Borysthenio . . . amne'; 'collis . . . Heliconii' at Catull. 61.1 is another example.

34 **clade rubens:** rivers red with the blood of soldiers are a commonplace of the poets; v. de Jongh on Ov. *Tr.* 4.2.42.

36 **flumineis . . . altum:** contrast is enhanced by ringing the line with those words that express difference of kind or quality: so at 1.260 'rura . . . pontus', 2.116 'degener . . . decorum', 2.233 'praeteriti . . . futuri', 3.140, 4.606 'aruorum . . . aequor', 6.401 'terrenum . . . undas', and in this book 158 and 515 below. The device is of course found in other poets: Pl. *Most.* 509 'uiuum . . . mortui', Lucr. 1.457 'aduentu . . . abituque', *Aen.* 8.485 'mortua . . . 'uiuis', Hor. *Carm.* 4.5.39 'sicci . . . uuidi' and *Ep.* 1.5.20 'contracta . . . solutum'. In a number of these examples the lines are not end-stopped and the sense flows over from the previous line and continues into the next; and yet the opposition between the first and las word of the single line is felt and exploited for rhetorical effect. Cf. Hübner 587.

37-9 The contrast was not lost on Plutarch (74): 'he who had sailed about this sea with five hundred ships was flung upon a single skiff'. Florus, who of course had read Lucan, describes Pompey's flight from Brundisium in similar terms:

'turpe dictu modo princeps patrum . . . per triumphatum a se mare lacera . . . naui fugiebat', 2.13.20. But whereas Plutarch and Florus rather obviously contrast past with present, Lucan, in a pathetic paradox, stresses that Pompey is *still* lord of the sea (for all the good it does him).

37 **Corcyra**, an island, must here mean the waters around it.

38 **Cilicum dominus:** Cilicia had been the chief haven of the pirates whom Pompey swept from the seas in 67 BC (cf. 26n). If Pompey indeed settled some of these pirates in Calabria, as Servius says in his note to Vir. *Geor.* 4.127, then he is their 'lord' in the further sense of patron.

39 **exiguam . . . alnum:** for a general discussion of encompassing, or bracketing, word order in Latin poetry see T.V. Pearce in *CQ* 16. 1966. 140-71. Caspari (83ff) noted Lucan's fondness for the pattern in the early books, especially the first three, and its near absence from the truncated tenth. In this book it does not appear to be so uncommon. The smallness of the ship is frequently mentioned for pathetic effect (at 258, 565, and cf. Florus 2.13.51). But Plutarch says that Pompey went to Lesbos in a good-sized merchantman (74). *Alnus* 'ship', is an innovation of Lucan's, but a natural development from Vir. *Geor.* 2.451 'undam . . . innatat alnus'.

uector is in strong contrast with *dominus.*

pauidus, along with *trepidum* 35, keeps up the emotional state as described in 5-7; it helps to form a thematic link with the description of Cornelia at 44.

40-62 In this section Lucan has before his eyes the model of Ovid's Ceyx and Alcyone of *Met.* 11.710-28; v. R.T. Bruère in *CP* 46. 1951. 221. Lucan aims at a more passionate account of a watching wife; he uses apostrophe and alliteration, and even the tricolon crescendo (56f) to raise the emotional temperature. Ovid's treatment was not unsympathetic, as Brooks Otis has argued, *Ovid as an Epic Poet* (ed. 2, 1970), 275, but the smoothness of his narrative lacks the seemingly personal involvement of Lucan's long address to Cornelia. (And as usual Ovid intrudes with his own jokes and word plays, which tend to make the story less immediate.) But in the last analysis Ovid may have been cannier; he does not claim to wish to move us, but to entertain us (not so easy a task, after all). But Lucan does want to impel his reader in a certain direction, as he most plainly admits at 7.207-13, where he lays claim to a vividness that must shatter the reader and make him a Pompeian. To do this Lucan pulls out all the rhetorical stops and often ends in frigidity (for example, at 589 below).

40 **conscia . . . litora:** the inhabitants of the island are probably at the back of Lucan's mind, but we need not hesitate to see some degree of personification as at 5.461f 'prima duces uidit . . . tellus', and 197 below. The meeting of husband and wife was hinted at in the last line of the fifth book, 'instabat miserae,

Magnum quae redderet, hora'.

secretae P, -a Ω: the majority reading is unexceptionable, because *secreta* would be an attributive epithet, while *conscia* is predicative; moreover, *secreta litora* is almost a standing phrase (v. Ollfors 1.121). But *secretae*, which Bentley conjectured before P's reading was known, is to be preferred. The number and case of epithets are often changed by scribes to make them agree with the nearest noun; at 7, for example, one Ms records as a variant *trepido* for *trepidum*. So in this line the presence of *conscia* and *litora* work against the preservation of *secretae*. (And if *secreta* were the original reading, it may be asked why a scribe should alter it to the less obvious *secretae*.) The elision of *ae*, which must always be regarded as a special case, is supported by 74 below (v. Leo, *Plautinische Forschungen* (ed. 2, 1912), 334-60).

41   **iubet**, without an object as at 2.632 (v. *TLL* 7.2, 577. 64ff).

43   **stares** implies defeat, but the victor sits, as Postgate observed; cf. 440f.

43-5   The first half of the sentence, as far as *habet*, forms a tricolon, with pleasing variety in the number and voice of the three verbs. *Omnis* in the last clause points to a partial close; v. 734n.

44   The jumpy dactylic rhythm of the line underscores the sense. *Exagitant* looks back to *exanimat* 8 in sound, shape and position, while *trepida* recalls 35; such echoes suggest the sympathy of husband and wife.

45   **Thessaliam**: 'thought of the battle in Thessaly, i.e. Pharsalia'. Latin poets often use the simple noun where English prose requires the fuller expression, 'the thought of . . .'; so at *Aen.* 2.562 'subiit deserta Creusa'. Cf. 285-6n. Since Pharsalia is in Thessaly, Lucan uses both words to designate the battle; so in English we speak of Waterloo alone, to mean the battle fought there (cf. *Leucada* 5.479 and 510 below). The sense of *habet* is hard to define: 'dwells on' Haskins, 'is filled with' Postgate, 'present' Riley; Lucan may be here at fault for the imprecision.

46   **rupis . . . abruptae** is an example of etymological word play beloved of the poets. One of the earliest Latin epitaphs, 'sepulchrum hau pulchrum pulchrai feminae' CIL 1.1007, in which *se-* was probably reckoned to be the equivalent of *sine,* shows the figure's influence (v. Lejay, *Histoire* (1922), 137). 'Mere poetical assonance', as Munro calls it at Lucr. 1.826, does not do justice to such examples as 2.134 'cecidere cadauera' or 4.373 'uires rediere uiris'. For 'rupis . . . scopulos' cf. 4.452 and Eur. *Ion* 274.

46-7   Duff follows Postgate in regarding *que* as unnecessary, at most a sign of hendiadys 'to the peak of a steep cliff at the shore's edge'. This is reasonable, but does not take into account the agility of heroines. Ariadne in Catull. 64. 126-8 mounts a rock to gaze after Theseus, and then she runs into the surf, perhaps to pursue him

When Ovid wrote Phyllis's letter to Demophoon he recalled this, and had her climb rocks and wade into the breakers for a view of the sea: 'scopulos fruticosaque litora calco,/ quaque patent oculis aequora lata meis/ . . . prospicio' (*Her.* 2.121ff); he clarifies this action a bit further on, 124-30, where *prospicio* answers to *prospiciens* here, and 'qua primas porrigit aequor aquas' is Lucan's *extrema litora.* So Phyllis is to be pictured as gazing out to sea either from a crag or from the beach, and, upon sighting a ship, she wades into the surf. This latter passage influenced Lucan; his Cornelia is sometimes on a rock as at 5.780, sometimes on the beach; *que* has a slightly disjunctive force, 'or'.

48   **prima uides**, simply as a phrase, recalls Ov. *Her.* 5.63. The triple alliteration in the middle of the line is noteworthy; it is also found at 2.253, 559, 3.297, 620, 660; 6.180; 7.44, 704.

49   The sentiment of this line is attractive (cf. 591). That Lucan had some psychological subtlety is charmingly shown at 2.348f, where Cato's wife, Marcia, resents Cornelia's being allowed to accompany Pompey to war.

50   **uestros** refers to Cornelia and the Mytilenaeans. Although *uester* can be used for *tuus*, as Housman showed in *CQ* 3.1909,244-8 = *Papers* 2.790-4, such an interpretation would hardly be suitable here (cf. Postgate in *Hermathena* 18.1914-19.91-8, esp. 94). Bentley gave the correct punctuation of the line in one of his copies of Lucan, now kept in the British Library.

51-2 'only evil news of the war . . . ': in both Greek and Latin the notion 'only' need not be expressed in cases where English requires it. Examples are numerous: *Il.* 8.228, Ter. *Ph.* 184, *Haut.* 228, Caes. *B.G.* 1.33.4 ('only the Rhone'), Catull. 44.21, Vir. *Geor.* 1.192. There are useful discussions by Nipperdey-Andresen on Tac. *Ann.* 13.3., Camps on Prop. 3.2.26, Kenney on Lucr. 3.144, and Summers on Sen. *Ep.* 15.2. Duff's translation of Lucan is especially good at noticing this ellipse.

52   **rumorque sinister**: for unreliable bad news from the front as a wife's daily food see Aesch. *Ag.* 864-76 and Prop. 3.12.9ff 'illa quidem interea fama tabescit inani . . . '

53   **perdis tempora**, faulted by Heitland (lxxx), is nevertheless a good Ciceronian usage (cf. *De Or.* 3.146), found also in Ovid at *A.A.* 1.504. Apology, however, is unnecessary, for language cannot be expected to stand still.

54-5 As at 61f the final alliteration carries over into the next line.

55   **crimen deum**: for Pompey's condition as a reproach to heaven see 800n. **notauit** = *conspexit*, an Ovidian usage (Langen on V. Fl. 2.312).

56-7 This description is dramatically delayed until Cornelia herself can make out that what she sees is Pompey. Only then do we too see him, and still through her eyes. She first notices his face, and then his clothes, which is the natural order. But the description remains purely physical. We may compare the meeting of Achaemenides and the Trojans at *Aen.* 3.590-5. There too a human wreck is vividly described (by Aeneas), but *miseranda* at 591 immediately goes beyond the physical sight and points to the emotional response of the viewer. Lucan's *crudele* at 55 is not on the same level of sympathy. He prefers to shock with the picture of a great man in rags. The description is a tricolon.

56 **deformem pallore ducem**: soldiers are tanned, so this is the pallor of fear, disgraceful in a general.

57 **canities** is meant to make a pathetic appeal. Pompey was in fact fifty-eight, and about four years older than Caesar, but Lucan likes to make him out to be much older and so more pitiable.

atro: that dust (but after a sea voyage?) should be dark is not in itself remarkable (cf. *Aen.* 9.33), but here the addition of the epithet is prompted by a desire to point up the contrast with the whiteness of his hair. We may compare 2.220 'sanguine caeruleum torrenti diuidit aequor' with Eur. *Herc. Fur.* 573 'Dirce's white stream shall be bloodied', and 1.243f 'nigrae morsu robiginis enses . . . fulsere aquilae' with *Othello* I.2.59 'Keep up your *bright* swords for the dew will *rust* them'; so too 9.843f and Getty's defense of *nigrum* at 1.615. For a general discussion see Norden 395f.

58 **nox** 'unconsciousness'; v. *OLD* sv 6a.

59 **animam** G, **-um** Ω: the masculine is not correct in the light of 4.370 'clausitque animam' of a draught of water, and of Ov. *Met.* 7.604 'animam laqueo claudunt'.

60 **riguerunt corda**: the perfect tense describes instantaneous effect as at *Aen.* 1.84 'incubuere mari', and in Lucan at 1.246 and 9.289; metrical convenience moreover contributes to the use of the tense. *Corda*, used of one person, is apparently found for the first time in Lucr. 6.14.

61 **spe mortis**: Lucan uses similar turns of phrase very elliptically; at 5.130 'spes ueri' is 'hope of learning the truth' and at 7.270 'spem mundi' is 'the world you hope to win'. The genitive is therefore objective.

62 **litoribus** is ablative as at 7.860.

uacuas: the adjective is constantly attached to *harena* or *litus*, for the ancients tended to find beaches less agreeable than we do; they were seen as little deserts, fit for cremations (cf. 743f), and not as resorts (the sea coast is another matter). As an 'epitheton constans' therefore *uacuas* is almost colourless, and there is no justification for seeing in it either a reference to lack of defense (cf. 'uacuo mari', Tac. *Hist.* 3.47), or to the absence of a welcoming party as comm. Bern. took it.

64 The sentiment of the line looks to the commonplace of silent complaint against a tyrant or taskmaster, here Fate; cf. 1.257-9 and 2.20 with adn.'s note; Sen.

Suas. 6.4; *Oct.* 511f; St. *Th.* 1.169; Tac. *Ann.* 13.16.7; Aesch. *Ag.* 449.
tacitos 'stifled' as at 1.247 (cf. Heinsius 505).

65   **permisere sibi** sounds a note of Stoic self-restraint.

66   **eram:** Virgil once admits *erus* into the *Aeneid* at 3.324, and there the every-
     day word is specially employed to express the force of Andromache's contempt
     (cf. Williams (1962) ad loc.). Ovid, when he uses the same word at *Met.* 8.853,
     also maintains the word's force and stresses the depravity of Erysichthon in
     selling his daughter, Mestra, to successive bidders, who thus become her *eri.*
     The word is also found sparingly in the *Heroides,* where the genre is a consider-
     ation. Seneca allows *era* in tragedy, perhaps on Ennius's authority, in addresses
     of servant to mistress (e.g., *Med.* 426, *Ph.* 267, 733). Thus *erus* and *era* can be
     said to have a place in the higher genres, but careful writers have preserved the
     words' nuance. Here there is no particular reason for *eram,* and it is probably
     no more than metrical convenience that has suggested its use.
     quam = *at illam;* so at 3.730 *qui* is *et ille,* and cf. 4.466, 6.250, 7.764 and 845,
     9.911.

66-7 **pectore ambit** is a bold phrase for 'embrace', illustrated by Ollfors (2.29) with
     similar uses at 4.648f, Petr. 91.9, and V. Fl. 1.762.
     refouet: the whole action clearly looks back to Anna's embracing Dido at *Aen.*
     4.686, 'semianimemque sinu germanam amplexa fouebat', and with it is ming-
     led recollection of Ov. *Met.* 10.186f, 'excipit artus . . . te refouet', in which
     Apollo holds Hyacinth.

68   **coeperat:** the subject is Cornelia, but Lucan is inclined to change subject un-
     expectedly; so at 3.713f Tyrrhenus is the subject, though he has only just been
     named as object in the previous sentence. Virgil too could make an unannounc-
     ed shift of subject, as Pease illustrates on *Aen.* 4.532; but Lucan does it very
     often and sometimes obscurely, as at 167 *consulit.*
     in summum reuocato sanguine corpus: 'loss' of blood was regarded as the cause
     of fainting; cf. Ov. *Her.* 3.60 'sanguinis atque animi pectus inane fuit' and *A.A.*
     1.540 'nullus in exanimi corpore sanguis erat'. Chafing the limbs was therefore
     the remedy recommended by Celsus, *De Med.* 3.26. *Summum* means 'at the
     surface' and the phrase recalls Ov. *Met.* 2.235 'sanguine . . . in corpora summa
     uocato'.

70-85 Heitland trenchantly called this speech abominable, lxiv n.14, and it is unlikely
     to fall upon sympathetic ears nowadays. But to do the sentiments it expresses
     justice, it should be observed that they suit the context, and, more importantly,
     they illustrate the poet's concern for noble passion. In the first place Pompey's
     admonition, that mourning be reserved for his death, is prospective of the action
     of the book, and so it is an example of anticipation (12n and 712n). Secondly,

the reference to his death and to Cornelia's love for him more naturally prompts her reply than does the speech which, for example, Plutarch puts in his mouth at 75. Albeit the modern reader is unmoved by Pompey's appeal, is it fair to find the address in 74, or the social attitude that lies behind *deformis* in 81 repulsive? It was noted above that Racine too sought a high emotional isolation for his personages to brood within, and that the nobility, as portrayed by both poets, are ever conscious of and so identify themselves with their rank, the claims of which are paramount (cf. Auerbach 331 and Introduction 23). A review of a few other passages will make Lucan's attitude plain. At 5.343 Caesar thus rebukes his rebellious troops: 'humanum paucis uiuit genus', and at 538f a plebeian cloak is said to be unable to conceal his native pride. At 6.376-80 the river Titaressos scorns to mix his noble Stygian waters with the less well-born Peneus (and a similar but joking conceit will be found in Cic. *De Leg.* 2.6). In a finely expressed paradox Lucan says that the basilisk, whose Greek name means 'princeling', knows his station: 'in uacua regnat basiliscus harena', 9.726. Back amid the human race, more or less, the witch Erichtho is charmed as much by the nobility as by the number of anticipated corpses (6.584-6), and especially in the seventh book the gulf between nobles and commoners is stressed, e.g., at 598 and 760-2 (cf. Servius on *Aen.* 11.3 'est haec consuetudo apud poetas ut a plebe segregent duces'). And finally in this book, at 736, Pompey's *plebeium funus* is a pathetic insult to the man. In short the modern reader is again confronted with an aspect of baroque sensibility (cf. 207-9n). We are here reading the literature of a noble society, from which effective power had been withdrawn to be bestowed upon upstarts of various classes. (But Lucan's own family, it is worth noting, had only recently been ennobled.) The well-born therefore placed compensatory weight upon inherited rank. Very relevant to this passage is the speech of Cornelia at 5.764f, just before she is shipped off to Lesbos: 'sorte frequenti / plebeiaque nimis careo dimissa marito'. She loves Pompey, but one consideration as important to her as affection is the vulgar disgrace of this seeming divorce. Thus that Pompey's attempt to console his wife here should begin with a reminder of her station and ancestry — 'proles tam clara Metelli', 410 — is, for the age in which the poem was written, both natural and appropriate. He appeals to her not to act *infra dignitatem.*

71   **inmodicos** explains why Pompey may be said to rebuke his wife; her grief has passed reasonable bounds (and yet all Lucan has described is her fainting). Pompey's address is in accordance with a Platonic injunction to refrain from excessive expressions of joy or sorrow and to behave in a decorous manner amid grief, *Leg.* 5.732c. Pompey's *deformis* and Plato's εὐσχημονεῖν are both

93

an appeal to good manners.

uoce is a pleonasm common in all levels of Latin; see Löfstedt 2.185. Ignorance of this led to the following comment of Arnulph, a commentator of the late twelfth century: 'uoce, non uerbere, sicut quidam non uxorii'.

72   It was the practice of Greek poets who used the dactylic hexameter to begin and end speeches with complete lines. A number of Lucan's speeches, including this one, conform to the practice, but no pattern emerges. But for Virgil's careful variety see Norden 135f.

73   Women are quite as conscious of their lineage as men: 'illustris femina iactat auos', Prop. 2.13.10.

74   **frangis** was explained by Postgate as meaning *frangi sinis*; the idiom is very common: see Housman on 1.103 and 3.485 (both passages had been cited already by Postgate), and *Papers* 41, Dilke on St. *Ach.* 1.6f, Fordyce on Catull. 64.305, Goodyear on *Aetna* 77, Kenney on Lucr. 3.490 and *CR* 27.1977.181, and Fraenkel *Horace* (1957), 215, n. 2.

      aditum 'avenue', governing a genitive, is found first here in poetry, then at St. *Ach.* 2.90; but the construction was well established in Cicero (v. *TLL* 1.701.11-23).

      mansurae in saecula famae sounds the first note of a theme important in this book (it will be discussed in the introductory passage on 577-710). The whole phrase was borrowed by Corippus, a sixth century poet deeply indebted to Lucan, *Ioh.* 8.467.

75-6 Postgate recognised how much Lucan draws upon Ovid in this passage, which is a variation upon *Tr.* 4.3.71-80. There Ovid encourages his own wife to face Fate with courage. Ovid's experience is immediate, Lucan's borrowed.

      laudis . . . unica materia is a good instance of the distributional figure, ἀπὸ κοινοῦ : the words form a single thought yet each member of the sentence is allotted a part of the phrase. Housman expounds the principle in less obvious cases at 9.232f, and especially at 5.680f, where he offers examples of a dependent genitive preceding its governing noun, as here. Plainly *laudis* has been pushed to the head of its sentence and line for emphasis.

      hoc: the sense 'your' is well developed in the Silver age; cf. 5.685 and V. Fl. 1.749, and 7.441 as explained by Leo, *Ausg. kl. Schr.* 2.231f. A representative list may be consulted at *TLL* 6. 2704.35-74, esp. 68-71. The loose but emphatic style of declamation encourages the usage, and leads Lucan once at least into imprecision; at 7.451 *hoc caput* refers to Caesar, but he has not been mentioned.

      sexu appeared for the first time in a higher genre in Seneca's *Oedipus* 53; Lucan introduced it to epic.

cura Markland, **iura** Ω: Housman explained the phrase *legum iura*, which is the reading of all the Mss, as meaning 'ut leges iura sua retineant'; his careful discussion is ignored by *TLL* 7.2, 681.78. But Markland's emendation gives better sense, and the error is common: cf. St. *Th*. 3.351 where ω's *cura* has been replaced by *iura* in ς, and Livy 2.36.6 where M's *cura* is so altered by a third hand; (on the other hand, at 763 below the lemma of comm. Bern. reads INCURIA for *iniuria*, and at Manil. 2.744 *cura* has expelled *iura* from the chief Mss).

legum and **arma** form a concealed doublet (cf. 26n), meaning 'public affairs at home and abroad'; cf. *Cons. ad Liu.* 49f 'nec uires errasse tuas campoue foroue/ quamque libet citra constituisse domum', St. *Silu*. 1.2.267 'qui leges qui castra regant'. A wife's duty is private, and directed toward the home (so Telemachus had told his mother), and her husband.

76 **unica materia** is recalled at CE 2103.9f. The sentiment of the line is something of a commonplace; Summers (13, n.2) cites Sen. *Phoen*. 386, and *Ep*. 66.27, and St. *Th*. 3 705. The famous *Laudatio Turiae*, however, of the final years of the first century B.C. shows that the commonplace was founded on experience. For *materia* 'opportunity' see *OLD* s.v. 8.

erige mentem: for the metaphor see Lejay on Hor. *Serm*. 2.3. 150, and for *mens* with the sense *animus* 331n.

77-8 Cortius well compared Sen. *Herc. Oet*. 359 'amat uel ipsum quod caret patrio lare'.

78 **maior** here and often puns on Pompey's nickname *Magnus*; Lucan likes that name for its metrical convenience and its impressive connotations. But it is worth noting that in his own lifetime, if Cicero's letters are a guide, he was usually called Pompeius. For the pun on the nickname cf. Ov. *Pont*. 4.3.41 'quid fuerat Magno maius?' and the fragment of Livy quoted on 91; Manilius has the same conceit of Alexander at 1.770, 'Magno maxima Pella'.

79-80 The defection is not historically founded, but Lucan wants to stress here Pompey's solitary state amid disaster, and so magnify Cornelia's devotion.

senatus is in apposition to *pia turba*. Unless *pia* is ironical (and it is hard to see how it can be), the phrase has been borrowed with incomplete success from Ov. *Tr*. 5.3.47 'pia turba poetae' (which is itself borrowed from Ovid's master, Propertius, 3.13.18, 'matrum . . . pia turba'). Mme. H. Fugier observes of this expression that it betrays an imperial attitude to the Senate, now seen as a body whose devotion is owed to one man (cf. *Recherches sur l'Expression du Sacré dans la Langue latine* (Paris, 1963), 383). Lucan is clearly setting one woman's devotion against the fickleness of men, hence the emphasis on *sola* in 81, and the contrast between *tua pietas* in 77 with *pia turba*.

80   **discessit**: a verb commonly takes its number from the nearest subject word (cf. for Lucan Oudendorp on 1.422, and Bentley on Hor. *Carm.* 1.24.8). **Magnum**: the rhetorical figure whereby the speaker names himself and uses the third person is called ἔμφασις, though its Latin name, *adfectus*, shows another aspect of its emotional effect (cf. Norden 266 and Introduction 23). Since children and the simple tend to speak of themselves in the third person, this device is at home in pastoral, e.g., Virg. *Ecl.* 9.53f, and it is common in Herodas, a writer of mimes (cf. Kroll on Catull. 6.1). But the grand and self-absorbed figures of the tragic stage also use the figure, notably Sophocles's Ajax and Seneca's Medea; but even Homer had Achilles speak in this fashion at *Il.* 1.240. One historical example is telling; Pollio reported that Julius Caesar had said 'G. Caesar condemnatus essem' (Suet. *D.J.* 30.4). Lucan's Pompey is rather given to the figure. At 81 *marito* is another type of *adfectus*, in which the speaker emphasizes his relationship to the one addressed; cf. *Aen.* 4.478, 9.484-6.

81   **sola** is emphatically placed to stress its contrast with *tanta* in the previous line (see 116f n); initial alliteration enhances this.

82   **uetitus**, a favourite of Lucan's, is a poet's way of saying 'unable' (*nescius* with the infinitive is another); for its construction with the passive infinitive cf. 7.316 'uetita uirtute moueri'.

83-4 **tu . . . meo** are emphatically placed at the beginning and end of the sentence.

84-5 **uiuit . . . perit** also bracket the sentence, and their position at the main caesura of their respective lines, along with the pause before and after each, emphasizes the contrast in sense. Cf. 1.289f, and 706f below.

85   **quod defles illud amasti** is one of Lucan's characteristic *sententiae*: it concludes a passage in only four words, like 'felix se nescit amari' at 7.727 (cf. Bonner 268). By the middle ages it had deservedly achieved proverbial status, and even found its way into Petrarch's *Africa* 1.330 'quod non sumus illud amamus', again a closing *sententia* (cf. Sanford *AJP* 55.1934.4). There seems to be an inherent impressiveness in this concluding cadence of four words; examples are collected by G. Saintsbury in *A Second Scrap Book* (1923), 256, n.1.

86   **uocibus his** is a phrase taken from the small change of epic style; cf. *Aen.* 9.83, Ov. *Met.* 9.674, V. Fl. 1.302 and in Lucan at 7.296, 262 below and 9.215.

87   **gemitu rumpente querellas**: the poetic use of *rumpo* 'break out into' was initiated by Virgil following a Greek idiom (v. Langen on V. Fl. 1.508 and Austin on *Aen.* 2.129). Similar is the passive *rupta uerba* at 5.152f and *rupta*

96

uoce at Tac. *Ann.* 6.20.1.

88 **o utinam** is found in Tibullus but as usual Lucan probably owes it to Ovid (*Her.* 11.21, *Met.* 1.363, 8.501).
in omitted by P. Though Lucan follows Virgil in omitting prepositions with verbs of motion (170n), here its absence in P is accidental, (as also at 315, because it has been swallowed up by the m of *membra*). Such omissions are common: v. Bentley on Hor. *Serm.* 1.2.88 and 2.1.2, Wagner *Quaest. Verg.* 14.4, Clausen in *AJP* 70.1949.311 and 76.1955.52.

89 **infelix coniunx** is no mere rhodomontade, for a widow could be regarded as unlucky, especially the widow of the younger Crassus. Cicero speaks in this way of Fulvia at *Phil.* 2.11, and we may compare Apul. *Ap.* 92.
laeta 'bringing joy to', so Langen on V. Fl. 1.30, but there may be the sense 'propitious' as at 585.

90 **bis nocui mundo** stuck in Petrarch's head, for he recalls it at *Africa* 3.417 'sic nocuit mundo uiuens moriensque Medusa'. In general he sought to avoid direct recollection of classical authors (which is not itself a classical procedure), and he is said to have wept when a friend pointed to a Virgilian tag (but see 85n).
pronuba . . . Erinys: the notion is illustrated copiously by Burman on Ov. *Her.* 2.117 'pronuba Tisiphone'.

91 Comm. Bern. tell us that the sentiment is owed to Livy, bk. 112, now fr. 46 W-M: 'uicit, Magne, felicitatem tuam mea fortuna. quid enim ex funesta Crassorum domo recipiebas nisi ut minueretur magnitudo tua?'. The sentence from *me* to *deos* forms a tricolon crescendo, since the last member is only one thought subdivided into complementary halves – men and gods – for the sake of the doublet (v. 26n).

92 **Assyrios . . . casus**: for the sense see 25n. Assyria is a poet's geography.
ciuilia 'of civil war', see *OLD* s v 2b and 505 below.

94 **causa melior** is a common expression in the context of civil war; so at Sen. *Phoen.* 384, Vell. Pat. 2.49.2 (of Pompey), and Tac. *Hist.* 2.77. Lucan uses this or similar phrases at 2.531, 4.259 (paradoxically of Caesar), and 7.349. He properly looks to the legal sense of the phrase (cf. Cic. *De Or.* 1.44), as well as to its moral connotations. Pompey's cause was vindicated when Augustus 'restored' the old form of the republic. It is worth noting that Velleius Paterculus, who had served under Tiberius and supported the principate, admits in the passage cited above 'alterius ducis (Pompey) causa melior uidebatur'. (That Augustus 'restored' the republic is questioned by F. Millar in *JRS* 63.1973.50-67; he is answered by P.A. Brunt in *PBSR* 43.1975.25,

n.102, who lays the correct emphasis on Velleius's phrase at 2.89.3, 'imperium magistratuum ad pristinum redactum modum . . . prisca illa et antiqua rei publicae forma reuocata.' This last is a sentence that sums up the preceding remarks, not, as punctuated by Millar p. 64, an ablative absolute referring strictly to the increased number of praetors.)

94-5 The interjection *o* is common with the vocative in Greek, but in Latin it is a sign of heightened appeal (KG 1.48, nn.3, 4; LHS 26, n.e).

95-6 **hoc iuris in:** the same construction at 6.496f; it is owed to Ovid, *Am.* 1.1.5.

96 **inpia**, which recalls Pompey's appeal to her *pietas* at 77, economically suggests that Cornelia regards her marriage as itself a breach of faith.

97 **miserum** sc. *te;* Lucan commonly omits the pronoun: 2.495 *me*, 728 *te*, 6.244 *me;* 137 below *uos* and 215 *te.*

98 **sed**, used to mark a corrective addition, is illustrated by Mayor on Juv. 5.147 and in the index to vol. 2, p. 443; for the relative clause cf. Ov. *Met.* 5.381 'sed qua nec acutior ulla'.
mollius of the sea as at *Aen.* 8.726 and Ov. *Her.* 18.88.

98-9 **mollius . . . certa . . . paratior:** in the midst of the comparatives *certa* may retain its force as a positive, but it is also possible that it is lent comparative force by its neighbours, as seems to be the case with *ferus* – which, however, has no comparative – between *maior* and *inmanior* at 1.479f; Vollmer, in a dubious note to St. *Silu.* 2.2.153, cites *Th.* 3.454.

99 **certa fides regum** anticipates the treachery of Ptolemy, and the loyalty of Deiotarus.
totus closes the enumeration; v. 734n.

100 **sparge:** by Lucan's time this verb was no more than a drastic synonym for *iacere*, as is clear from 9.748 'spargere signa', and *Herc. Oet.* 1317f 'sparge . . . telum'. Cf. 203n.

100-1 **armis** is dative as at 10.80 'tempora . . . dependit amori'.

102 **tuas . . . iaces:** overuse of apostrophe leads to sudden awkward shifts of addressee; v. 513-5n. *Iaceo* can refer to the dwelling-place of a person, as at Ov. *Pont.* 1.7.5. Cornelia ought to know where Julia is buried, but she does not know where her troubled ghost is, (but see Bruère *CP* 46.1951.235, n.95). Morford observes that this address recalls Julia's apparition at the beginning of the third book, where she prophesied disaster to Pompey at the start of a voyage; now too just before a voyage she is ominously recalled (80f).

103 **ades** suggests that ghosts must, like gods, be present to be effective.
exige poenas recalls the phrase at 21f, where it was her husband who was paying a penalty.

104 crudelis Ω, -es V: of course penalties can be cruel (cf. *Aen.* 6.501 and Ov. *Met.* 2.612), but it is not clear that the epithet here deserves to be postponed and emphasized; Housman saw that there was more point to its being vocative. **paelice** was the term used of Cornelia by Julia at 3.23; so here Cornelia accepts the charge to assuage the ghost, a neat touch.

105 tuo must be stressed when read aloud.
iterum refusa is an example of a common pleonasm discussed by Löfstedt, 2.178; cf. 1.74 'repetens iterum', 391 'rursus redeuntis'; 5.207 and 7.719.

106 cunctorum certainly includes Pompey and the maidservants, but may hint that the shore is now thronged with Mytilenaeans. Lucan's scenes are rarely intimate, and an audience is essential for his characters.
soluit is causative, 'she made their eyes melt'.

107 duri: the *duritia* of not weeping is copiously illustrated by Bentley on Hor. *Carm.* 1.3.18; cf. 9.50 'mala uel duri lacrimas motura Catonis'.
flectuntur: the three weighty syllables, called a molossus, are well placed to hint at the gradual shift in Pompey's feelings.

108 Thessaliae Ω, -a V: the grounds for choosing between the variants are set out at length in *Mnemosyne* for 1979. In brief, the ablative is supported only by 5.266 'pars iacet Hesperia'; the other ablatives cited by Housman are irrelevant, because common. On the other hand, the locative was in Lucan's day a vanishing case, and was always rare when used of a region. For these reasons the majority reading is here retained. Guyetus saw that 'sicca Thessaliae lumina' must mean 'quae in Thessalia sicca fuerunt'. This somewhat strained syntax finds a small measure of support in 'uigiles pectore curae' at 161 (though *uigiles* has a verbal force not found in *sicca*).
confudit 'blur', see Housman on 7.322; the line is imitated by Corippus *Ioh.* 8. 332 'lumina confundunt lacrimis', where *lacrimis* certainly helps. But Ovid speaks of grief-stricken features as 'confusos uultus' at *Tr.* 3.5.11; the sense is plain from the context. Juvenal uses *turbo* in the same sense at 6.8. The perfect tense of the verb is the majority reading. One Ms, P, gives the present. J. Willis in *Latin Textual Criticism* (Urbana, 1972), 166f notes that there is a tendency to alter other tenses, often the perfect, to the present. Thus at 9.332 P reads *effundere*, which is unmetrical. The perfect here may be instantaneous (v. 60n), and its use alongside the present is in any case unexceptionable (v. Francken on 6.237, and Cortius on 6.541).
lumina Lesbos: alliteration closes the scene. *Lesbos* boldly balances *Thessaliae*, and must mean 'the scene on the beach at Lesbos' (cf. Ribbeck 120f).

INTRODUCTION TO LINES 109-158

A moment of emotional equilibrium has been struck in the scene just past. The dramatic difficulty for the poet is to move away from this moment without bathos. One of Lucan's devices, as we shall see, is to address his characters or comment upon the action just passed in his own person (692ff); but here quickly, in a single line, he introduces a Mytilenaean welcoming party, who offer shelter. The immediate purpose of the section is to disturb, but not violently, the balance just struck. But its function in the book as a whole is to be one of tragic contrast, for we may compare the selfless generosity of the Mytilenaeans with the perfidy of Egypt. In the poem as a whole it fills out the picture of Pompey, by showing how much devotion he could command even in defeat.

This devotion is historically attested by Plutarch, *Pomp.*75, but Postgate rightly noted that the historical Pompey would refuse the offer of hospitality out of fear of treachery (xxxi n.1). Even Lucan's Pompey is no less astute (cf. 145f); but here Pompey is not so coarse as to hint at betrayal, and Lucan can develop the sad courtesy of the situation. Between Plutarch and Lucan there are again national differences of approach to the narrative: the Greek describes a philosophical discussion between Pompey and Cratippus on providence, a good Stoic theme which Lucan might have treated. Yet he prefers to develop in a highly romantic vein a theme adumbrated at 7.712-25 where the Larissaeans offer to help the general (cf. Val. Max. 4.5.5 for Pompey's noble refusal). This is another example of Lucan's foreshadowing technique, although the Larissa episode is quite complete in itself. Here the theme is treated more discursively for the sake of contrasts within the book, and for the opportunity of an emotional tableau on the beach.

Throughout this section unity of tone is maintained by the use of a metaphor drawn from mercantile affairs. It appears in 111 *pignus seruasse*, 112 *deuotos . . . foedere muros*, 126 *fidem*, 128 *mundi nomine*, 130 *pignore*, 141 *praestas . . . fidem*, and lastly at 190f *pignus depositum*. It is a simple enough device, enhanced by the echoes, in Pompey's response to the Mytilenaeans, of the terms of their own offer. These will be noted as they occur.

109   **pleno iam litore** may be an allusion back to the empty shore of 62. At any rate it is a very abrupt means of moving from the intimacy of what has gone before to the public demonstration which follows.

110-1   **maxima gloria**: the theme of glory (see introductory note to 511-710) picks up Pompey's admonition to Cornelia at 718 and further links these scenes. The untempered superlatives (*maxima, semper, tanti, cuncta*) are

100

characteristic of Lucan's attempt to achieve sublimity by the rhetorical device called *auxesis* or *magnificatio*. Pompey's faithfulness, which is here touched upon, is developed not only for its pathetic appeal to the reader, but as a foil to the licence of Caesar and Cleopatra in the tenth book.

112-4 **tu . . . tua** neatly ring the apodosis.

quoque 'as well as Cornelia'.

muros stresses the defensive capabilities of the town, and suggests that Pompey no longer has the initiative in the war.

113 **uel** in the sense 'even, just' does not appear to be common in epic. Virgil has it in speeches at *Aen.* 11.259 and 430, Lucan in a narrative passage at 7.29; see LHS 502.

113-4 **una nocte tua** is a curious expression to which 1.520 'nox una tuis non credita muris' and St. *Th.* 12.366f 'quae temeraria quaeris nocte mea?' are roughly similar.

114-5 This allusion, albeit highflown, to the tourist industry may seem strange, but it is nevertheless a compliment to Pompey and an assurance of his death-less fame. The theme is resumed and elaborated movingly at the close of the book (821f and 851-8); cf. also 9.950ff and 10.15-19 where visits are paid to Troy and Alexander's tomb by Caesar. For more general discussions on sightseeing Sandys on Cic. *Or.* 5, Munro on *Aetna* 565-98, and Tac. *Ann.* 2.54 may be consulted (Virgil contracted a fatal sunstroke while visiting Megara; *uita Suet.* 35).

adoret is also used of devotion to Pompey at 7.708.

116-7 The opposition in sense between *nulla* and *omnia* is reinforced by their initial position in the line. This pattern of emphasis is not uncommon in Lucan: cf. 1.142f, 510f, 3.3f, 5.496f, 6.281f, and 80f above or 344f below, 10.490f. Similar are Lucr. 1.455f 'seruitium . . . libertas', Hor. *Ep.* 1.10.1f, Ov. *Met.* 2.827f, 15.256f, and St. *Th.* 9.263f.

omnia = *cetera omnia*, v. Shackleton Bailey on Prop. 2.1.57.

magis = *rectius* (so *TLL* 8.59.84).

118 **haec iam crimen habent** is pointedly recalled at 517 by the treacherous Pothinus. For the transition-formula *quid, quod* see Tarrant on Sen. *Ag.* 265.

118-9 The punctuation of these lines is owed to Grotius. In this sentence the two clauses must in English be connected, for example by putting 'while' before the second; this is not uncommon in Latin poetry as Summers shows on Ov. *Met.* 8.486 and Duff on Juv. 1.107-9; cf. Hor. *Carm.* 3.9.21f and Ov. *Tr.* 3.4.21f. In all these examples the rhetorical contrast between the clauses is heightened by the asyndeton. (Fraenkel (2.287) does not seem to have observed the contrast, which Weise's paraphrase with *autem* brings out.)

120	certa loci: *certus* here means 'having sure knowledge of' and it first takes the genitive in literature at Ov. *Met.* 13.722; cf. 7.31 'fati certus'.

certa loci: *certus* here means 'having sure knowledge of' and it first takes the genitive in literature at Ov. *Met.* 13.722; cf. 7.31 'fati certus'.

noto litore: the point seems to be that Pompey's comrades will expect him to be at Lesbos rather than any where else; *certa loci* supports this. The reason of course is Cornelia's presence there.

fatum: cf. Curtius 5.1.8 'pristinam fortunam reparare'.

121 This phrase, chiastically disposed, is recalled at 10.18 'auro cultuque deum'. But the scene which Lucan probably intends us to recall is that described at 3.114-68 where Caesar robs the state treasury in the temple of Saturn in Rome. By way of contrast Pompey is here offered what Caesar would take. (Dio relates that Caesar despoiled the temple of Hercules at Tyre as a penalty for the harbouring of Cornelia and Sextus; 42.49.2.)

122 **si . . . si**: the disjunctive force of the repeated particle is characteristic of old Latin, but Lucan is here indebted to Ovid, *Her.* 10.93 'si mare si terras'; v. Munro on Lucr. 4.783.

ista: Virgil's use of this prosaic word recommended it to later poets. For its extended sense, 'this of mine', see 545n.

124 This line, though printed by Duff, is probably not Lucan's. It is not found in any Ms which is reckoned independently to transmit the text, and it contains a verb form, *habeto*, which Lucan does not use. (So at 6.152 an interpolator gives himself away by using *absque*.)

125-7 The paradoxical sentiment, designed, as usual, to close a speech, is echoed by Pothinus at 534 where a more self-seeking policy is enunciated. Courteously the Mytilenaeans suggest that it is Pompey who may fail them. Housman in his note to 6.248 gives other instances in Lucan of the overlogical use of *ne*. So too at 6.724f 'mortis munus eripitur . . . non posse mori' *non* is over-precise; the gift of death is the act of dying, and the clause would make sense without the negative. But Latin writers commonly with verbs implying removal see the result of removal in negative terms: 'the gift of death is removed; result: he cannot die'. This is all carefully set out in KS 2.2.227 and by Nutting in *AJP* 52.1931.53ff. In the present sentence the charge is contained only in the words *uideare . . . miser*; but *detrahe*, a verb of removal, prompts the writer to express the result in negative form, hence *ne*. In a note to 4.398f Housman discusses some less obvious examples of the idiom; in all cases there is, as he observes, an underlying sense of *ademptio*; but the usage is too widespread to justify his charge of *orationis negligentia*.

126 **fidem secutus** 'gain the protection of' is a phrase with legal overtones; see

TLL 6.664.75-84, but Fraenkel lists the present line at 680.18.
damnasse 'reject' is a sense common in Silver Latin (see *TLL* 5.17.52-84, esp. 68f to 18.3). The chiastic arrangement 'felix secutus . . . damnasse miser' further enhances the contrasting sense.

127 **pietate**: much of this book is concerned with examples of loyalty and the effect of civil war on the practice of the virtue. In the early part of the book Cornelia, the Senate, the Mytilenaeans, and king Deiotarus all exemplify it. But in the middle portion the Egyptians and Septimius betray it. At the end however Cordus and the poet himself show their *pietas* towards Pompey.

128 **laetus in aduersis** is to be taken as a phrase. To take *in aduersis* with *esse fidem* is weak on three counts: first, the word order is against it; secondly, the paradox of rejoicing amid misfortune is rhetorically attractive and finds support from St. *Th.* 10.227 'gaudet in aduersis'; and thirdly, the absolute assertion of *esse fidem* is diminished in impact if it is qualified.
laetus . . . gaudens: words of similar sense ring the line; for the opposite device see 36n.
mundi nomine contains a mercantile metaphor, 'on the world's account'; see Heitland xc. Lucan's imagination moves grandly from the particular (*uirorum* is just the Mytilenaeans) to the universal in *mundi*.
gaudens: Servius on *Aen.* 3.300 says 'notandum sane finitum esse uersum participio quod rarum apud Latinos est, apud Graecos uitiosissimum'. Since the word which called forth the observation is *linquens* Servius is assumed to be talking only about the nominative singular. The matter is discussed by W.R. Hardie in *CQ* 10.1916.35-8 and he observes that in *Aen.* 1 the ratio of such line endings is 1:252 but in *Aen.* 8 it is 1:731, which bears Servius out. But in the *Pharsalia* the ratio in the first six books is 1:272. Further examples in this book are at 152, 229, 244, 316, a ratio of 1:174.

129 **nullum toto**: similar emphatic juxtapositions at 2.146 *uni cuncta,* and 147 *semel omnia*; 4.379 *nobilis ignoto*; 187 below. The bracketing word order of *nullum . . . solum* keeps the clause from straggling.

130 **pignore** picks up *pignus* from the Mytilenaeans' speech at 111.

132 **adfectus** is not used concretely to mean 'loved one' until Apuleius, so here it refers to Pompey's good-will, as at 9.1100.
cari penates: looks to *lares* at 113; the line end is found at 7.346.

133 **hic mihi Roma fuit**: for the sentiment cf. 263n and Tac. *Hist.* 3.84 'proprium esse militis decus in castris: illam patriam, illos penates'.

133-4 What Pompey is here made to say is untrue, for he had gone to Amphipolis first, but Lucan ignores this in order to place emotional considerations before policy (in despite of ancient sailing practice).

puppem dedi, as Burman noted, is a curious expression; to it *TLL* compare V. Fl. 7.545 'daret in proelia tauros' and of course 194 below.

134   **saeui Caesaris iram** is echoed at 765.

135   Here Pompey recalls the Mytilenaeans' words at 111 and 125.

136   **tantam ueniae materiam** is Pompey himself, since he could be handed over to Caesar.

137   For the omission of the emphatic pronoun *uos*, as well perhaps as *me*, see Housman *Papers* 2.884. Postgate restored the older punctuation of the text. **fecisse nocentes**: at 118 the Mytilenaeans remarked that they were guilty. In this line Pompey makes that notion clearer by stating that it is he who has made them so. The phrase *facere nocentem* is somewhat paradoxical, in that the *nocens* is usually the agent of the crime, but this phrase rather implies that he is passive, and that his guilt is due to circumstance or to association. The notion is first found in Seneca (*Med.* 280, 499, *Phoen.* 367f), and it is very common in Lucan (2.259, 499 (of Cato), 7.260, 488, and 484 below). It occurs only once in Statius, *Th.* 11.176. Its significance in a work on civil war is undeniable; indeed it is part of Lucan's success that he so keenly feels the shared and universal guilt of civil war. Statius, whose epic theme is similar, scarcely stresses to the same degree the criminality of fratricidal war, and this may be counted a failure of imagination.

138   **fata agitanda** is an unusual phrase — *OLD* s.v. *agito* 3c quotes only this instance — and it is explained by comm. Bern. to mean 'experienda fortuna est per totum mundum'. Pompey means to say that he cannot stop in Lesbos, but must pursue his destiny over the globe. The phrase is doubtless owed to *Aen.* 11.694 'agitata per orbem'.

139   **heu** is only a sigh; cf. Housman on 5.354, Shackleton Bailey 218, and *OLD* s.v. 2. **nimium felix**: for the phrase see Pease on *Aen.* 4.657. **aeterno nomine** takes up a point made by the Mytilenaeans. They hope to be famous, and Pompey confirms the hope. Lucan himself will hold out a similar promise to Cordus for his loyalty at 782.

140   **populos regesque** is one of Lucan's commonest, and grandest, phrases: cf. 5.49, 754f, 7.56, 300.

142   Pompey's quest recalls that of Homer's gods, who are said to visit earth to look over men's good or bad behaviour (*Od.* 17.486f). **fas . . . scelus**: the emphatic nouns ring the line, but *scelus*, coming second, is therefore the more likely alternative. *Fas* is here loyalty, as at Tac. *Ann.*

15.54.5; cf. *OLD* sv 4.

quibus in terris . . . **ubi** is as pleonastic as Catull. 63.55 'ubinam aut quibus locis'.

143 **uotorum extrema**: in expressions of this sort the chief emphasis falls on the adjective used as a noun: these are his very last prayers. Cf. 2.272, 9.420, 10.467 and Knox-Headlam on Herodas 1.67.

144 **Lesbo** stands for the inhabitants of the island as at 3.185f; see Housman on Manil. 4.602.

146 **non exire uetent** shows understandable caution, but the tragic irony of it will only become clear after Pompey is at the mercy of the Egyptians.

147 **mutare putares**: for the assonance see Housman on 4.219, to which may be added 2.25 'fugiente rigentia', 7.69f 'tuorum castrorum', and 9.792 (cited by Housman on Manil. 2.938). The indefinite second person singular, used to soften an hyperbole, is found in epic at *Aen.* 8.691, 11.528, and Ov. *Met.* 11.126, as well as in Lucan at 1.493 and 9.412. For this formula see E.R. Curtius *Ges. Aufs. zur romanischen Phil.* (1960), 143.

148 **tellurem patriaeque solum**: here *que* has a limiting and explanatory function, for *tellurem* alone might be too vague; so too at 1.35, 7.347, 545, 190 below, and Ov. *Fasti* 2.508 'patrias artes militiamque colant'; see Kenney on Lucr. 3.346.

149 **plangitur**: the third person singular is the oldest form of the passive and it is regularly used as an impersonal; cf. 4.151 *paretur*, 243 *itur* and 366 below (LHS 287f).

infestae dextrae recalls the gesture of the Larissaeans at 7.724f.

150-3 Housman follows Cortius and Francken in taking both *Pompeium* and *illam* as subjects of *discedere*; his note implies that *Pompeium* could only be the object of *ingemuit* if *discedentem* were supplied from the infinitive.

151 The usage of *ast* is discussed by Austin at *Aen.* 2.467. Lucan is traditional: he always sets it before a pronoun beginning with a vowel.

152 **uidere** 'regard, look upon' as at 7.398f 'crimen ciuile uidemus tot uacuas urbes'. The subject of the verb is *populus*, which can have its verb in the plural because of the inherent notion of plurality; this is called 'constructio ad sensum', and is very common with *pars* (v. Langen on V. Fl. 2.554). But usually the progression in number is from singular to plural, as at 1.239-42, 484-6, 7.102-4.

153-4 **mariti uictoris**: for the *-tor* noun used as an adjective, a common construction, cf. 472.

154-5 **si peteret, uix poterant**: the protasis is past unreal, so the pluperfect subjunctive might have been expected; but in fact the imperfect is the original

105

tense and so is found not infrequently, e.g., Juv. 4.85 and 7.69; see S.A. Handford *The Latin Subjunctive* (1947), 123-5. As for *poterant* in the apodosis, both the mood and tense of this particular verb are usual even in the past unreal sentences (LHS 327f).

matres: of course Cornelia's acquaintance would have been limited to the ladies of the community.

156   **hos . . . hos:** if two different groups of people are meant, then the distribution is, as Housman says, feeble. If, on the other hand, the same group is designated by each pronoun, then the anaphora lacks force, since *pudor* and *probitas* are much the same, and we expect greater difference between the subjects, as at 4.116f and 6.189 'illum tota premit moles, illum omnia tela'. But at 7.551 Lucan writes 'hic furor hic rabies hic sunt tua crimina', where, despite the third member, *hic* is everywhere the same place, and there is no real difference between *furor* and *rabies*. Thus 'hic furor hic rabies' is as careless as 'hos pudor hos probitas'; in both passages the pronouns refer to the same people. For the constant conjunction of *pudor* and *probitas* compare Afranius *Epist.* 8, Catull. 42.24, Cic. *De Rep.* 3.18, Hor. *Epode* 17.40, and St. *Silu.* 2.1.39f (where, echoing Lucan, *modestia* is again in the list). See also R. Lattimore *Themes in Greek and Latin Epitaphs* (Urbana, 1942), 296.

157   **animi** Bentley for the *summissanimis* (or variants) of the Mss. Housman accepted Heinsius's *animis*, but in the plural *animus* regularly means 'courage or pride', as at 347 and 544. The choice is discussed fully in *Mnemosyne* for 1979.

158   **stantis adhuc fati:** does this descriptive genitive attach to *coniuge*, which is to be understood ἀπὸ κοινοῦ, or to the unexpressed subject, Cornelia? The former course is not without difficulty, for it is not clear that 'stantis adhuc fati coniuge' could mean 'cum coniunx stantis adhuc fati esset' (so W.B. Anderson in *CR* 41.1927.31). It is moreover very hard to believe that such a genitive would depend upon a single ablative word so as to describe a kind of attendant circumstance. Until a support is found for that interpretation, it is far easier to apply the phrase to the unexpressed subject word, *Cornelia*: 'she, of yet unfallen fortune, lived as if her husband were beaten'. This usage can be found in Livy at, e.g., 30.37.9 'nouem annorum a uobis profectus post sextum et tricesimum redii', where 'nouem annorum' depends upon the unexpressed *ego*; (cf. Weissenborn-Müller on 30.26.7). Likewise at Juv. 3.48 'mancus et extinctae corpus non utile dextrae' Duff assumes that the adjective and genitive depends upon the unexpressed subject, *homo*. So too at Suet. *Nero* 20.1 'quamquam exiguae uocis' and

106

57.2 'extitisset condicionis incertae', and Sen. *Dial.* 12.5.5 'exploratae iam firmitatis' some noun or pronoun, unexpressed, governs the descriptive genitive.

stantis . . . uicto: for the bracketing structure see 36n. This praise of Cornelia is deserved; Plutarch dilates upon her virtues in *Pomp.* 55. But in Lucan's hands it is not praise for its own sake. There is in the first place, as Haskins saw, an implied contrast with the meddlesome wives of some provincial governors (for which see Mayor on Juv. 8.128, but Pilate's wife is ignored). And more importantly Lucan shifts for a moment our pathetic concern from Pompey to his wife in order to prevent tedium. Since she will have an important part to play later in this book, as well as in the next, the poet makes an opportunity for focussing on her.

INTRODUCTION TO LINES 159-201

Pompey and his entourage set off from Lesbos with no goal in sight. Lucan handles the indecision with skill. He opens the section with a sun symbolically half set. Then he has Pompey enquire of the helmsman about steering by stars, a Virgilian reminiscence. That query is subtly posed and answered. For Pompey wants only to know the way either to Syria, the gateway to Parthia, or to Libya; clearly Egypt is no part of his plan. But in contrast to his vacillation, the helmsman lives in a world securely fixed. In his reply he introduces Egypt, a place, at that, to be passed by.

159-61 The sun is half set. Servius in his note to *Aen.* 11.183 tells us that Asinius Pollio had observed how Virgil adapted his descriptions of the times of day to the mood of the action. Comm. Bern. show a similar sense of the pathetic opportunities thus opened up in the note to 4.49: 'uariis incertus motibus aer: prout erat caelum, ita gerebatur et bellum'. But apart from the pictorial representation of Pompey's declining fortunes in the present passage, Lucan is alluding to a famous remark of the young Pompey to Sulla, his master, to the effect that more men saluted the rising than the setting sun (Plut. *Pomp.* 14 and Pease on *Aen.* 4, p. 390).

159 **pelago** may be ablative or dative with *demissus*, there is no way of deciding. **Titan** for the sun was introduced into Latin poetry by Cicero; it is a favourite with Ovid and Seneca (v. Pease on *Aen.* 4.119 and W. Kranz *Philol.* 105. 1961.290-5).

160 Silver age poets were eager to vary and elaborate descriptions of times and seasons, e.g. Lucan 6.570f where he describes midnight as 'the time when the sun ushers in the noonday beneath our hemisphere'. Often, obscurity

107

is inevitable. As such things go, the present case is not bad.

si quibus does not necessarily call into doubt the existence of the Antipodes; it is just a relative at 3.151 and 9.78; for its coupling with the simple relative see Prop. 2.24.47f, 4.1.105, and *Herc. Oet.* 1854-6.

61-7 The subjects and predicates in these lines deserve careful attention, because they show how loosely abstract Lucan's writing can be. Pompey's *curae* are said to approach cities as well as *mentes* and *arua*; that is, in his wakeful concern he notionally approaches nations and kings to find out their disposition. Then his *labor* casts off dismay and he (an abrupt change of subject) enquires about the stars. Like *curae, labor* is an instance of metonymy such as is found at 2.704f, 4.660 *uictoria* = 'Romani uictores'; 6.487 'ira leonum = leones irati', and 718 below. For other writers see Kenney on Lucr. 3.344f, Shackleton Bailey 279 and on Prop. 3.13.55 and Williams on St. *Th.* 10.288-92.

61 **pectore**, as the word order dictates, is to be taken with *uigiles* and not with *adeunt.* The leader sleepless with care for his charge is a commonplace from Homer on: see *Il.* 2.61f, Soph. *Oed.R.* 65, *Aen.* 8.26-30, Lucan 2.239f of Cato, V. Fl. 1.295f, St. *Silu.* 1.4.55 'uigiles curae' again, Claud. *In Eutr.* 1. 362f; Cicero has a good joke on the theme at *Ad Fam.* 7.30.1, concerning the consul-for-a-day Caninius, who never slept during his consulship.

62 **adeunt** is almost a technical term for approaching gods or their shrines (so 6.772f), and here it implies that Pompey is humbled.

63 **uarias regum mentes** should recall to mind Cornelia's wish at 98f. It also foreshadows the untrustworthiness of Ptolemy. Tacitus speaks of the wavering allegiance of barbarians at *Hist.* 3.48.

63 **mundi**, like *orbe* at 603, means 'part of the world'.

66 **fessos** suggests fruitless worry, as Servius observes on *Aen.* 8. 232.

67 Lucan is here reworking *Aen.* 10.159-62, a sketchy interlude in which Pallas asks Aeneas about the stars which guide their journey. But Aeneas has a goal, while Pompey only gradually builds up to his real question, 'can we get to Syria or Libya?' *Saepe* in 165 shows that after some thought he asks one question and then relapses into brooding silence; then another followed by silence; and so on, until the helmsman begs for clear orders. The certain fixity of stars and their movements well contrasts with Pompey's indecision. Similar are the reflections of Seneca in the post-Neronian *Octavia*, 377-90, and Catull. 5.4-6. But as Riley fairly complained, the helmsman's answer is frigid and misplaced in the extreme.

68-9 For the expression of finding a sea-path by the stars see Housman on Manil. 4.280.

170   quotus ignis looks a curious expression, but if we recall Horace's 'hora quot;
            est' at *Serm.* 2.6.44, where the answer required is clearly an ordinal number
            then we can begin to grasp what Lucan means. The fact of the matter, how-
            ever, seems to be that no one star in the constellation would have been used
            for guidance (see Gundel in *RE* 9A1. 1043.6-29). Thus Lucan must be put-
            ting into Pompey's mouth a question that reveals his ignorance of steering.
            (The designation of stars by a letter of the Greek alphabet is modern prac-
            tice.)
            Libyam . . . derigat: for the accusative of goal without a preposition see
            Landgraf in *ALL* 10.1898.391-402; he observes that Lucan follows Virgil's
            lead in commonly using the accusative alone and he cites 1.686f, 5.9, 534,
            7.477, and 845 below.

171-2   Pichon acutely observed that Lucan has adapted Virgil over two lines (221,
            n.7). He has taken from *Aen.* 3.515 'tacito labentia caelo', and has applied
            the epithet to a word synonymous with *caelum, Olympi* in 171, and then
            he has used the rest of the phrase in 172.
            seruator is here used unusually in its radical sense 'watcher'; cf. *seruet* 169
            and see Langen on V. Fl. 1.18.
            Olympi 'heaven' is illustrated by Langen on V. Fl. 1.4.

172   **fluunt labentia** is redundant but expressive of the unchecked movement of
            the stars.

174   **mergitur,** used of setting stars, is illustrated by Housman on Manil. 2.949.

175   **axis:** Duff is the first to propose the translation 'pole-star', and certainly
            this helps the modern reader (at 3.219 he gives pole-star for *Cynosura* also).
            In this he is followed by the *OLD*. But this is not accurate. Reference in
            antiquity to this star is very scant, limited, it seems, to no more than three:
            Vitr. 9.4.6, pseudo-Eratosthenes *Catast.* 3, and Eudoxus F 11 in Laserre's
            edition. The reason for this rare attestation is that navigators had no pre-
            cision instruments and so used no one star in the two Bears to guide them.
            The Greeks sailed by Helice, large and bright, the Phoenicians by Cynosura,
            smaller and more accurate. Only astronomers were concerned about the
            existence of what we know as Polaris, the Pole-star. *Axis* in Lucan is a
            vague word meaning 'quarter of the sky' and it is given precision by an
            epithet, e.g., *Hesperium* at 3.359 to signify West; so at 2.586 *medius axis*
            is the torrid zone, and at 4.62 it plainly means East. Ovid is probably the
            initiator of the usage; so *TLL* 2.1638.38f. Here *axis* has no qualifier, but
            it is given precision by the following relative clause. Thus at 176 *hic* is an
            adverb, not a pronoun, and means 'in this northern quarter of heaven'.

Pompey's helmsman sails by the Little Bear (of which constellation Polaris is the brightest star), as he goes on to make clear, but in this line he speaks vaguely of the North.

inocciduus is first found in Germ. *Arat.* 64 and *Anth. Lat.* 426.6 (a poem of the Claudian age). Lucan is by no means as fertile as Ovid in producing words of this sort (see Owen on *Tr.* 1, p.100f and E.J. Kenney 'The Style of the Metamorphoses' in *Ovid*, ed. J.W. Binns, pp. 124-6); but he has to his credit *indespectus* at 6.748, *inredux* at 9.408, and a word with a future, *inmaculatus* at 2.736.

177   (and parts of **193-9**): the translation is from L. Casson, *Ships and Seamanship in the Ancient World* (Princeton, 1971), reproduced by the kind permission of the Princeton University Press. In both instances Casson praises Lucan's accuracy, a welcome change from the scorn heaped upon his numerous errors.

    surget: for the sequence of a future in the protasis to a present in the apodosis see Housman on Manil. 1.469 and cf. 365f below.

178   **curuantem litora Pontum:** similar descriptions are found at Manil. 4.626 'curuata per undas litora' of the South-east corner of the Mediterranean, Silius 15.173f 'sinuatos gurgite ... / anfractus pelagi' of the Riviera, and Hor. *Carm.* 1.33.15f 'Hadriae curuantis Calabros sinus'.

179   **quidquid** has the sense *in quantum* as at 3.294, 365 below, and 9. 523f (see Housman's *Lucan*, p.333). It is used with the same sense by Livy at 7.32.6 and 21.54.8 (see Housman on Manil. 3.324).

182   **excipit:** for the sense see *OLD* sv 16; the use without an object is rare if the verb has spatial sense.

    contenta had been used of a constellation by Manilius at 1.503 'haec contenta suos in uertice flectere gyros'.

183   **uagari:** used of heavenly bodies this verb and the adjective *uagus* mean no more than that the object appears and disappears; see Housman on 7.425, on Manil. 2.71, and the illuminating note of Fordyce on Catull. 64.271.

185   **quo pede:** there are two *pedes;* see Baehrens on Catull. 4.20f. Thus a precisian would regard *quo* as a solecism for *utro*; but the licence is found in Virgil at *Aen.* 12.726f, and it is not uncommon later: cf. Luc. 1.126 and 7.259, 3.589 with *utrasque* in 590, and Duff on Juv. 8.196.

187   **solum toto** gives a common sort of juxtaposition: 3.230, 6.249, 9.246, 522f. Cf. 129n.

189   **pelago caeloque:** the case is ablative of means; 'pelago est nauigatione, cursu, caeli obseruatione' says Francken, and the phrase picks up 168f. As Lucretius says, sailors 'nil aliud nisi aquam caelumque tuentur' (4.434).

190   **cetera da uentis:** that is to say that his flight is to be headlong; cf. Aesch. *Pers.* 480f and the scholiast's comment there.

          comitem pignusque: comm. Bern. is confused by *que*, thinking it additive. But it is in fact explanatory (v. 148n), and *pignus* harks back to 111 and 130.

192   **at** has not so much an adversative force here, but is used to introduce an immediate consequence, as at 3.683; see Housman *Papers* 3.1229, and *OLD* sv 2b.

193-9: for this description of the ship's turn from a run to a reach, see Casson, cited at 177.

195   We do not know what place Lucan has in mind, whether we read *Asinae* with the majority or *Sasinae* with PG. The ancient commentators were quite as baffled as we are to-day. Emendation is risky, for it is always possible that Lucan may have fancied the place (under whatever name) may have existed, even if it did not; cf. Bourgéry, *RPh*, ser. 3, 2.1928.39.

196   **hos dedit . . . tenet hos:** the chiasmus lends a grace to this bit of technical description. For the second *hos* one would expect *illos*, but Lucan likes to repeat the pronoun, as Oudendorp showed on 7.503. This was originally a usage of comedy but Virgil brought it into the high style, e.g., at *Aen.* 10.9f; see LHS 181f.

197-9   The description is attractive and lively. The sea perceives the change of direction, and the ship looks a different way: the personification is unobtrusive and effective. It is amazing that the Dutchmen Heinsius and Burman could ask 'what sound?'.

198   **pelagus:** the proper object of *secante* would be *aequora*, but the poets avoid the colourless pronoun *is* (see 14n), and have recourse to synonyms. The classic example is *Aen.* 1.246 'it mare proruptum et pelago premit arua sonanti', where *pelago* is *mare;* see Housman on 1.102 and Shackleton Bailey 33f. For the ship 'looking' cf. V. Fl. 1.423; Melville in *Omoo*, ch. 7, says that the bows are in sailor language called eyes, and indeed eyes were often painted on ancient ships.

199   This is the only simile in the book. It is cast in the form of a negative comparison, for which see Austin on *Aen.* 2.496; not unusually in such forms of comparison, the term of comparison itself – here 'ease' or 'skill' – is omitted. Both the form and substance of the simile recall *Aen.* 5.144-7.

200   The more obvious sound effects were eschewed by the Silver Latin poets; Quintilian's disapproval was therefore shared (*I.O.* 1.5.72). But Lucan has a couple of lines in which sound and metre underscore sense, e.g., 1.215 'perque imas serpit ualles', 238, 629, 2.219, 5.160, 6.714f, 7.44, 10.318 'praecipites cataractae'. Here the line runs in dactyls to the third foot cae-

sura, but the rest of the line is as spondaic as it can reasonably be. The choice of consonants seems also to be pictorial.

201 This line is a reworking of Ov. *Tr.* 1.9.1 'detur inoffenso uitae tibi tangere metam', but Lucan extends the meaning of *inoffensae* and uses it as a passive.

INTRODUCTION TO LINES 202-255

The mission of King Deiotarus to Parthia is impossible to establish historically, and even its poetical purpose is, at first sight, unclear. Lucan may have in the back of his mind some recollection of the embassy of Lucilius Hirrus before Pharsalia (see Caes. *B.C.* 3.82.4). Or it may be that Livy knew, or thought he knew, that the king was despatched upon some such mission. This is not however a problem of the first importance, for Lucan is cavalier in his approach to history, and he would be surprised to learn how sharply his poem has been criticised for its historical shortcomings. But his distortions are rarely arbitrary, and tend rather to serve some end within the poem. For example, the well-known exaggeration of the difference between the ages of Caesar and Pompey at 1.129-35 is no more than a device for arousing the reader's sympathy for the older general who, Lucan fancies, is at the close of his distinguished career; comm. Bern. did not miss the point in saying 'subtiliter detrahit Caesari, quod senem uicerit'.

Another example comes from the carefully composed opening of the seventh book, 14-16. There Lucan identifies Pompey's first triumph with the defeat of Sertorius; it was in fact his second. It may be suggested that this error arose out of a desire to connect Pompey's first great success in arms with the defeat of a fellow-Roman, in short, to hint that he won his spurs in civil war. This would then form a contrast to the end of his career. However that may be, it is certain that, in giving a different account from Plutarch, *Caes.* 32, of Caesar's vision at 1.186ff, Lucan is motivated by a desire not to offend against epic propriety. In general then, it may be said that Lucan is not captious when he chooses to rewrite the past.

What end might he have had in view here? Up to now the reader has been given several examples of conspicuous *fides* and *pietas* towards Pompey. Cornelia and the Mytilenaeans are eager to join their fates to his. And at the beginning of this section Sextus and the Senate (*turba fidelis* 205) also come up. Deiotarus serves as another instance of high loyalty. It was noted at 140 that Lucan likes to join the words *populi* and *reges*; the Mytilenaeans are a *populus*, and so Deiotarus is cited as a *rex*. His loyalty is historically attested. In the dialogue *Brutus*, 21, Cicero calls him 'fidelissimus atque optimus rex' and in the eleventh *Philippic* oration he

112

stresses the king's connexion with Pompey and the Roman state (34). But the speech which Cicero delivered privately before Caesar in defense of Deiotarus is naturally more cautious; emphasis is laid upon his loyalty to Rome, and his personal attachment to Pompey is played down. At any rate, Lucan has good precedent in choosing Deiotarus as a type of loyalty. Within the economy of the eighth book the king's ready service and unhesitating devotion stand in sharp contrast to the devious perfidy of Ptolemy. One final consideration: it is now made clear that Pompey's intention to go to Parthia for help, which was no more than a hint at 169, has taken more definite shape. All taken in all, the section is not as pointless as it has seemed.

It is characteristic of Lucan's epic technique that the first four lines of the passage are no more than a sketch for setting the scene. There is a certain abruptness about 202, which is not mitigated by its elegance (internal alliteration, chiastic pattern of verbs and their objects, and a Virgilian placement of the verbs at the beginning and end of the line). For all that, it remains a breathless transition from the night interlude which precedes it. Moreover the reader is unable to visualise just where or how the meetings Lucan mentions take place, for Lucan himself is not much interested in such matters. Description in Lucan must have some use; so at 5.125f where he gives a pretty enough account of Delphi and the seeress Phemonoe roving about the woods, the charm of the *locus amoenus* is only stressed to contrast with the tremendous events that follow. Likewise at 4.196-204 the fine account of the truce in Spain is foil to the coming treachery (cf. Ribbeck 105). In the present case Lucan clearly felt that there was no need to be specific about the locality or means of meeting on the high seas. Since he has not troubled to fix the scene in his mind or present it clearly to his reader, the writing is here obscure in its details. But the general import is clear, and emendation is not called for.

203   sparsus: 'in longinquas regiones missus uel pulsus', Langen on V. Fl. 2.595; cf. V. Fl. 6.656 *spargitur* 'he is sped away', and 100n.

204   adsequitur is not common in verse, though it is found at 2.652 meaning 'pursue'.

204-5   primusque . . . natus: the centre of difficulty can be located in the phrase *a litore Lesbi.* It must have a vaguely temporal sense, 'after leaving Lesbos'. For this we may compare *Aen.* 10.148 'ab Euandro castris ingressus Etruscis'. Now in this passage it is Aeneas who leaves Evander and goes to the Etruscan camp; he performs both actions, whether implied or stated. But in the passage under discussion, Housman, who was followed by Duff, assumes that Pompey is the one who is referred to in the phrase *a litore Lesbi*; this is very hard, since the subject of the sentence is *natus*, Pompey's younger son

Sextus. If Housman's interpretation is correct (and it has not been accepted in the translation) then Lucan has written elliptically indeed. It is truer to the Latin to assume that Lucan has forgotten the true course of events, and imagined Sextus as going to Lesbos and then setting off to join his father.

206   **neque** here means *ne . . . quidem* 'not even', a usage apparently first found in Vir. *Ecl.* 3.102; see *OLD* s.v. *neque* 2b. *nec* is more commonly used with this sense, especially in the Silver age (v. Langen on V. Fl. 4.200), but the dactylic form has been preferred to open the line, as at *Aen.* 2.71.

207-9   Lucan voices a like sentiment when Pompey leaves Italy at 2.730 'adhuc ingens populis comitantibus exul'. For Lucan it is not enough that greatness should be in ashes, but that, paradoxically, it should still have about it all the trappings of state. The sentiments of 37-9 are comparable.

208   **sceptra . . . tenentes**: Lucan treats the present participle as if it were a noun; so *habitans* at 6.293; the usage is Senecan, as Summers points out in his excellent introduction to the *Select Letters* (1920), lix-lxii; see also LHS 156.

209   **exul** is so placed that great emphasis falls upon it. The word comes as a shock after the previous, high-sounding line. To Roman ears *exul* implied a disgrace, for exile was the extreme penalty of the law for a citizen (Cicero for example could never bear to use the word of himself but always spoke of his 'departure', and Ovid, though he calls himself an exile to awaken sympathy, is at pains to point out that legally he was relegated, not exiled).

211-38   The speech abounds in the place names so close to Lucan's heart. But the listing of Eastern tribes is neither an ornament nor a display of ill-founded knowledge. As in the similar speech of Pompey to Sextus at 2.632-48, the roll-call is designed to impress the reader with the vastness not only of Pompey's influence but of Rome's dominion. The only way to bring it home to the reader that this is a world war is to name the peoples who might be expected to take part. But of course this is all part of Lucan's vision, not an accurate catalogue (see 223n).

211   **quando amissus orbis**, sc. *est.* Heitland complained about Lucan's awkward inelegant manner of omitting the auxiliary verb (cviii). But Leo lists examples drawn from the poets of the Golden age, and observes how few examples there are before Lucan, except in Virgil! He goes on to say that Lucan omits *est* with the passive ten times in the first book, but concludes that Statius is the boldest innovator (185-90).

212   **fidissime** strikes the keynote of this section.

213   **populosque** 'of the nations'. It is well known that poets are addicted to the distributional figure ἀπὸ κοινοῦ. If the present line were written out in prose

it would read 'temptare Eoam fidem et fidem populorum qui etc.'. The
second *fidem* can be dispensed with. Then, as not uncommonly happens,
the case of the remaining noun, *populorum*, is altered. Metrical convenience is commonly the reason for the alteration. This process is not always
recognised. Catullus, for example, writes at 67.35 'de Postumio et Corneli
narrat amore', which means 'de Postumi amore et de Corneli amore narrat';
at *Serm.* 1.2.1-2 Horace writes 'ambubaiarum collegia, pharmacopolae' for
'pharmacopolarum collegia'; Valerius Flaccus has at 2.580f 'tumulos prae-
labitur Ili/ Dardaniumque patrem' for 'Dardaniique patris'. Lucan offers a
few examples too. At 7.633f he writes 'illic per fata uirorum/ per populos
(= per populorum fata), hic Roma perit'; at 7.776 'pectore in hoc pater
est, omnes in Caesare (= in Caesaris pectore) manes'; and at 9.51f 'Cornelia
nautas (= nautarum)/ priuignique fugam tenuit'. So Vir. *Geor.* 4.559f.
bibentes: Roman poets commonly designated barbarian peoples by naming
the rivers they dwelt near and hence were supposed to drink from; the conceit however is as old as Homer, *Il.* 2.824f; see *TLL* 2.1964.39-66, and
especially E. Norden *Kl. Schr.* (1966), 184.

215 **Magno** is again the figure 'emphasis' discussed at 80n.
   quaerentem fata is characteristically obscure.
217 **totum mutare diem** is discussed in appendix I.
   superbo is explained by 1.10, for the Parthians had no fear of Rome after
   the defeat of Crassus. Lentulus will use the arrogance of the Parthians as a
   counter argument to Pompey's at 346.
218 **Arsacides** is not found before Lucan, and it is taken up by Tacitus, *Hist.* 1.
   40. In the plural it means 'Parthians', as *Cecropidae* means 'Athenians' or
   Labdacidae 'Thebans'. But here and at 409 in the singular it refers to the
   Parthian king.
   foedera: there is no evidence for an actual treaty, but Lucan may be recalling the Parthian embassy to Pompey in Syria in 63 BC; so A.W. Lintott in
   CQ 21.1971.501, n.14.
219-20 **per Iouem . . . per magos:** the anaphora is purely verbal, since *per* in each
   case has a slightly different sense.
221 **Armenios . . . Geticis:** these epithets cohere a little better than Virgil's
   'Partho torquere Cydonia cornu/ spicula' at *Ecl.* 10.59f or 'spicula torque-
   bat Lycio Gortynia cornu' at *Aen.* 11.773. Both poets mean only to say
   that orientals are archers, and that the best gear comes from the East.
222 **cum Caspia claustra** is a noteworthy triple alliteration, such as we find in
   the first line of the poem, at 4.110, 490, 251 below, and 10.321.

222-5   Weise's punctuation is followed here for its smoothness. In 222 *si* has the sense *si quidem* 'since', a polite usage, common in prayers, e.g., Catull. 76. 17 and 19, For protases that bracket the apodosis see 837-40n.

223   **aeterni Martis Alanos:** this reference is an anachronism, for the Alani did not come into prominence in Roman foreign affairs until well after the civil wars; see A.B. Bosworth in *HSCP* 81.1977.222.

225   **tutam trepidos:** as at 5.381 'trepidam tutus', juxtaposition and alliteration point up the contrast. Ctesiphon was the true capital, but Babylon, as at 1.10, has always sounded more romantic.

226   **arua . . . ultima:** either the epithet is used as a noun as at 10.273 'per ultima terrae', or this is an instance of the distribution of a noun and its epithet over two clauses; see Housman on Manil. 1.270, where some of the examples are of the epithet following the noun.

227   Burman observed that this whole vaunt is a lie to history, but Lucan is hinting at a comparison between Pompey and Alexander, that he will develop in his funeral eulogy at the close of the book. Whatever the truth may be about the extent of Pompey's eastern campaigns, for which see Florus 1.40. 31, he was commonly held to have seen India. At Petr. 123.239 he is called 'saeui repertor Hydaspis', and Ampelius says at 47.5 'sub hoc . . . duce ad Indicum oceanum et rubrum mare usque peruenit'.

229   **tamen** when used as a connective particle regularly stands at the head of its sentence or clause. But, when used as the correlative of *quamuis,* it properly stands before the word it modifies. Housman has fully illustrated in his notes to 1.333 (where several of his examples are drawn from Munro on Lucr. 3. 553) and to Manil. 4.413 how frequently *tamen* shifts its position, if *quamuis* is dropped, generally towards the head of its sentence or clause, as here. In a sense, it is reasserting its function as a connective, though logically it is still being used as a correlative particle.

230   **nostris uos:** pronouns tend to cluster together, but their juxtaposition is none the less pointed; cf. 1.279 'tua nos faciet uictoria ciues'.

231   **solusque:** Burman felt that 'solus et e . . . ' would be *numerosior* but Housman notes at 3.405 and at Manil. 5.614 other instances where *et* is not postponed for the sake of a dactylic opening.

232-3   The alliteration at the close of one line and at the beginning of the next shows that Lucan had an ear for the powerful, if not fine, phrase. Cf. 69f and 9.230f.

234   **iras:** the plural commonly means 'martial ardour'.

236   **excedat . . . ripam:** Ovid was the first poet to use this verb as a transitive; see Getty on 1.497.

116

237   **Pellaeum:** a favourite epithet of Lucan's; here it refers to Alexander, who was born at Pella, capital of Macedonia. But at 298 it means 'Macedonian'; it is also used to refer to Alexandria or to the kings of Egypt.

237-8   **uincite . . . uinci:** for Lucan's fondness for word-play on the active and passive of this verb see Bonner 265f. The imperative is a lively replacement for the conditional protasis, as at 183f. The concluding phrase of Pompey's speech, 'uinci Roma uolet', is paradoxical and provocative. The turn of phrase is found in Livy 2.59.2 'non enim uincere tantum noluit . . . sed uinci uoluit', Ovid *A.A.* 1.666 'uinci . . . uolet', and Sen. *Tro.* 279; Mayor lists numerous parallels to the sentiment on Juv. 4.69 'ipse capi uoluit'.

239-40   It was a commonplace that servile or inconspicuous dress preserved the prominent from harm: cf. Tac. *Hist.* 3.73 and PLM 4.80.5-6 'cum sonuere tubae iugulo stat diuite ferrum/barbaricum: tenuis praebia ('safe-conduct') pannus habet'.

240   **raptos:** the cloak is not asked for or simply taken, but grabbed. The word describes Deiotarus's haste and willingness to obey (as well as the heated atmosphere of the poem).

241-3   These lines were faulted by Heinsius, and Burman concurred in the judgment, saying that they have a monkish smack about them. But the obtrusive moralising is typical of the declamation schools and Lucan never avoids a chance to open a satiric vein. (Moreover since these lines are imitated by Dracontius, a fifth century poet, it would have to have been a very early monk indeed who could interpolate the lines; see Hudson Williams in *CQ* 41.1947.105f.) For other such intrusive moral commonplaces we may compare the polemic against wealth at 3.114-22, the praise of the pauper's life at 5.527-9, the praise of Ammon's simplicity at 9.515-21, and the denunciation of asps in Italy at 9.706f.

244   **relinquens** 'have nothing to do with, avoid, ignore' as at 4.42 'hoste relicto'. The sense was illustrated by Housman, *Papers* 2.854. Postgate failed to grasp the point that Pompey avoided Ephesus and went round the seaward side of Samos. Duff of course gets it right here, at 247 and at 9.1003.

245-6   **spumantia** 'covered with foam' as at *Aen.* 4.135; more logically, the past participle also has this sense, as at Cic. *Diu.* 1.13 'saxa spumata liquore'. **paruae . . . Sami** is treated by Postgate as one of the geographical inaccuracies so typical of Lucan, and Roman poets generally (lxxxvii). See also Leo 202. Granting that poor Lucan has erred again, the reader may notwithstanding wonder why the large island of Samos has been called small. The point seems to be that Lucan chooses to fancy the lands or cities small as at 251 and 259, and the waters wide as at 248 because Pompey is a trembling passenger in a little boat (39 and 258). In a word, the epithets are chosen for pathetic force, and Lucan seeks to arouse in us an emotional response to Pompey's plight, not to satisfy our knowledge of geography.

249   **conpensat** is 'conpendio abbreuiare', says *TLL* 3.2049.77-83, and it cites the usual parallel, Sen. *Phaedra* 84; at 9.685 Lucan uses the uncompounded form of the verb in the same sense, 'pensabat iter'.

249-50   The *locus classicus* for a description of this optical illusion on shipboard is Lucr. 4.387-90; on the other hand, *recedo* is very common, as in the English idiom.

250-1   **nec ausus adit** = 'et non-ausus adit', where the negative notion in *nec* applies only to the participle and not to the main verb; see Housman on 7.504f.

251   Phaselis was a byword for wretchedness; see Knox-Headlam on Herodas 2.57. The pathos is underlined by the triple alliteration, and enhanced by apostrophe and the verbal contrast between *parua* and *Magnus* in 252. (But of course it would have been imprudent to enter a fortified city.)

253   **exhaustae populis**: the ablative of the thing removed is found first in Cicero and Lucretius; see *OLD* sv *exhaurio* 5.

253-4   **maiorque . . . fuit** is a frigid conceit.

255   **Taurum Tauroque**: the repetition is designed to connect clauses or phrases and avoid the unwelcome forms of *is* (see 14n); we should say 'he sees Taurus and Dipsus pouring from it'. The device is found in Virgil, *Aen.* 1.325 'sic Venus et Veneris contra sic filius orsus', in Horace, *Ep.* 1.10.33 'reges et regum . . . amicos', and in Ovid it is a mannerism: *Met.* 4.89, 170, 296, 7.225, 447, *A.A.* 1.27, 225, 3.11, *Am.* 1.10.19, 2.11.36. (It is worth noting that the turn of phrase is found in Homer in such phrases as 'Priam and the sons of Priam' at *Il.* 4.31, 35, 47.)

INTRODUCTION TO LINES 256-327

When Pompey left Lesbos he had fixed upon no destination, but in conversation with the helmsman he hinted at a preference for Parthia. This hint was realised with the despatch of Deiotarus thither on embassy. Now however a proper decision is to be made at a meeting of the Senate in exile.

The speech of Pompey urging an appeal to Parthia is, in Postgate's words, a vivid and vigorous declamation. Indeed it had to be for Pompey's sake, and for Lucan's. We know from Quintilian (*I.0.*3.8.33) that this particular deliberation was a school exercise; if it became so after the publication of the *Pharsalia*, that would

118

show the poem's success. But if it was already a theme when Lucan was writing, then he would have been faced with a tradition of arguments that his audience could be expected to know; the poet's task would be to surpass all known efforts. At the same time this speech must, in the context of the eighth book, fail; for failure is central to Lucan's portrait of Pompey. Thus the speech is not so strong throughout as Pompey's situation demands. This is his position: he requires of a suitable ally (*deceat* 278) two qualities, military power and trustworthiness (*uiribus atque fide* 277; cf. Sallust's *uirtus et fides* in *Cat.* 20.2 and *Iug.* 74.1). Now both Ptolemy and Juba are unreliable, and Pompey has no doubts about Parthian might (290-305); but, just when he ought for the sake of his argument to assert that they are loyal, he wishes aloud that he had not to rely on them (306). His own word *fiducia* is tauntingly echoed by Lentulus in his reply at 362 and especially 447. Verses 309-10, as Housman observes, reassert Pompey's intention to try the Parthians, but at 311-16 he again hints at bad faith and digresses. He returns to the main argument at 316, and *sed* must be emphasized when read. Pompey manages to pull his case together again in time to close on an epigram. But this self-defeating middle section is an attempt to demonstrate even further the vacillation we have hitherto witnessed. Lucan deliberately weakens the argument by letting Pompey voice his own misgivings; at the same time the poet displays his own lack of concern for verisimilitude; for, if he had cared to do so, he could have represented Pompey's doubts by way of interior monologue or by an 'editorial' comment (cf. *Aen.* 1.208f).

Pompey's situation is highly pathetic, for he is reduced to relying on his sense of personal glory (316-21); that salved defeat and will sustain Pompey's spirit in his dying moments. But, just as he acquiesced against his better judgment and hastily attacked at Pharsalia, so here his wavering will lead to his death in Egypt.

256   **hoc** is taken by Postgate to be ablative, referring to the action of *pacem praestitit*. It is however more likely to be accusative, and prospective of the infinitive *consultum (esse)*; this usage is illustrated by Vahlen 1.111f, and the accusative is so used at 4.719 'hoc metuens . . . timeri'. The nominative *hoc* is used at 5.529f 'hoc . . . contingere . . . potuit . . . trepidare', Sen. *Ep.* 52.3 'et hoc multum est, uelle seruari', Cic. *De Leg.* 2.38 'hoc . . . interfuit antiquum uocum conseruari modum'.

259   **ad profugum collecta ducem**: Pompey's exile began when he fled Italy (2.608 and 730); Lucan harps upon it to arouse sympathy (cf. 7.703 and 209n). There is no strictly analogous use of *colligere ad* before the present (at Sen. *Phaedra* 1113 *ad* has final force).

260   Cortius faulted this line because Syhedrae is not the sea port of Selinus; in

Lucan this is not a telling objection. The important point is that Syhedrae fulfils, as 'mittitque . . . recipitque' suggests, a requirement uttered at 145f. The reduplicated *que* is noteworthy just because the words connected are not juxtaposed, as at 262 for example. (This type of separation is not, unfortunately, discussed by H. Christensen in *ALL* 15.1908.165-211, but it is not uncommon: *Aen.* 5.619, Tibull. 1.9.20, Ov. *A.A.* 1.3, V.Fl. 1.55, St. *Silu.* 3.5.63; so Grotius should not have proposed to delete the first *que* from 6.616 'facilesque aditus multique patebunt'.)

261   **tandem** stresses that uncertainty of destination is now at last on the point of resolution.

263   **instar patriae** looks to the commonplace that a city is its people, but in the context of civil war it also shows that this is the legitimate government in exile. It should be recalled that historians of the principate admitted the force of Pompey's case (see 94n). Livy has a similar sentiment at 9.4.11 where Lentulus says of the army trapped at the Caudine Forks 'hic patriam uideo'.

263-4 **in litore nudo/ in Cilicum terra**: it cannot be said that in general where prepositions are repeated the second phrase is more concrete or pointed than the first. Lucan however tends to give greater precision to the second phrase at 6.216 'in caput atque oculi laeuom descendit in orbem' (of an arrow), at 6.734 'per busta . . . per funera' (where *funera* are corpses). So here the shore is unprotected, but worse, the land is Cilicia, whose once piratical natives would welcome a chance to pay back their conqueror (see 38n). *Litore nudo* is 'the bare strand' of *Paradise Lost* 1.379.

265   Burman observed that since *res nouae* means 'revolutionary activity' its usage here is hard to explain. But at Livy 1.8.6 'auida rerum nouarum' the sense of the phrase cannot be 'revolution'. In fact, context controls connotation, and *res* is a vague enough word to adapt itself to its surroundings, even in common phrases (so Summers on Sall. *Cat.* 51.26). Nor is it unusual for less common phrases to have quite different meanings depending on the context; see Madvig on Cic. *De Fin.* 2.64 and Housman on Manil. 2.617.

266-7 **non omnis . . . cecidi**: '*omnis* suppose l'idée de facultés ou d'éléments qui entrant dans un total; *totus* présente l'objet ou la personne dans son unité': Lejay on Hor. *Serm.* 1.9.2. We may compare 5.742 'totus adest in proelia Caesar'. Pompey's boast recalls (almost certainly an accident) Hor. *Carm.* 3.30.6 'non omnis moriar'. For this use of *omnis* see Munro on Lucr. 2.53 (and for *totus* 1.377).

268-9   **cladesque receptas excutere**: the metaphor here recalls the Libyan elephant of 6.208-10 who shakes off the darts stuck in his hide.

269-71 As at 118f, Lucan coordinates two clauses where the first is logically subordinate (so Housman on 2.294). The paradox in *ruinae erigere* is a neat one.

270   **plenis reddere fastis** is explained by adn. thus: 'fuit enim septies consul; ideo plenis fastis, hoc est, ipsius nomine signatis'; cf. *Laus Pisonis* 9 'pleni numeroso consule fasti' (the work is Neronian, and used to be attributed wrongly to Lucan).

272-3   That Pompey's naval arm was still unimpaired is asserted at 37f. In May of 49 BC Cicero told Atticus that Pompey felt possession of the sea was to be the key to success, *Att.* 10.8.4.
        mille and *millies* replaced the native Latin *sescenties* for a large indefinite number from the time of Terence on; see Wölfflin in *ALL* 9.1896.177. Lucan has chosen the number to recall the traditional number of ships that sailed against Troy (see Fraenkel on Aesch. *Ag.* 45).

273-4   The form of expression is imitated by Florus, 2.13.65 'sparsae magis quam oppressae uires', referring to the Pompeians in Africa; so in Lucan 9.245 'Emathium sparsit uictoria ferrum'. For Florus's debt to Lucan see Westerburg in *RM* 37.1882.35-49.

274-6   Plutarch says that Pompey and his counsellors were realistic enough to consider help from any source (*Pomp.* 76), but that will hardly do for an epic poet. Lucan's Pompey magnificently disdains anything less than royal aid. The sentiment 'me . . . tueri fama potest rerum' may sound incredible, and yet Caesar himself says that he was prepared to follow Pompey to Egypt despite his few troops 'confisus fama rerum gestarum' at *B.C.* 3.106.3. Pompey is ever aware of the power of his name and reputation to stir men to arms in his support (cf. 2.633f and 9.90-2), but at an early opportunity Lucan had shown that Pompey was only a *nominis umbra,* 1.135.

277   **Libyam Parthosque Pharonque** is attractively varied in expression: a country, a people, and a place. Pharos (Egypt) comes last in the list because it will be preferred, though Pompey does not know it.

278   **quemnam** refers to the notion latent in *regna* and in the three preceding proper names, viz. the king. Few forms of sense construction are commoner: see Mayor on Juv. 14.241, Munro on Lucr. 4.934, and Diggle on Eur. *Phae.* p.119. Even as early as Caesar *B.C.* 3.106.1 'propter necessitudines regni' *regnum* was not far from meaning *rex*; this overlap in sense is complete in Lucan, cf. 3.145 and 313 below, St. *Th.* 12.380, and Löfstedt *comm.* 112.

279   **arcana ... expromam ... mentisque quo:** for nouns and clauses as equivalent objects of the same verb see 3.55f, 4.694-9, 6.454-9, 7.5f, and in this book 594ff and 729ff.

280   **mentis pondera** is, in this sense, like Sen. *Med.* 390 'quo pondus animi uergat'.

281-2   Egypt, which will at length be chosen, is the first to be rejected (so Ehlers 547). Velleius Paterculus tells us that Pompey was in fact the one who was eager to go to Egypt, 2.53.1. *Ardua*, repeated from 239, suggests the contrast between Deiotarus and Ptolemy. But Pompey does not so much doubt the king's loyalty as his ability to sustain it, as *robustos* shows.

283   **anceps dubii:** one of the epithets is, if strictly considered, unnecessary, but it has been added not only to stress the point but to balance the line, giving each noun a qualifier. Norden discusses this common practice of the poets (384 and 396). These epithets, as it happens, are often found together; see 2.447f, 4.770f, 9.581f and Tac. *Ann.* 4.73.4.

285-6   **multus ... in pectore ... Hannibal** for 'the thought of Hannibal' is copiously illustrated by Leo, 39; cf. 45n. For the use of *multus* see *OLD* sv 6.

286-7   **qui** can only refer to Hannibal, who Lucan says stains the Libyan royal house with his blood and contaminates Juba's Numidian ancestors (there is no surviving evidence of this charge). In Rome bastardy entailed neither civil disability nor social disgrace, and Spurius is no uncommon *praenomen*. (But nevertheless attested bastards among the nobility at Rome are surprisingly few; see Syme *Papers* 2.510-17). It is therefore unlikely that Lucan is saying that Hannibal's blood flowed illegitimately in Juba's veins. What he probably means is that Hannibal is a collateral relative, and that is sufficiently alarming to a Roman. With *contingit* we should understand *sanguine* ἀπὸ κοινοῦ.

287   **supplice Varo** will be tauntingly recalled by Lentulus at 346.

288   **Romana = res Romanae = Roma,** a grand and metrically useful synonym found at 341, 545 and often.

289   Pompey dismisses Egypt and Libya, and boldly commands his Senate to head East with him. He gives the reason for this plan after having stated his point of view. (That Parthia was not an unreasonable choice is asserted by Justinus 42.4.6; cf. *RE* 13.268.62ff.)

        quare agite: Lucan elides a long into a short syllable only in the first foot; see Hosius's *index metricus*, p.392.

290-4   Pompey argues that Parthia is in effect a world of its own, and to carry this point he lists its constituent elements: land is *recessus*, sea is *Oceanus*, and sky *polus*. The clauses form a tricolon crescendo, and 291 is a golden line.

292 **polus** was used to mean 'sky', by the figure synecdoche (and by analogy to πόλος) as early as the tragedian Accius; see *OLD* sv 2. The phrase *polus alter* is discussed in appendix I.

293 **mare discolor unda**: *unda* is best taken as an ablative defining *discolor*; if it is taken as nominative (and *discolor* would then agree with it), the phrase in apposition to *mare* draws too much attention to itself. Pompey is only trying to show that Parthia has its own sea; *discolor undă* would stress the fact that the sea is an unusual colour, Red.

295 **celsior . . . fortior**: it is hard to see why the comparative is used, and Duff has ignored it. It may simply be the case that Lucan uses it as a form more emphatic than the positive; the comparative is so used in later Latin. The height of cavalry is stressed by Virgil, *Geor.* 2.145 and Manil. 5.636f.

296 **tendere neruos** is picked up by Lentulus at 383.

297 **segnis** governs an infinitive from Horace on; cf. *Carm.* 3.21.21, Ov. *Tr.* 5.7.19. **incerta** is tauntingly recalled at 373.

298-300 Parthian might has been described in general terms, so now Pompey gives particular instances of their victories. Burman saw that 298 could not refer to Alexander, but rather to some defection from one of his successors; comm. Bern. says 'quod ab Arsace Seleucus occisus est'. The subsequent allusions are equally vague, and may be unfactual. Lucan simply wants to give the reader a notion of vast eastern empire, won by the bow.

298-9 **fregere sarisas Bactraque** is not an example of true zeugma, since *fregere* suggests a verb of similar meaning, e.g., *uicerunt*, for Bactra and Babylon.

299-300 **murisque superbam Assyrias Babylona domos**: such interlaced apposition is discussed by Norden (116f), by Leo on *Culex* p.37, and by Vahlen 1.119f. There are few examples as extended as this, for most are confined to the type found at Vir. *Geor.* 4.168 'ignauom fucos pecus'. But at 6.350 'Emathis aequorei regnum Pharsalos Achillis' is an exact parallel. For the sense of *domos* see *TLL* 5.1, 1973, 40-72.

300 **nec pila timentur**: the sentiment is found at 10.47f.

301 **Parthis** is dative of agent; the history of its use with the simple passive is sketched by LHS 97, and further examples in Lucan are given by Dilke on 7.511f.
audentque: Fraenkel warns at *Horace* (1957), 219, n.4, that it is crude and misleading to speak of the copula as endowed with adversative force. Rather it is the context which colours it with this sense. Lucan is very fond of the usage, as a glance at Mooney's *Index*, p.224 shows; cf. 620n.

302 **Scythicas** means 'their own', as comm. Bern. observed, for Roman poets tend to regard all eastern tribes as much the same.

123

Crasso pereunte is a tactless allusion (in fact he was not killed in battle), but it paves the way for the doubts Pompey voices at 306 and their resolution at 326f.

303-5 The construction of this sentence deserves close attention. It is a sort of logical argument, each step of which fills one line, and its conclusion is divided into two cola for epigrammatic point. The alliteration is throughout remarkable, and stresses the sinister skill of Parthian archers. The first two lines are symmetrically constructed thus: A b V a B and a b V A B (a true golden line). Each step of the argument emphasizes some quantitative point: *solo, multo, parua*. The diction is made vivid by the use of *stridula* (a word coined by Virgil), and there is a mild personification in *fidentia*, an old and common military metaphor (see *Il.* 4.303, Aesch. *Pers.* 55, Eur. *Hel.* 154, Vir. *Geor.* 3.31).

303 **nec** is to be analysed into its logically component parts, *et* and *non*, but unlike *nec* at 250 the negative word stands next to the word it modifies, *solo*; see Housman on Manil. 4.738.

304 Ulysses used poisoned arrows to kill men, *Od.* 1.260, but their use is unknown in the *Iliad*, a sign of Homer's disapproval. In general the device was deplored, along with archery itself (see 385-6n), but in the *Aeneid* a Trojan uses poison against an animal (9.772) and the Lydian Ismarus is so armed at 10.140.

306 This admission of his own misgivings, though quickly suppressed, will prove fatal to Pompey's case and Lentulus will worry this very point at 362.

308 The sentiment is not unlike *Il.* 3.440 'we too have gods on our side'.

309-10 **reuolsos excitosque** = 'reuellam et effundam, exciam et inmittam'; similar are 2.395 'sparsas extendere partes', 409 'Eridanus fractas deuoluit in aequora siluas', 7.159, 846, below 789-90, 844 and 846. This compendious idiom is common in the poets and in historians. These lines are an example of theme and variation. The second line is cast in the 'quasi-golden' pattern, a b V B A, and *ortus* gives more definition to the whole sentence. Like *raptos* at 240, *reuolsos* is characteristic of the violence of Lucan's language.

311 **quodsi**: 'If *quodsi* is prosaic, Propertius is to be pitied; he uses it at every turn'; Gildersleeve's lively note to Persius *Prol.* 12 is substantiated by Axelson 47ff and LHS 571.

313-4 This sentiment is re-echoed at 594f.

314-6 **feram solacia . . . fecisse**: the syntax is Ovidian, cf. *Met.* 5.191f; so at 354-6 below the infinitive is explanatory.

315 **orbe . . . alio** is explained by Housman in his note to 309f to mean 'other than our own'. See appendix I.

315-6 **nihil . . . pie**: in the first clause both the subject and verb, *socerum fecisse*,

124

must be understood ἀπὸ κοινοῦ from the second. Other examples of this sort of distribution are collected by E.J. Kenney in *CQ* 8.1958.55. Anaphora, *nihil . . . nil,* is used instead of a copula, as at 318f.

316   **sed** resumes the argument left at 306.

        cuncta reuoluens . . . uenerabilis fui: logically considered, the participle does not harmonize with the main verb. But there is no need to accept Guyetus's conjecture 'si . . . reuolues' because such lapses from strict logical expression can be pointed to not only in Lucan (e.g., 2.571f, 9.1019f, and see Postgate on 8 above) but in other writers: Catull. 116, Tac. *Hist.* 3.38 (with Summers' note) and *Ann.* 15.67.8. (Moreover, since *Aen.* 9.391 ends with the phrase 'omne reuoluens' it is likely that Lucan has casually recalled it here, but has failed to assimilate it to its new context.)

321   **abit . . . redit**: a defence of this, the reading of the Ms tradition, against Lachmann's conjecture, *redi,* is to be found in *Mnemosyne* for 1979.

322   **Roma, faue coeptis**: this phrase is uttered by Caesar, when faced with Rome herself at 1.200, where the name comes at the end of his prayer to form a powerful climax. Here the address is abrupt. *Coeptis* as usual implies a bold or risky undertaking; see Pease on *Aen.* 4.642.

325   **et nostris miscere malis**: *nostris* is here just the Romans, for at 7.654f Pompey refused to involve nations in his personal ruin.

INTRODUCTION TO LINES 328-471

     Lentulus now replies to Pompey's proposal in a speech 'too long by half, but good in spirit' (Heitland, lviii), and puts forward a plan of his own. As for the facts, Plutarch records that it was Theophanes of Mytilene, Pompey's companion and panegyrist, who opposed his scheme (76). Lucan chooses Lentulus, not only because he had appeared in a patriotic light earlier at 5.15-47, but because it better suits the *Romanitas* of the poem to exclude a Greek sage and pretend that the Senate still freely discussed such matters. The speech fulfils Cicero's requirements in *De Or.* 2.335: Lentulus argues mainly from considerations of *honestas* and harps upon the baseness of Pompey's plan (so *uirtus, nobilitas* 329, *dignus* 330, 347, *pudor* 349, 390, 419, *uir* in a strong sense 367, 385, 396, *uilis* 393). In fine, Lentulus urges 'intuta quae indecora' (Tac. *Hist.* 1.33).

329   **uirtutis stimulis** appears at 7.103, where it is apposite applied to soldiers in the sense 'spur to valour'. Here Duff's translation is what the context requires, but the phrase is not really at home, especially with the verb, *praecessit.*

330   **tulit . . . uoces**: epic poets were always in need of periphrases meaning 'say', and this one seems to be coined by Lucan; see *TLL* 6. 542.83-4.

modo consule: Latin naturally allows an adverb to modify a noun; see Fordyce on Catull. 4.10. Examples from Lucan are collected by Hosius in his *index*, p.386b.

331-45 Lentulus begins his speech with a barrage of questions, all intended to be unanswerable. The variety of pauses is noteworthy, though in 339-41 the stop at the penthemimeral caesura is overworked. But in reading we naturally treat 'quid . . . amor' as one colon, whereas the following question is broken into two cola, an apodosis and its protasis.

331 **sicine** makes its first appearance in epic here. This lively word, expressive of disillusioned reproach, is found in Catullus's epyllion, 64.132 (and also at 77.3) and in Propertius, for whom see H. Tränkle, *Die Sprachkunst des Properz und die Tradition der lateinischen Dichterschprache* (1960), 156. But somewhat surprisingly neither Virgil nor Ovid have the word. Now Ovid was not in principle opposed to the vivid suffix, *ine*, as *huncine* at *Her.* 16.305 shows (if it is accepted that Ovid wrote the double *Heroides*). Livy used *sicine* in his history, an elevated genre, at 6.16.2, and Seneca has it at *Phaed.* 864, which would certainly have removed any scruple Lucan might have felt about using it in epic.

332 **una dies**, used to stress the suddenness of fatal reversals, has a history stretching back to Homer. In the following examples it should be noted that some other word denoting quantity is also present, often indeed juxtaposed, and it is perhaps this rhetorical opposition as much as the nature of ancient warfare which prompted the phrase: *Il.* 6.422 'all in one day went into Hades's house', Aesch. *Per.* 431f, Soph. *Ant.* 14, *El.* 1149, 1363, Eur. *Herc. Fur.* 510, Herod. 5.92η, and for comedy, where as in tragedy the conventions of the stage would encourage the turn of phrase, see E.W. Handley on Men. *Dysc.* 186f. In Latin we meet what is by now a commonplace at Lucr.3.899 (and in his note *ad loc.* E.J. Kenney collects sepulchral examples) and 5.999f, at Prop. 2.20.28, 3.11.70, Ov. *Am.* 1.15.24 (an echo of Lucretius), and at Severus fr. 13.10 Morel. Lucan's reflection on the effect of Pharsalia is similar to Plut. *Pomp.* 73, who speaks of a single hour. While the expression in Greek is always just a dative of time, the genius of the Latin language encouraged personification. In the examples cited above *dies* is always the subject of the verb (cf. Livy 9.39.11 and Sen. *Med.* 423f). In *Elementi Plautini in Plauto* (1960), 101-4 Fraenkel suggested that it was the designation of days as *fasti* and *nefasti* which tended to endow each with its own personality.

332-3 **secundum Emathiam lis tanta datur?**: the scholiasts rightly note that the language is legal (e.g., Cic. *Pro Rosc. Com.* 1.3, Val. Max.2.8.2). This is unobjectionable in the present context just because a civil war was a *causa*, in which one side or the other had stronger legal claims; see 94n and Postgate on 7.870; *damnauit* at 332 also contributes to the legal tone. Lucan's work bristles with legal metaphors, as Heitland (xc) and Fraenkel (2.283f) demonstrate. This is due to his legal training and practice at the bar, as well as to the pervasive legal knowledge in Roman life; see Kenney on Lucr. 3.971 and in *YCS* 21.1969.243-63, and A.G. Lee's index to his commentary on Ovid *Met.* 1, sv 'metaphor, legal'.

334   **uolneris auxilium**: the metaphor is resumed at 352.

334-5   **solos . . . pedes**: the bracketing word order, and the alliteration with *Parthorum* give bite to the expression. Too many have assumed that Lentulus alludes to the swift retreat of the Parthians; but of course he is speaking of an act of abasement as at 7.372. Postgate compared Sen. *De Clem.* 1.21.2 'ex alto ad inimici pedes abiectus'.

335-9   The construction of this sentence merits close analysis because it reveals an unhappy combination of nicety and flabbiness. It begins and ends with noun phrases, chiastically arranged: 'transfuga mundi' and 'Parthorum pedes'. These phrases are the most emphatic in the sentence, and the other lines flesh out these bones. The sentence as a whole also forms a chiasmus: noun phrase, participial phrase, the predicate, another participial phrase and then the closing noun phrase. The two participial phrases are strongly alliterative, and indeed every element of the sentence is weighted. But for all that there is an impression of flaccidity, due, it seems, to the end-stopping of the three central lines, and to the insufficiency of the lone finite verb, *quaeris*, to support the superstructure. In fact *quaeris* is the least emphatic word in the sentence, and so Lucan has devalued completely the role of the main verb by enmeshing it among phrases, none of which is subordinate to it in sense or in emphasis. The structure and emphases of the first sentence of this book are similar. There is here no integration, only accumulation. It is the sort of construction which could never (or but rarely) have come from the pen of Virgil or Ovid.

335   **transfuga** is pointed because it finds no place in epic (or indeed in poetry, though Statius has a feeble imitation of this passage at *Silu.* 1.2.203-5). *Mundi* is puzzling, and Duff's translation has been diffidently retained. At *Met.* 6.189 Ovid could fairly describe Latona as 'exul mundi' because he had already pointed out that heaven, earth, and sea had rejected her (188). Lucan embraces the entire conceit, but with rather less justification; his expression shows how it appealed to his sense of grandeur.

337   **aliena sidera** is discussed in appendix I. The phrase is similar to Petr. 79.1 'alienaque litora quaere' (PLM 4, p.90).

338   The last depravity will be apostasy from the state rites, especially from loyalty to the hearth. Horace levels this same charge against the soldier of
Crassus, now orientalised, and 'oblitus aeternae Vestae' at *Carm.* 3.5.5-12.
culture is chosen over the nominative because the short final e is metrically
handy. The device is found in Greek tragedy, and there are examples in
Callimachus (see KG 2.1, 50, and fr.24.9, 599P). It enters Latin with
Catullus (44.1, 77.1) after whom it is not infrequent: e.g., *Aen.* 2.283, 10.
327 and 811, Tibull.1.7.53, Pers. 3.28f. Examples are collected by Postgate on 643 below, and by Housman on 5.583 (cf. too his *Papers* 283); see
Langen on V. Fl.1.392 and 4.468.

341   **si seruire potes**: the view had been expressed in the *Aleadae* of Sophocles,
fr. 85P, that impiety, committed with a view to gaining power, might be
preferable to slavery. Here Lentulus argues that Pompey will not only give
up Rome's religion, but for all that he will only be a slave. *Potes* means 'if
you can bring yourself to . . . '; see Fordyce on Catull.68.41.

341-6   The text of these lines is discussed in *Mnemosyne* for 1979. At 345 all the
Mss read *extolletque*, and so there is no stated subject word in the whole
of the sentence. To remedy this Housman proposed *rex tolletque* at 345.
Lucan however never begins a line with a monosyllable after which there
is a pause, nor is the lack of an epithet for *rex* stylistically satisfactory.
Thus the text is to be left as transmitted, and the subject must be understood from the context, viz., 'the Parthian' (and not necessarily the king),
as adn. explains.

342-3   **auditu** suggests 'quid si uidisset', as adn. well observes. The contrast is
pointed up by *uidit* in the next line.

343   The hyperbaton in this line, in which a phrase is enmeshed within another
phrase, is illustrated by Housman *ad loc.*, and in the *addendum* to Manil.
1.429. From the adduced examples it may be observed that generally, as
here, an epithet at the third foot caesura agrees with a noun set at the end
of the line; so at 5.800 'fertur ad aequoreas, ac se prosternit, harenas'. See
Postgate in *CR* 30.1916.142ff.

344   The line looks back to 7.584 and 206 above. For the play on *uidit* and
uidebit cf. 4.605f, 7.683f and 9.242f. Here the verbs are emphatically
placed at the beginning and end of their lines.

346   **Pompeio supplice** throws back in Pompey's face his own argument against
approaching Juba at 287.

347   **nil . . . dignum** brackets the line for emphasis.

349   **patimurne** seems to be a deliberative indicative (LHS 308). (At *Aen.* 2.322

and 4.534 Austin and Pease respectively make out a case for a true indicative, not a deliberative; so too Fordyce on Catull.1.1.) At *Aen.* 3.367 'quae prima pericula vito?' the mood is used as a deliberative; cf. Mayor on Juv. 4.130 and Langen on V. Fl.5.285.

349-50   **pudoris . . . uolnus** is close in meaning to 'pudoris funera' at 4.231f. Lentulus is now setting about a reply to Pompey's paradoxical final remark, and the repetition of *uindicet* makes this clear. Thus *clades* refers to the civil war, especially to Pharsalia. Lentulus observes that Pompey was chosen as leader only for civil war, *ciuilibus armis*, and so that he has no authority to bring in the Parthian as an ally, if only to extinguish the inimical race. The following sentence, 'quid . . . latentes', is not at first sight easy to harmonize with this, and Burman honestly admits 'obscura haec mihi'. But the progression of thought is not broken. *Spargis* in 353 has the metaphorical sense 'broadcast' and 'uolnera nostra' in 352 means 'the wounds we Romans have given each other'. Once the Parthians learn of the disastrous losses sustained among the Romans they will cross the Euphrates with a view to the final eradication of the Roman name. This sense is analogous to that at 1.9 'gentibus inuisis Latium praebere cruorem', which Duff (alone?) takes to mean 'to give to hated nations the spectacle of Roman bloodshed'.

352   **nempe** is not found in Virgil. Lucan admits this lively particle, common in Ovid, to speeches, where it naturally belongs, and once to the narrative at 4.388.

353   **spargis** 'spread word of' also at V. Fl.1.96ff.

354   **transire** is used absolutely at 7.647 and here it refers to crossing the Euphrates. At Tac. *Agr.* 15.4 (and in the letters of Erasmus) it is used to mean Channel crossings.

354-5   **solacia . . . admittere**: see 314-6n.

356   **ciui seruire suo** is an epigrammatic paradox: a citizen cannot be a slave to a fellow-citizen.

357-8   The careful placement of *ducentem* and *sequentem* stresses their opposed sense.

358   In Greek *Euphrates* is of the first declension. The dative singular is in η, and the Latin ablative singular reflects this by using long e. So too with *Ganges* at Ov. *Fas.* 3.729. See Housman *Papers* 2.833.

359   **solus** is not strictly true, for Ptolemy sent no troops to either side, a point made by Pothinus at 531f. The fact however is not material to Lentulus's case for it was indeed unlikely that Orodes would have helped Pompey in defeat.

129

361   **auditi** 'heard of' is discussed by Fordyce on *Aen.* 7.196.

362   **fiducia** is tauntingly echoed from 306 where Pompey wished that he had not to rely on Parthian arms. Now Lentulus will demonstrate that after all they are not even good fighters.

364   **mortis amator** and its kindred expression *uelle mori* are typical of Lucan's passionate commitment to showy (not easeful) death: cf. 4.147,280,485, 544,6.246. Death for him is a goal to which a man can form the strongest attachment. Statius, Lucan's constant imitator, also strikes this note; see *Th.* 9.674f, 10.677, 804; 12.679. See Schnepf 387f and W. Rutz in *Hermes* 88.1960.462-75. (The notion is found in the anonymous poem *De Bello Aegyptiaco* 46 'trahiturque libidine mortis'; if the poem is by Rabirius, then it predates Lucan. See PLM 1, p.218.)

365-6   **quidquid . . . ibitur** is a construction analogous to 179-81. The use of the tenses is hard to find parallels for.

        ad Eoos tractus mundique teporem is a coupling of abstract and concrete, for *teporem* means 'partem tepidam'.

        emollit 'enervate' is a sense first found in Livy; see *OLD* sv 2b. At 2.593 Sophene is called *mollis*, and adn. remarks that this is due to the heat. *Clementia* is first used of weather by Grattius; see *OLD* sv 2. The influence of climate upon character was assumed in antiquity, and the notion is by no means discredited to this day. Full references to the chief examples will be found in Mayor's note on Juv. 10.50, Summers on Sen. *Ep.* 51.10, and Page on Eur. *Med.* 826f. Most relevant to the present argument is Hippocrates *Aer.* 62 in which Asians are said to be less warlike than Europeans because their climate lacks extremes, and is mixed.

367-8   **laxas uestes et fluxa uirorum uelamenta** offers a distinction without a difference, though the second element adds an important new notion in *uirorum*: it is the fact that such clothes appear on men that disgusts. Gellius noticed that the Latin epic poets permitted themselves such reflections upon State enemies, and he cites from Ennius a reproach put upon the Carthaginian army, 'tunicata iuuentus', that is relevant here; *N.A.* 6.12.7. The dress of orientals was long remarkable in the West because of its abundance and looseness, which prompted moral censure; it was taken as a sign of unmanliness; cf. Diels-Kranz *Die Fragmente der Vorsokratiker* 2.408, Arist. *Ves.* 1087-90, Manil. 4.750, Apul. *Flor.* 6. At 2.593, cited in the previous note, *mollis* is explained by comm. Bern. as referring to the fact that men there cover the whole body. Seneca's *Ep.* 114 remains a fascinating account of Maecenas, whose dress was taken as a sign of his morals: loose. So here Lentulus treads the path of well-worn commonplace.

368	**uides** brings the whole disgusting picture before our eyes. The verb has the force of a warning; see Dodds on Eur. *Ba.* 337.
369	**inter** = *in*; see González-Haba in *Glotta* 42.1964.198.
370	**arua solo** is an example of *adiectio* discussed at 198n.

superabilis may have been coined by Ovid at *Tr.* 5.8.27. *Hosti* is dative of agent, a usage common with adjectives of this formation; see Roby 1146.

371   **libertate fugae** is emphasized by enjambment and by its position at the head of the line. Lentulus wants to stress this precondition of Parthian superiority.

tumebit is presumably attracted into the future, though the sense could be 'where the ground will prove to be hilly'. At any rate Lentulus is countering Pompey's claims at 295.

372   **aspera** is chosen to show how unsuited the soft Parthians are to campaigning in rough country.

nec per opacas is an unusual rhythm for Lucan, though analogies can be found in other poets; see Hellegouarc'h 219-21.

372-3   **opacas . . . tenebras** is an otiose expression which however is exactly like 'gloomy dark' in Eur. *Ba.* 510. The epithet may have been chosen for the sake of emphasis, or, as is more likely, to balance the epithet attached to *iuga.* For all that, it is still not clear what produces the darkness. Since no-one chose to fight by night, it is more likely that Lucan refers to the darkness of woods or glades; so Ov. *Met.* 1.475 'siluarum tenebris' and Florus 1.39.6 'tenebras saltuum'. And up to now Lentulus has been talking about topography, not the time of day. But the obscurity of expression is real and culpable.

373   **incerto**, referring to poor aim, rebuts Pompey's assertion at 297.

374   **uiolenti uorticis** is the descriptive genitive; see 21n.

375   **totum** G, **tota** Ω: in the present context there is good reason to say that a man will not fight through a whole summer day; this seems more pointed then to observe that he is wholly drenched in blood (for *tota* of the majority of Mss is probably acc. pl.) The hyperbaton, *totum . . . diem* is very much in Lucan's manner; see Nutting in U.Cal.Publ.Class.Phil. 11.1932. 268n. It is reasonable to suppose that an original *totum* was altered out of the common desire of scribes to confine the reference of a word to the line in which it is found; so at 3.748 *missi* and 5.703 *Hesperiis* (indeed few alterations are more common).

376   **exiget** 'pass time'; see *OLD* sv 6 and Mayor on Pliny *Ep.* 3.1.1.

378   **aut**: the negative idea is carried over into this clause, as at 1.286f and

2:360ff; see *TLL* 2.1568.4-11.

379 **erit** 'will prove to be' as at 1.31 and 9.782 *sequetur*; see Housman on 10.390 and Manil. 2.432.

380 The whole line is an example of increasing cola, with change of number and gender in each. Similar patterns will be found at 1.110, 2.199, 7.424, 551, and 765 below. Earlier examples are Lucr. 5.1397 and Ov. *Am.* 2.12.3, 14. The omission of *est* is a characteristic economy.

381 **melior** is first construed with the infinitive here; cf. 482 below.

cessisse loco quam pellere: the qualities so scornfully mentioned by Lentulus — skirmishing, scattered retreat, ubiquitous ranging — have successfully countered conventional methods of fighting from the time of Tiridates (cf. Tac. *Ann.* 13.37.1). Sir John Moore introduced guerrilla tactics in the British army during the Peninsular War, and T.E. Lawrence preserved this type of fighting among the modern heirs of the Parthians. *Loco* is to be understood ἀπὸ κοινοῦ with both infinitives. The perfect infinitive, *cessisse,* is probably no more than a metrical eke, though it can be argued that it has developed a timeless aspect on analogy to the Greek aorist. Virgil is the first to combine this tenseless perfect infinitive with a present at *Geor.* 3. 435f (see Norden 147 and KS 2.1, 133f). Tibullus and Ovid greatly favoured the usage, for many perfect infinitive forms are well suited to the end of a pentameter line (see Wölfflin in *ALL* 11.1900.513 and Bednara *ALL* 14.1906. 575ff). Lucan has such combinations at 3.368f, and 417-21, in addition to those cited by Postgate in his note on this line.

382 **inlita tela dolis:** at 303-5 Pompey had mentioned how effective were these poisoned arrows. Lentulus bluntly damns the device as unmanly. After *inlita* one expects a concrete word for poison, but the bold *dolis* passes an unequivocal moral judgment. (So at Soph. *Aj.* 1245 σὺν δόλῳ κεντήσεθ' 'you will stab us with guile'; δόλῳ alone would be adverbial, but σύν shows that it is instrumental.) Guile moreover is usually taken to be a sign of or a defense against weakness (cf. Plato *Legg.* 6.781a).

Martem comminus: the adverb is used adnominally; see 330n.

384 This reprehensible tactic is also described at 7.515f 'nusquam rexere sagittas/ sed petitur solus qui campis inminet aer.' *Ferre* is to be understood ἀπὸ κοινοῦ as the object infinitive of *permittere.*

uolnera: Virgil was apparently the first to say 'wound' for the weapon that is about to inflict one at *Aen.* 2.529, and then commonly (see U. Hübner *RM* 117.1974.350-7). This once vivid metaphor becomes worn with use: Sen. *Herc. Oet.* 160, Lucan 3.568, 7.619, St. *Th.* 7.270, and 11.53. But thanks to alliteration the vividness is here retained.

385-6 **ensis . . . gladiis** ring the sentence for emphasis. Lucan stands alone among Latin poets in his indifference to the distinction which throughout the language was felt to control the use of these synonyms. The table in *TLL* 5.2, 608 tells its own story. In the *Aeneid* Virgil uses *gladius* only four times, in the books which may have been composed towards the end (9, 10, and 12). Ovid was less scrupulous, and so here too, as in other matters, may prove to have been Lucan's guide; in the *Metamorphoses gladius* appears thirteen times, against forty occurrences of *ensis*. In his tragedies Seneca is careful to use *gladius* only six times (its anapaestic form is no bar); *ensis* of course does not appear in his prose. Even after Lucan the poets avoid impropriety and hesitate to overuse the prosy word. But Lucan uses *gladius* forty-six times, and *ensis* only nine more. This must have been conscious policy, and it was probably adopted out of a desire to enliven epic diction by abolishing its remoteness. The reader would be affected more by the common word. Hence too the frequency of *cadauer*; see 438n and the Introduction p. 14.

uirorum is emphatically placed as at 367 and 1.165. It points to the age-old contempt which the front line fighter feels for the archer, distant, concealed and protected. The earliest example is at *Il.* 4.242 (and cf. 11.385 for Diomede's rebuke to Paris); see D.L. Page *History and the Homeric Iliad* (1959), 278 and G.S. Kirk *Homer and the Epic* (1965), 202. The later hoplites found archers no less despicable, and so the taunt is found after the heroic age (cf. Aesch. *Pers.* 239f, Soph. *Aj.* 1120-3 and fr. 427 and 859P (abuse of Trojans)). Lycus depreciates Hercules's accomplishments with the bow at Eur. *Herc. Fur.* 160 (and see Wilamowitz's edition, vol.2.44). Finally, Plutarch records a Spartan's chagrin at being killed by a 'womanly archer' (*Mor.* 234e). But Latin taunts are rarer, perhaps because the Romans' traditional enemies in the West were not bowmen and because later their own foreign auxiliaries used the weapon (see J. Harmand *L'Armée et Le Soldat* (1967), 76f). There is only, apart from this line, St. *Silu.* 3.2.126, though the later Greek writer, Procopius, thought it necessary to defend the use of archers in the Roman army of Belisarius (see Gibbon *Decline* ch. 41, n.14 of Bury's edition).

nam is here a transitional particle meaning 'but' or 'indeed'; see *OLD* sv 4 and cf. Ov. *Met.* 8.530, and 5.749 above.

proelia prima: the final alliteration enhances the contempt. But as Farnaby noted Lentulus is incorrect, for camels brought up fresh supplies of arrows. For *prima* 'the first part of . . . ' see LS sv IIA.

387 **exarmo** is first found in poetry at Sen. *Phoen.* 482, and 5.356 above.

388   **manus** is genitive, *fiducia* being supplied ἀπὸ κοινοῦ. It implies not only physical courage, but close combat (cf. 382 *comminus*).

       fiducia, a key word throughout these paired speeches, reappears from 362 where Lentulus began his attack on Parthian reliability and prowess. Its repetition marks the close of the section (as for example do *belli* and *bellum* at 1.158 and 182).

390-4   **temptare . . . sepulchrum?**: Lentulus here answers Pompey's argument of 314-6, that death in Parthia might be preferable to death in the West. The sentence is well constructed with many t's to point up the taunt. The *ut* consecutive clause is tripartite, each section having a different subject and varied number, but all linked by emphatic soundings of *tua*, *tibi*, and *te*. An index of Lucan's imagination is the narrowing focus: *toto orbe, barbara tellus, uilia busta,* from hemisphere to grave (see 546n). After the preceding enjambment, the adjective phrase which fills a whole line has a closing effect.

393   **incumbat** is strangely rare outside the sepulchral inscriptions themselves; cf. CE 191.1, 1039.3.

       busta: the plural is not unusual of one man's tomb; cf. Prop. 2. 13.38, 3.16, 24, Ov. *Pont.* 1.2.150, and 5.670 above (Housman illustrates the analogous use of *monimenta* at Manil. 4.685).

394   **inuidiosa tamen** implies *quamuis* with *parua ac uilia* in 393. But to whom would Pompey's tomb be an object of envy? Surely to Crassus. But Lucan has not used the dative case after *inuidiosa*, and has chosen to write an ablative absolute, *Crasso quaerente.* This is done for metrical convenience. Exactly analogous are Tibull. 2.3.17 'illo . . . gestante . . . occurrens', Ov. *Met.* 8.409f, and Juv. 1.69f 'quae molle Calaenum/ porrectura uiro miscet sitiente rubetam'.

       quaerente: the sense is illustrated by Munro on Lucr. 1.332 (and 4.705), and Housman on Manil. 5.275; see *OLD* sv 2.

395   **leuior**, transmitted by PGU, suits better the preceding *incumbat* than does *melior* of MZV. The substitution is common; cf. 9.938 (G), Hor. *Serm.* 2.7.19 and *Carm.* 1.24.19 (which is cited by Donatus on Ter. *Hec.* 603 with *melius* against *leuius* of all Horace's Mss). (Moreover, since *sors melior* begins a line at 9.330, the reading here may be due to recollection, a common source of variant reading. The scribe of antiquity often knew the text he transcribed very well, unlike his mediaeval heir.)

       mors ultima poena: for the phrase compare Ov. *Her.* 10.82 'mors minus poenae . . . habet', CE 507 'poenam non sentio mortis: poena fuit uita', Quint. *I.O.* 6.2.23f and Sen. *Dial.* 12.13.2. At 7.470 Lucan says that death is the *poena* 'quae cunctis . . . paratur'.

397-404 The sexual activities hinted at in these lines are discussed by Housman, *Papers* 3.1183. The argument put forward by Lentulus seems to have foundation in fact, for Plutarch tells us that it was this very consideration of insult to his widow that prompted Pompey to change his mind (76). Romantic Plutarch stressed the point, but for Lucan it is just one among many. The reason is clear: Theophanes in Plutarch is trying to sway Pompey alone, but Lentulus is addressing a meeting of the Senate.

Venus quae . . . polluit leges . . . thalamique patent: the syntax is harsh but not unexampled. In Latin poetry it is not so uncommon for an independent clause to be tacked on to a relative clause, if its content is related to the content of the relative clause. Often what links the two clauses is that they have a subject word in common; for example, *Aen.* 6.283f 'ulmus . . . quam sedem Somnia . . . / uana tenere ferunt foliisque sub omnibus haerent'; see Munro on Lucr. 1.720, and Vahlen 1.166. The present instance is more harsh but finds an analogue in *Aen.* 5.286-9 'Aeneas . . . tendit . . . in campum quem . . . cingebant siluae mediaque in ualle theatri circus erat'. The sentence has nevertheless rhetorical balance: *polluit* is answered by *nefandi,* and *innumeris coniugibus* is picked up by *inter mille nurus.*

399-400 **innumeris . . . coniugibus** is the harem; cf. V. Fl.7.236.

399 **leges et foedera** is borrowed from 2.2.

401 **epulis uaesana meroque**: dinner (especially in the case of the later Christian meal) was assumed to be the prelude to vice (see Min. Fel. *Oct.* 9.6).

402 **non ullis exceptos legibus** was explained by Postgate in *CQ* 1.1907.217f; he compared the reason ascribed to Solon for his not legislating against parricide: he hoped the crime would never occur. Equally relevant is Plato's discussion at *Legg.* 8.838 of the unwritten law against incest; he argues that the temptation to such a crime is too rare for it to be specifically forbidden. As Postgate went on to point out, *exceptos* is a legal term meaning 'specially mentioned'; see *OLD* sv *excipio* 4.

audet was first restored to the text by Oudendorp, who recorded his changed opinion in the 'omissa et corrigenda ad notas' of his edition.

403 The tyrants of the Greek stage were characteristically promiscuous, and Lucan borrows the trait (see Denniston on Eur. *El.* 945, and cf. *Suppl.* 452-5).

404 **iacuere** is presumably a gnomic perfect (see 30n). For incest as an eastern vice see Stevens on Eur. *And.* 171ff, as well as Mayor on pp. 206f of his notes to Tertullian's *Apologeticus.* Catullus 90 brings the theme into Latin.

405 **sacrataque pignora matres** is a pattern of apposition first found perhaps at

Lucr. 5.1284. Housman gives further examples in his notes to 3.106f and Manil. 2.23 with its *addendum*. The development of the meaning of *pignus* is discussed by Merrill on Pliny *Ep.* 1.12.3.

406-7 The point of the allusion to Oedipus seems to be that his crime was unique and unintentional; how much worse therefore are the frequent and conscious incests of the Parthian.

apud gentes is a legal phrase consciously repeated at 420.

non sponte was stressed at Soph. *O.C.* 521ff.

407 A line composed of only four words is found in Homer from time to time, and then in Callimachus, presumably as an ornament of style (e.g., *Hymn.* 3.171, 216). Ennius brings the weighty pattern into Latin (e.g., *Ann.* 183, 191, 223, 303V), and from him it is inherited by the Latin poets generally (e.g., Catull. 64.115, and see Winbolt 227f). We find examples in Lucan at 1.653, 4.461, 680, 6.340, 386 (a spondeiazon), 809, and 7.394. Müller holds the view that the very paucity of examples argues that the poets did not see the device as an elegance. But four word lines are not easy to compose, and they are especially hard to bring off in the developed hexameter which eschews words of four or five syllables at the close. It is easy *not* to write a four word line. Müller's view therefore is unlikely to be correct (574).

410 **proles tam clara** stresses sharply the contrast between Cornelia, a high-bred Roman lady, and the degenerate (*sanguine mixto*) who will debauch her.

411 **stabit** is a shocking word, for it is properly used of servants and of prostitutes (see Owen on Ov. *Tr.* 2.310).

411-12 Lentulus has said that Cornelia will be *millesima coniunx,* only one out of many wives, but he goes on to qualify this by saying that her dignity will subject her to particular attention.

413 **stimulata** Ω, **-ante** V: the choice, sometimes obvious (but not so here) between participles is also offered at *Aen.* 2.114, 12.506 and 746, *Moret.* 32, Ov. *Her.* 6.143, Luc. 5.421, 582 below, 10.135, St. *Th.* 12.364.

414 **quo . . .** : this final clause does not represent any purpose in the mind of the subject of the sentence, but rather a purpose present to the mind of the speaker or writer, which prompts him to make the remark.

416 **trahitur** is a vivid present; the whole passage conforms to the rules of *descriptio*, as laid down in the treatise *Ad Her.* 4.51, for instance.

cladis . . . uetustae: five years before! Lucan inadvertently is speaking from the point of view of Nero's reign.

417 **haereat** is a jussive subjunctive used to replace a conditional protasis. For a discussion of this lively alternative see Blase in *Glotta* 11.1921.161ff. Another example in Lucan is at 10.191f. The sense of *haereat* 'lodge in the mind' is illustrated in *OLD* sv 7c; usually an indirect object is stated, but not at Ov. *Met.* 12.184, Sen. *Ep.* 123.9, *De Ben.* 3.5.1, or Quint. *I.O.*1.1.5 and 11.2.34.

418 **ab rege** is a set phrase in which *a* is almost never found; see Neue[3] 2.846f.

419 The thought of these lines re-echoes 1.10f.

420 **populos** is often used by Lucan specifically of Italians, or more precisely still of Romans; this was noted by Haskins on 2.314, and by Housman on 1.511. It seems also to be the sense of the word at 804 below.
socerique tuumque is a pattern of coordination close to Ovid's heart, but infrequently imitated after him. Lucan has one more example at 5.48; see Christensen in *ALL* 15.1908.173.

422-6 The articulation of this sentence is worth scrutiny, for it is a good example of Lucan's skill in handling a sentence that extends over several lines. Enjambment is employed throughout, there is unobtrusive subordination in the *nequa* and *dum* clauses, and the second infinitive clause dependent upon *debuerant* is compactly bound into a whole by the encircling *Arctoum . . . latus.*

423 and 426 **duces** and **ducum**: for the repetition see 575n. The present instance is vexing because the words do not refer to the same leaders. *Duces* are living Romans, *ducum* are the dead Crassi.

425 **nudare** is common in military contexts; see *OLD* sv 4.
perfida continues this book's emphasis on loyalty, but in this context it answers Pompey's demand at 277 for *fides* in his allies.

426 **in tumulos prolapsa ducum** has been generally misunderstood by modern students of the poem. As was said in the note to 423 *ducum* here are the Crassi, who were never (so the story went) buried. Lentulus would have the ruins of Susa and Babylon serve as the tombs of these Roman generals. *In* therefore has final (or perhaps consecutive) force, a not uncommon usage illustrated by Oudendorp on 2.151   by Heinsius on Claud. *In Ruf.* 1.151, and by Owen on Ov. *Tr.* 2.409; see *OLD* sv 21. Of commentators who notice that a paraphrase is wanted, Farnaby and Cortius are seised of the sense; of translators Thos. May is correct with 'Till . . . Susa and . . . Babylon/ Had fallen for tombs'.

430 **de qua . . . triumphis** is to be taken as a single phrase, as Housman showed on 9.299; cf. Florus 2.13.88 'de Gallia triumphum trahens'. The adnominal use of the prepositional phrase is illustrated by Munro on Lucr. 2.51, and by Housman on Manil. 4.64.

432 **umbra . . . confixa sagittis**: 'Deiphobus appears all mangled in Virgils Ghosts

137

yet we meet with perfect shadows among the wounded ghosts of Homer',
truly noted Sir Thos. Browne in *Urne-Buriall,* ch. 4 (if, that is, we follow
the Alexandrian scholars in rejecting *Od.* 11.40). After Homer it was the
fashion to fancy that a shade bore the marks of its last agony (though Lucan's
striving for pathos has blinded him to the fact that Crassus was not killed by
arrows). Collections of instances are made by Heinsius 559, and by Norden
on *Aen.* 6.446 (to which may be added Ov. *Met.* 10.49, V. Fl. 1.49, Tac. *Ann.*
1.65, and Lucian. *Nec.* 10). Dante could portray the special bodies of the
saved in Purgatory as bearing the wounds of life (for example, Manfredi at
3.108 'Ma l'un de' cigli un colpo avea diviso') because the Evangelists so
describe the risen body of Jesus (e.g., S. John 20.24-9).

433 funera 'death', see *TLL* 6.1605.13.

434 nudae 'unburied', see *OLD* sv 5.

436-7 quae . . . duces cannot, Postgate says, mean that the headless bodies of
chieftains were lugged around the walls, for that would be an 'uninstructive
and profitless proceeding'. This is to assume that, when committing an
outrage, men seek either instruction or profit. (Though profit there doubtless was, but of a magical sort.) Moreover in Latin the genitive or ablative
with *truncus* always expresses the part missing (e.g., Vir. *Geor.* 4.309f, Ov.
Met. 15.375f, V. Fl. 3.444f, Sil. 10.310, and Mart. 2.83.3); so here the
Latin reader must have taken *ceruice* with *trunci* to mean 'headless'. *Lustrarunt* means 'go round' as at *Aen.* 11.190 and 5.416 above (cf. Housman
on Manil. 3.321), not 'purify' as it is classified in *OLD* sv 1a, (though puri-
fication may have been at the back of the Parthians' mind). In this book
the allusion to the beheading of the Crassi must glance at Pompey's fate.

437 ubi = *locus ubi;* see Housman on 6.355 and especially 1.405.
nomina 'bearers of great names', as often; see *OLD* sv 17.

438 cadauera is largely avoided by Augustan poets, and if used at all it serves
a special effect; see Axelson 49f. Virgil uses it of beasts at *Geor.* 3.557 and
of the corpse of the wild man Cacus in *Aen.* 8.264; Ovid uses it of plague-
stricken dead at *Met.* 7.602 and thrice in his invective poem, *Ibis.* Lucan
however does not hesitate to use it indiscriminately, and on two occasions
plays on the etymology of the word, 2.134 'cecidere cadauera', and 6.822f.
He thus raised the word to currency in epic – his ape, Silius, uses it often –
and this was entirely on his own initiative. The reason for this is suggested
in the Introduction, p. 14.

438-9 Tigris . . . reddidit: it was a common, if erroneous, fancy in antiquity that
Tigris was one of those rivers which hides its diving flood. Lucan had earlier alluded to this curiosity of natural history at 3.261-3. For a discussion

of literary borrowings that surround the matter see *CQ* 28.1978.241f.

440-1   **in media socerum . . . Thessalia:** the word order is pictorial, a not uncommon device, found for example at 3.583, 4.14, and 6.792; cf. *Aen.* 8.608 'aetherios inter dea candida nimbos', Hor. *Carm.* 1.5.1, and Ov. *Met.* 4.184 'in mediis ambo deprensi amplexibus haerent'.

      sedentem refers to the victor on his tribunal; cf. 7.19 'sedit adhuc Romanus eques'.

441   **quin respicis** is a vigorous turn of phrase, brought from common speech into epic by Virgil; see Austin on *Aen.* 4.99.

445   **gurgite . . . amnis:** Borneau suggests that Lucan here has in mind the curved projection of Nile's delta which thrusts up into the sea (127, n.3). *Summouet* certainly hints at the magistrate's lictors, who thrust aside bystanders. *Gurgite* is taken to mean 'mouth' in *TLL* 6.2364.13f, but Duff's 'channels' is unexceptionable. The phrase *gurgite septeno* is borrowed by both Silius, at 1.197, and Claudian, *In Ruf.* 1.185 of the Nile's mouth.

446   **terra suis contenta bonis** is not as ethical as it sounds; rather it hints that a self-sufficient country, with no need of imports, is strong; so Dionysius of Halicarnassus speaks of Italy at *Ant. Rom.* 1.36.3. Lentulus avoids all discussion of Egyptian power, and so sounds this dim commendatory note. Indeed the close of the speech is rhetorically weak.

447   **Iouis** in the sense 'rain', without a clarifying epithet, seems to be unique.

448   **sceptra tibi debita:** Aulus Gabinius, a proconsul in Syria and a henchman of Pompey's, had restored to the throne the present Ptolemy's father, the twelfth of that name, commonly called the 'Flute-player'. Ampelius says that Pompey was appointed the boy's guardian (35.6).

451   Tac. *Ann.* 14.1.1 'uetustate imperii coalita audacia' voices a similar opinion.

452   **adsuetos sceptris** recalls Sen. *Tro.* 152 'adsuetas ad sceptra manus'.

454-5   **quantum . . . habes:** this sort of apostrophe is discussed in the Introduction, p.15.

455   **uicta est sententia Magni:** 'sheer prose' said Postgate, but with the precedent of Ov. *Met.* 9.517. But Postgate did not appreciate that Lucan in this blunt way stresses the freedom of the debate; in the old Senate even a Pompey could fail to carry his point. Moreover the plain statement has ominous overtones; cf. 'superat sententia Sabini' at Caes. *B.G.* 5.31.3.

456-71   This section is an interlude between the long rebuttal of Lentulus and Pothinus' brilliant harangue. Meanwhile Lucan treats the reader to speculation on the birth of Venus, and to some clever star lore. Once again straightforward narrative is avoided.

456 Cypro is dative of goal, an uncommon use of the case with placenames; Heitland (civ) gives further instances in Lucan, but none is a proper name. (For Virgil's practice see Page on *Aen.* 12.256.)

457 cui is an example of abbreviated comparison, called 'comparatio compendiaria' found also at 2.138, 7.101, 144, 9.762f.

458-9 Paphian Venus was the object of Tacitus's interest at *Hist.* 2.2-3, for short digressions were part of the historical tradition; cf. Sallust's account of the brothers Philaeni at *Jug.* 79. Lucan's scepticism also suggests an historical source.

459 si fas est, supply *credere* from *credimus*. The intransitive (or absolute) use of *coepisse* 'to have a beginning' is illustrated in *OLD* sv 4; see too Duff on Sen. *Dial.* 11.1.1.

462 transuerso uertitur seems owed to Manil. 3.308. Examples of the simple form of the verb following the compound (often, but not here, with the same sense) are collected by W. Clausen in *AJP* 76.1955 49ff, and by C. Watkins in *HSCP* 71.1966.115-9.

463 tenuit is here a technical term, illustrated by Housman on 3.181-3.
montem is here used of a vast structure, the lighthouse at Pharos. It was built in three stages, and rose to 135m; see *RE* sv Pharos, 3.

464 infima is not common in poetry for the usual *ultimus*. Lucan's description tallies with that of Callimachus, fr.384.48 P.

467-9 The usual sort of periphrasis, here for the autumnal equinox. Lucan is following the unreformed calendar. In fact (and in accordance with the Julian reforms) Pompey reached Egypt in mid-July (Postgate, lxxvii).

468-9 die, noctique and hibernae uerni are pointedly juxtaposed.
solacia 'compensation' is also found in Tacitus; see Furneaux on *Agr.* 6.3.

471 In this line Lucan alludes to the dropping of the wind towards sunset. He has in the back of his mind *Aen.* 3.568 'fessos uentus cum sole reliquit', but, in his desire to cast his model into the shade, he has given a cosmetic treatment to the Virgilian simplicity. By the use of metonomy *Phoebus* is used instead of *sol*, and drooping sails present a vivid picture in place of the simple *reliquit*. (Moreover Lucan has used *languent* in a slightly different sense with each subject word, as Riley and Duff observed.) This tendency to outshine the model is worth illustrating briefly. At 9.349 'uentosa perflantem marmora concha' he is imitating *Aen.* 6.171 'caua . . . personat aequora concha'; but Lucan's epithet for *concha* is choicer, and his word for sea, *marmora* (an almost certain emendation), is the rarer. But just as Ovid was his constant study, so is he the poet to be surpassed. Does Ovid's figure of Inuidia at *Met.* 2.792 scorch the grass? Then Lucan's Erichtho must blast seeds (6.521). Does Inuidia poison cities with her breath (*Met.* 2.794f)? Let Erichtho waste the very atmosphere (6.522). Much of the excess of Silver Latin poetry is generated by this sense of a need to go beyond what had been thought or written hitherto (see Ribbeck 91 and Fraenkel Pathos 2.243=25).

INTRODUCTION TO LINES 472-576

Lentulus has won the day, and so Pompey sets sail for Egypt. This section treates of the reaction to his arrival in the royal court. Lucan omits all mention of Pompey's embassy to Ptolemy to request aid and shelter (so Caes. *B.C.* 3.103.3). Postgate felicitously calls this telescoping of historical detail 'synthetic concentration'. It is characteristic of Lucan's feel for dramatic economy that he does not clutter his narrative (at its best) with detail that would weaken pathetic force. Thus Acoreus, who is first to speak and urges the honouring of former pledges, is not given a formal speech and this is a sure token of the futility of his plea. Instead, the reader is given a tour-de-force, the speech of Pothinus (well discussed by Bonner 286ff, especially the 'partes suadendi'). It opens with a cascade of epigrams, each as vicious and telling as its fellow (485-95). This gnomic preamble is persuasive just because the general reference of a maxim releases it in the hearer's mind from a given situation (such for example is the method of Ovid's Scylla in *Met.* 8.72f; cf. Hollis on 69f). Thus the maxim 'ius et fas multos faciunt . . . nocentes' is designed to cover the majority of cases, hence *multos*; but the question is not meant to be raised, whether it is applicable to the present case. Of course Pothinus implies that it does apply to Ptolemy, and that it is a base for action. After this generalised opening Pothinus moves to the particular situation, discoursing on Pompey's jinx, his selfishness, and the danger to Egypt of Caesar's attack. He closes as he began on a general note. His advice is accepted, and Achillas is appointed to kill Pompey. Just at this point Lucan breaks off for an impassioned denunciation of Egypt (542). Such extended outbursts are characteristic of Lucan, a sign of his involvement in the action of his own poem (see Introduction pp.15f). Abuse of Egypt was something of a commonplace, as Mayor shows in his introductory note to the fifteenth Satire of Juvenal. Although Lucan's jibes are unoriginal, in the context of this book they give an important contrast to the theme of loyalty exemplified by Cornelia, Deiotarus, and, above all, the Mytilenaeans. Now, at last, loyalty is disregarded and policy triumphs (539, 547).

As long ago as 1761 David Ruhnken urged classical scholars to disclose the debt

141

of modern writers to their ancient models in his Inaugural, entitled *De Doctore Umbratico*. If space allowed, it would be instructive to follow his advice in the case of Corneille, and cite his borrowings from Lucan in his tragedy of *Pompée*. Corneille plundered the *Pharsalia*, as he admitted himself, and in his *Examen* to the play says that the grandeur of his style is owed to this pillaging as well as to a close imitation of Lucan's mode of thought and expression. (On one occasion Corneille even went so far as to prefer Lucan to Virgil, which convinced the scholar-bishop, Huet, that a great poet was not for all that a sound critic; *Huetiana* 74, ed. 1723, p.177.) Comparison of the poets is instructive; in general Lucan is more pointed, which, in the speech of Pothinus, is an end in itself. Corneille was sufficiently impressed with the speech that he made of it the opening scene of his tragedy.

472 **rapido . . . per litora cursu** is an awkward phrase, since it does not cohere with the verb, *conpleuerat;* rather it describes a previous action of the spy's. In the translation it is treated as a sort of ablative absolute, 'after having made a quick ride along the beach'.

473 **hospitis** is ironical here but at 498 it may mean 'stranger'.
aduentu 'news of . . . '; so *Aen.* 5.664f 'nuntius . . . incensas perfert naues' means 'news that the ships were burned', and St. *Th.* 3.236f 'remeat portans inmania Tydeus ausa' means 'news of the terrible deeds'.

474 **consilii . . . tempus:** when *tempus* means 'opportunity' a gerundive can usually be understood with any dependent genitive; here *habendi*, and at V. Fl.3.419 'tempora sacri' *faciendi* (Strand 83).

475 The antecedent of *quos* is *monstra* in 474. But since the portentous figures are at least notionally men the relative takes its gender from the idea. Horace has the same expression at *Carm.* 1.37.21 'fatale monstrum . . . quae' where the relative refers to Cleopatra. Cf. 278n.

476 **senio** is more than old age; it connotes, as at 1.129-30, a degree of decrepitude as well; this is brought out by 'fractis . . . annis'. The description as a whole, especially *iam*, suggests that Acoreus's decency is not due to sincerity but to senile decay.

477 **hunc** (instead of a relative) is used to open a parenthesis at Prop. 3.12.30 and St. *Th.* 3.600; so too *eum* at *Aen.* 8.33.
custos Nili is assumed to be a reference to the Nilometer, which measured the river's rise and fall; see Strabo 17.48.
crescentis in arua: Lucan has the same phrase at 10.219 'quod crescat in arua', but the use of *in* to mean 'over' is hard to illustrate.

478 **uana sacris** mocks the animal-headed gods of Egypt, a standing joke to the

less ancient cultures of Greece and Rome. *Sacris* is an ablative of respect.

479   The meaning appears to be that while Acoreus was priest more than one sacred bull, called Apis, had lived out the span allotted by its mistress, Diana. This would mean that Lucan held a common but mistaken view that the bull was not allowed to live beyond a certain age (so too Pliny *N.H.* 8. 184-6 and Am. Marc. 22.14.7). The true state of affairs is set out in *RE* 1.2808.24-31 and by J. Gwyn Griffiths on Plut. *De Is.* 56, p.462.

482   **melior** is found with an infinitive in Persius also, 4.16.

483   **Pompeium ... Pothinus**: the heavily spondaic line, and the alliteration of the proper names (as at 10.103), point up the pathos of the contrast, which Duff has well expressed.

     leto damnare is recalled at 570 and 9.87. *Leto* is probably dative, as explained by Langen on V. Fl. 2.16, whose note Housman has in mind at 1.249. For this rare dative see Munro on Lucr. 6.1232.

484-95   Throughout these lines the varied sentence length and pauses within the line are very lively. For once Lucan abandons his cumulative technique and sets down simple nouns and verbs. This lack of adornment lends force and plausibility to the sentiments. Similar is the speech of Licinius Mucianus in Tac. *Hist.* 2.76f.

486   **fatis accede deisque**: that the gods favoured Caesar is known from Lucan's most famous line, 1.127. But the present sentiment is more general, and is found, for example, in Eur. *Tro.* 1008f 'With an eye on Fortune, you strove to side with her, and you refused to side with virtue', Caesar in Cic. *Att.* 10. 8B, Ov. *Pont.* 2.6.23 'turpe sequi casum et fortunae accedere amicum', and 2.3.10; see *TLL* 3.686.23ff. When Lucan praises the Massiliots at 3.303 he says they followed the cause, and not destiny (cf.2.705). Thus Manilius says at 4.96 'nec Fortuna probat causas sequiturque merentis'.

487   **cole felices miseros fuge** is a typical four word epigram (see 85n), here disposed chiastically to juxtapose the adjectives of opposite sense. Very similar is Sen. *Herc. Oet.* 122 'felices sequeris, mors, miseros fugis' (a line that should always be cited for sigmatism).

488   It is possible, but not necessarily the case, that *distant* has one sense with *sidera* and *terra*, viz, spatial separation, and another with *flamma* and *mari*, viz, essential difference. This would not be an example of zeugma, as that term is now understood, but of syllepsis; a clear distinction is made between these terms by H.W. Fowler in *Modern English Usage*, art. 'Syllepsis and Zeugma'. Verbs are often found doing double duty thus; so in Pindar *Pyth.* 1.40f τιθέμεν means 'take' with its first object and 'make' with its second

(see Jebb on Soph. *O.C.* 1356f); at *Aen.* 2.258f *laxat* means 'release' with *Danaos* and 'open' with *claustra;* in Hor. *Ep.* 2.1.7 'dum terras hominumque colunt genus' Wilkins takes the verb to mean 'dwell' and 'care for' with its different objects; in Tac. *Hist.* 1.37 'nunc et subiectos nos habuit tamquam suos et uilis ut alienos' the verb first means 'possessed' and then 'regarded'. Further examples may be found in Housman's note to 4.316-8 and the additional note to Manil. 1.792. Two points should be stressed. First, despite imprecise commentators, there is no zeugma in this usage, just because the verb naturally has the senses required of it with its different objects. Secondly, the distinction exists largely for the modern reader. Cf. the use of *quatitur* at 37 and *languent* at 471.

mari here is just the element water, a not uncommon usage.

490   **arces** in its present sense is illustrated in *OLD* sv 1c.

492-3   **facere ... facis** is an example of κύκλος, whereby the sentence begins and ends with the same word, as at 1.693f. For the sentiment we may compare Sall. *Hist.* 3.48.13 'omnis iniuria grauitate tutior est' and Sen. *Ag.* 115 'per scelera semper sceleribus tutum est iter'.

495   **saeua pudebunt:** the personal use of impersonal verbs is rare after Terence (see Ashmore on *And.* 481f and cf. *Adel.* 754 'non te haec pudent?'). Bentley emended the offending verb here, and Postgate thought it might be a recollection, suitably refashioned, of a line from early tragedy (which is unlikely in the case of a poet who read so little out of the way of Virgil and Ovid, Livy and Seneca). The fact is that *pudet*, of all the impersonals, is the one which most readily admitted of personal use. At any rate it is so used by Statius at *Th.* 3.61 'pudet ira fateri', and perhaps in a piece of late Republican verse as emended by L.Müller (433), 'qui non pudet et rubet' (an emendation not noticed by Morel in FPL, p. 174). We find it again in *Per. Ven.* 26 '(rosa) non pudebit soluere ruborem noto', but in later Latin the impersonals again were not uncommonly used as personal verbs; see Löfstedt comm. 46.

496   **annos** 'youth' as illustrated by Langen on V. Fl. 3.179 and *OLD* sv 6c; cf. 9.1087 'parcimus annis'.

497   **nec** = *ne ... quidem*; 206n.

498   **neu** = *et ne,* where the *ne* clause is parenthetical; that is to say, it does not describe the purpose of the subject of the main verb, but rather describes a purpose present to the mind of the speaker. Examples are given by Roby 1660, and he notes the rarity of the perfect subjunctive until after the Augustan age.

nos Ω, **te** VGmz: *nos* is preferable because it associates Pothinus closely with the king, as in 518 (Postgate). But at 520-4 Pothinus tactfully takes upon himself alone the burden of killing Pompey (cf. Pylades' use of change of number in Eur. *Or.* 1147-50). That Pompey might have intended to take personal control of Egypt was alleged at the time as an excuse for his murder; so Caes. *B.C.* 3.104.1

500   damnatae does not necessarily imply that judicial measures were taken, as Postgate supposed (xlvi, n.1).

503   nec 'also not, neither', another sense of *ne ... quidem*, for which *nec* is commonly used in Silver Latin (see 206n). The distinction is clearly elucidated by Duff in his note to Juv. 11.7; cf. *OLD* sv *neque* 2.

505   cum qua gente cadat recalls the sentiment of 7.711 'terras elige morti'. The desire to involve others in one's own ruin is illustrated by Costa on Sen. *Med.* 426-8 'mecum omnia abeant'.

     rapitur ciuilibus umbris means, as Housman saw, that Pompey is being claimed as *inferiae* by the shades of those killed at Pharsalia. A like sentiment is expressed by Cassandra in Sen. *Ag.* 741f 'quid me uocatis sospitem solam a meis,/ umbrae meorum?' Here and at 522 the verb stresses that everyone is in the grip of inescapable powers.

506   fugit:fugit: P omits the second *fugit* by haplography; the verb is erased in M and Z, the latter Ms filling the gap with *tonet*. This typical progression of error is illustrated by Heinsius on Ov. *Her.* 6.29, Housman Manil. I, *Preface* lix-lxvi, and Clausen on Pers. 1.111.

506-9   The period affords another example of Lucan's fondness for accumulation: each member is shorter than the preceding and each is made up of a main verb with a relative clause dependent on its object (for variety's sake each relative word is different). The period has a concealed doublet (26n), viz, the Romans, *senatus*, and the rest of the world, *gentes* and their *reges*.

507   pars magna is an exaggeration; at most ten senators died at Pharsalia (and for this reason that battle was less of a sore point with the nobility than Philippi). But Lucan is closer to the truth about the foreign dead, reckoned at 14,000.

508-9   metuit ... timet: the use of synonymous verbs in parallel clauses in one sentence is found in good prose, e.g., Cic. *Or.* 16 (Sandys) and *Acad.* 2.80 (Reid); we meet it in Lucan at 5.274f and 7.789-91. It is important to note this sort of thing in order to defend the text against suspicion; at 5.275 for instance *carne* has been proposed for *cerne*, to remove (unnecessarily) the synonym.

     gentes ... mixtas recalls 2.195 and 5.202. *Sanguis* here means 'slaughter' as at 10.7 'tui socerum rapuere a sanguine manes', and Sen. *N.Q.* 7.17.3 'cruenti quidam (comets) minaces qui omen post se futuri sanguinis ferunt'.

509 **deseruit**: but the desertion was mutual, see 532.

omnia is used as at 7.239 'in extremos quo (tempore) mitteret omnia casus' (might stake his all on a final cast) and 7.759 'promiserit omnia'.

mersit is fully illustrated by Housman *Papers* 3.915f.

510 **Thessaliae reus**: at 45 the place stands for the battle fought there. Pothinus now begins to shift the blame onto Pompey and to show that Egypt must preserve herself from guilt by association; hence the incidence of legal turns of phrase: *iustior causa, querella, crimen, poena.*

512 **in Magnum . . . querellae** is to be taken as a phrase, ὑφ' ἕν, as Housman shows at 9.299; cf. 7.725, and, for the use of *in*, 2.45. *Querella* is a legal term; cf. V. Max.9.10.2, Petr.15, and Tac.*Agr.* 41.1.

513-5 The shift of reference to Pompey in *maculas* and *facis* is abrupt after the address to Ptolemy in 512 (though there is no chance of a misunderstanding). Further examples of this stylistic infelicity, common to those who overwork apostrophe, are collected by Shackleton Bailey 171; from Lucan may be added 1.121-3, 7.23 (where *tibi* refers to an unaddressed Pompey), and in this book 102 and 806 (with its n). L. Håkanson treats of this in *Statius' Silvae* (Lund 1969), 43f.

sepositam semperque quietam is borne out by Petr. *Epig.* 79.4 (PLM IV) and by Strabo 17.53. Still, the remark is disingenuous at a time when Ptolemy was battling against Cleopatra (a point forgotten by Lucan rather than by Pothinus).

515 **uictori . . . cadenti**: words opposed in sense ring the line (36n).

516-7 **placuit . . . conferres**: the sequence is regular, as at 5.698f, because *placuit* is a preterite.

517 Earlier in this book the Mytilenaeans said 'haec (moenia) iam crimen habent' (118). Here Lucan uses a clear verbal echo to contrast their selfless loyalty with the timid perfidy of the Egyptian court. In this line *iam* is to be explained, as comm. Bern. saw, by the fact that Pompey has chosen Egypt as his refuge (515-7). With *quod* in 518 Pothinus opens a new thought, namely that the Egyptians owe Pompey nothing; because he urged long ago at Rome Ptolemy's cause, he had their good wishes at Pharsalia: so now they are quits.

518 **purgandum gladio** recalls 7.262 'gladio . . . exsoluite culpam'. After *maculas* (514) *purgandum* is emphatic and implies a ritual duty.

520 Pothinus cunningly uses now the first person singular to exculpate his master Ptolemy. But in saying 'quod fata iubent' he really blames destiny, whose unwilling instrument he claims to be.

522 **malueram** 'I could have wished' is illustrated in *TLL* 8.204.73; and the use

146

of the indicative to express unreality is explained by LHS 327.

rapimur absolves everyone. Cf. 7.487 'rapit omnia casus' and Sen. *Dial.* 1.5.8 'grande solacium est cum uniuerso rapi'.

523   **te** and **mihi** are brought to the head of the line for emphasis, even though this produces a tortured word order for 'dubitasne an mihi necesse sit te uiolare' (Housman).

525   **inermem**: Juvenal too calls thc Egyptians 'inbelle uolgus' (15.126).

527   **uires fateri** 'admit that our strength is not what it might be'; so at Ov. *Fasti* 6.19 'animum pallore fatebar'.

528   **Ptolemaee . . . Magni** stress as at 483 the sad contrast.

529   **bustum cineresque mouere**: tombs were of course inviolable, so by using a not uncommon conceit, that a concluded war is 'buried', Pothinus hints at some sort of sacrilege. *Mouere* means 'disturb' as at 791. For the conceit that war is buried with the warriors, see Housman on Manil. 2.879 with the *addendum; Oct.* 523f 'illic sepultum est . . . ciuile bellum' may be added.

531   It is strictly true that Egypt sent no troops to Pompey; those who did support him had been with Gabinius when he restored Ptolemy Auletes but had stayed on in the king's service, like Septimius; cf. Caes. *B.C.* 3.3.1, 4.4, and 10.402f.

    ante aciem: with this phrase should be understood *commissam;* the compendious expression is not uncommon, and has been fully illustrated by Vollmer on St. *Silu.* 1.3.16, and by both Francken and Housman on 6.145. Similar is 647 below.

    Nullis of course refers to only two armies; see 185n.

532   **Pompei nunc**: the monosyllable in the second longum of the second foot is discussed by Hellegouarc'h 197-207. His conclusions on its usage are that there is no pattern and that poets' practice is individual. Lucan and Tibullus are the least disposed to use the monosyllable at this point in the second foot to articulate the syntax (i.e., they were shy of setting there an emphatic word like *sed*).

    quae deserit orbis is recalled by Suetonius of Nero: 'talem principem . . . terrarum orbis tandem destituit', 40.1.

534-5   The close of Pothinus's speech is meant to recall, as at 517f, the loyal attitude of the Mytilenaeans, especially 125f. According to comm. Bern., Pothinus says that one must not fail in adversity those whose success one has shared, a sentiment found in Eur. *Herc.Fur.* 1220f. (And *aduersis* is dative of the neuter plural; see *OLD* sv *desum* 2.) Pothinus harps on the view that Egypt owes Pompey nothing.

536-8   The satire of these lines is patent. The postponement of *insueto* is especially well managed.

537   **rex puer** is a paradoxical phrase, in that kings ought to be mature and prudent. By this juxtaposition, Lucan neatly depicts a topsy-turvy world in which boys can have power over life and death.

538   **permittunt famuli** is also a paradox, couched in an epigram; one does not expect slaves to be the ones to grant permission. Again the thought is given point by postponing the telling word.

539   **perfida . . . tellus** alludes as much to the nature of the inhabitants, as to the topographical shallows.

540   The Syrtes are no where near Egypt (but cf. 444, and 862n). This sort of wild inaccuracy must be borne in mind when reading 543.

541   **exiguam . . . carinam** bracket the line (39n); *sociis* and *gladiis* are ablative with *instruit*, not dative as Postgate translated them. Together the ablatives form hendiadys (1n).

542-60   From the close of the speech to this point there have been just over six lines of narrative. Nothing is so typical of Lucan's epic technique, nothing sets him so far apart from all other poets in this genre as his tendency to abandon narrative for an editorial reflection upon events. So he appeals to characters in the poem, or in his own person denounces peoples and places, a manner both jarring and strident. But it may not be a manner either original or peculiar to him. The elder Seneca preserves for us in his *Suasoria* (6.26), a long fragment from the *Res Romanae* of Cornelius Severus, in which the poet, in his own person or at any rate in no dispassionate way, deplores the death of Cicero. This passage is well worth bearing in mind when reading Lucan's own reflections on the death of Pompey. It would seem that the more obviously declamatory poetry was inclined to this sort of personal utterance of the poet. There are notable examples in Lucan. The address to Caesar at the close of the seventh book (803-24) was reckoned by Macaulay, no mean judge, to show considerable power in its execution (amid an abundance of wretched bombast); and Sir Thos. Browne, who doted upon Lucan, paid the passage the compliment of frequent quotation in *Urne-Buriall.* In this book Lucan pours out his own views again at 692-700, and, with real inspiration, at 842-72. In the present passage the frequent shift in apostrophe is disconcerting, but an equally high incidence will be found in the emotional speech of Oedipus in Soph. *O.R.* 1391-1411 or in Prop. 3.7.

542-3   **Nilusne . . . Canopi** forms a tricolon crescendo, an especially imposing start to the denunciation.

543 **Pelusiaci . . . Canopi:** in a lecture delivered before the British Academy entitled *Flaws in Classical Research* – its relevance still intact – Postgate argued that this phrase would be a gross, albeit concealed, tautology if *Pelusiaci* means no more than 'Egyptian' (*PBA* 3.1908.9f). He argued that both words retain their proper sense and that they refer to the western and eastern mouths of Nile – a sort of universalising doublet. Housman however remained unconvinced. The reason for this is given in the remark of Servius on *Aen.* 8.165 'cum sciamus poetas uicinas omnes pro uno habere ciuitates'; so, he goes on to point out, Virgil can style Dido both Tyrian and Sidonian. The phrase was illustrated by Hosius in *RM* 48.1893.383.

544 **hos animos** is borrowed from Sen. *Tro.* 339 and becomes a common form of aposiopesis; e.g., Juv. 1.88f and cf. Heinsius on Claud. *In Eutr.* 2.134.

545 **iste** is used here with little or no reference to a second person, and so is a lively synonym of *hic.* This usage is not well illustrated at *OLD* sv 4; more examples can be given from the Augustan age: Hor. *Ep.* 1:6.67, *Aen.* 9.138f, Ov. *Met.* 11.667 (with Haupt-Ehwald's note). That *iste* is found at all in epic is due to Virgil (Norden 120, LHS 184). (The punctuation of these sentences seems first to be found in the Tonson edition of 1719, and Bentley too takes them as questions.)

546 As at 390-4 there is a gradual contraction of focus: *mundum, Romana, Aegypto, ensis* – from the world to a sword.

547 The guarantee which Lucan paradoxically fancies is made by civil war is that a man will at least die by the hand of a fellow-citizen (though *cognatas* refers to closer kin, here Caesar in 550).

549-50 **si . . . nefas** is connected by some editors with what precedes, and by others with what follows. An obvious objection to the latter course is the inelegant echo of 'tam claro nomine' by 'tanti nominis' in the apodosis. *Caesaris* (550) moreover clearly answers to *cognatas* (548) and so binds the *si* clause to the preceding sentence.

550 **Caesaris esse nefas** is similar to 2.264-6, 7.551 and 10.103. It was a truly imaginative stroke on the part of Statius to use this phrase of Lucan himself in the birthday poem, *Silu.* 2.7.100, 'sic et tu rabidi nefas tyranni'.

551 **caelo tonante** was rightly seen by Oudendorp to allude to a comparison, common in Lucan, of the civil war to the battle of gods and giants. In Lucan's imagination, the civil war was a disaster without precedent or parallel in history. All he could therefore liken to it was the myth of the battle on Phlegra's fields between gods and giants. This myth is spoken of at the very beginning of the poem in the dedication to Nero, 1.35f; it crops up again at 3.314ff

'tractentur uolnera nulla sacra manu . . . ' when the Massiliens beg to be left out of civil war. In the description of Thessaly at 6.410-12 it rightly holds a significant place. But the most impressive sounding of the myth is at 7.144-50 (cf. Introduction p.17).

552   **inseruisse** is recalled by Caesar at 9.1072.

         inpure ac semiuir are common terms of abuse; cf. Cic. *Phil.* 3.12.

553-6   The syntax of this sentence is obscure. There is only one verb, *erat,* and it must be used with two contrasted notions, the first expressed by *non . . . gener,* and the second by *Phario . . . Romanus.* And furthermore, as Postgate noted, the first notion has a concessive sense, 'suppose he were not'. (It would not be possible to understand from *erat* a jussive subjunctive in the first clause with concessive nuance, since the negative would have to be *ne* or *ut non.*) *Domitor mundi* is used by Caesar at 7.250 to address his army.

553-4   **Capitolia . . . inuectus:** examples of the use of *inueho* without a preposition are given in *OLD* sv 4 (to which may be added *Aen.* 8.714f. and Ov. *Met.* 11. 54). The line is recalled at 9.599.

554-5   The negative notion carries over all three *que*'s, in Lucan's usual way. But when the negative notion is dropped before *Phario*, there is no adversative particle to help the reader. Similar is 118f.

555   **uictorisque gener** is saved for last to give its sad irony full effect. Pompey had had a splendid career, but now one of his claims to fame will be that he was Caesar's son-in-law. (And yet in Aulus Gellius Fronto calls Caesar 'Pompei socer', 19.8.3, and this calls to mind a witticism of Talleyrand, recorded by Macaulay, *Letters,* ed. Pinney, 2.67f).

556   **Phario . . . Romanus** is picked up at 596.

         nostra is sympathetic and paves the way for Lucan's longing to serve Pompey, which he voices at the close of the book (cf. 7.865 'nostris ossibus').

556-7   **uiscera scrutaris gladio** is from Sen. *Med.* 1013 (if the passage is genuine).

         nescis . . . nescis is one of Cicero's happiest inventions, at *Parad.* 2.17. It recurs in Ov. *Met.* 1.514, and finds itself in St. *Th.* 3.704 and Mart. 1.3.3 as well. Epanalepsis is one of Lucan's favourite devices, and it lends greatly to his emotional power; cf. 1.203, 225, 347, 521, 7.304, 550, 555, 813, 9.200. Quintilian discusses the figure at *I.O.* 9.3.28ff; Summers has well said that epanalepsis and anaphora were the italics of the ancients (*CR* 19.1905.45).

562-3   **quem contra** attaches to *uecta.* The meaning and tense of *appulerat* have been faulted. It is true that the verb is used mainly of bringing a ship in to land, but that is only natural. Since Livy uses it of bringing a ship up to a wall, 30.10.3, and Cicero of approaching a rock, *Rab. Perd.* 25 and *De Or.*

2.154, Lucan might use it of one ship coming along another (where *applico* would be commoner). The tense of the verb implies that while Pompey was making for land (*petebat*) the ship had pulled alongside. Lucan then adopts the vivid present to describe the catastrophe.

564   celsa is something of a constant epithet of ships, as Pease illustrates on *Aen.* 4.554. Still, Lucan may be implying that Pompey's ship is bigger than the one that meets it.

565   malignum is explained by *uadis* in 566.

566   bímarem is an Horatian coinage dear to Ovid's heart. Lucan uses it in a different sense from that used by his predecessors, for here it means 'made up of two seas'. Lucan is not an innovator of language; he rarely coins a word, and rarely uses an old word in a new sense. It may be that he felt the language left him by Virgil and Ovid was sufficient for what he had to say, or he may also have seen that novelties might hinder comprehension during recitation.

567   adpellere is here intransitive (and so should find a place in *OLD* sv 4b). The reading of PU, *aduertere,* is an equally rare use of the intransitive, but it seems to be a scribe's recollection of Vir. *Geor.* 4.117 'terris . . . aduertere'.

568-71   non. . . praesagia derant is not the logical apodosis to the protasis, 'quod nisi . . . Magnum'. As Postgate explained it, there is an ellipse of the logical apodosis, viz 'Pompey might have escaped', except that it was Fate dragging him to the shore. So too there is an ellipse at 571: 'there were tokens for any of his companions to see, scil., if they had bothered to notice them'. (It is clear from 592f that Pompey's companions did not however bother to notice these tokens and only Cornelia was alarmed, 579.) This passage is now discussed by L. Håkanson in *PCPS* 25.1979.47; corruption of the tradition does not seem likely.

569   uicinia mortis is a common sort of phrase in Lucan; cf. 4.518 and 5.224. It is also found at Petr. 115.3.

574   uenturum: *fuisse* is to be understood. (In his note to Livy 9.4.6 W.B. Anderson seems to assume that *esse* would have to be understood, producing irregular syntax.)

574-5   classe . . . classem: it was Housman's opinion that repetition of the same word, even in adjacent lines, was largely excused if a full-stop intervened; see his note on Manil. 1.261. It may prove useful to categorize repetition in Lucan in a table, set out below. The most careless instances are on the left, the least (into which class the present example falls), on the right. Scattered examples are included from other poets; the *Thebaid* is significant in so far as it is a finished poem. The degree of carelessness is mitigated by the distance between the words repeated, their emphasis in the sentence, and by any change in case, number, or nuance of meaning.

Words or Phrases Repeated

at same place in verse		at different place in verse	
and same sentence	in different	and same sentence	in different
Aen. 1.432-6	Ov. *Met.* 7.234-6	*Aen.* 7.179f	*Aen.* 5.325-'
– 8.10-14	Luc. 4.741f	– 12.595f	Luc.1.657f
– 9.744-6	– 8.100-2	Luc. 1.25-7	– 8.574f
Luc. 1.388-91	– 8.106-8	– 1.167-70	
– 4.448-50	– 8.474-80	– 2.299-301	
– 5.546-8	– 8.493-6	– 2.334-6	
– 6.362-4	– 8.536-8	– 3.434-5	
– 6.507-9	– 8.590-2	– 4.19f	
– 8.244-7	– 8.625-31	– 4.788-90	
– 8.423-6	– 8.796-99	– 6.443f	
– 8.493-6		– 8.194-6	
– 8.570-2		– 10.229-34	
– 9.413-5		*Th.* 1.112f	
– 9.953-4		– 1.596-8	
Th. 2.682-5		– 5.691f	
– 7.394-6		– 8.354f	
		– 9.580-2	

The chief purpose of this sort of study is the defense of the text where it has been questioned on account of a repetition judged infelicitous. For example, Housman faults *ferro* at 3.435; but 4.19f and 6.443f show how little Lucan noticed such jingles. Some of the examples cited from the *Thebaid* have also been faulted, and yet they resist convincing emendation. There are numerous studies of repetition in the poets: e.g., Shackleton Bailey 9, Kenney *CQ* 9. 1959.248 (mainly Ovid, but with a general bibliograph), Johnson *Aristarchus Antibentleianus* (1717, on Horace), Vahlen 1.355ff, and Easterling *Hermes* 101.1973.14-34 (on Sophocles).

575   **classem** probably means 'fleet', for at 9.49 *puppes* are mentioned. Doubtless these came up with Sextus and the senators. *Classis* can however mean 'crew' as Fordyce observes on Catull. 64.53; so adn. understand *ratibus* at 3.691 (with which may be compared V. Fl.3.79f).

This section brings us to the climax of Pompey's flight, his murder, which has been hinted at throughout the poem. Pompey is stabbed by an Egyptian, and his head is lopped off, to be a pledge of Ptolemy's good faith to Caesar. Lucan's account is utterly personal and the book closes on a note of exaltation. He leaves out clogging details, for example, the fact that there were attendants in Pompey's skiff, or that Septimius had served under him. The omission of incident allows us to concentrate on the emotional state of the principals, and upon the poet's own moral revulsion. There is no digression into the anecdotal (cf. Schnepf 395). Lucan can once again focus on Cornelia, abandoned to grief and self-reproach, and on Pompey, calm and self-assured. This coupling-by-contrast is underscored by the repetition of a telling phrase, *iura sui* (612) and *iuris sui* (660), and by *patientius* (633) and *non patiens* (637). Cornelia's two outbursts are devised to raise the emotional temperature, which is kept down by Pompey's dignity; the second one separates the decollation from the actual murder, much as a chapter in an older novel is inserted to retard an inevitable and anticipated sequel, thus keeping the reader's attention on the stretch.

As early as 2.204f 'adhuc dubitantibus astris/ Pompeii damnare caput' Lucan had hinted at one of the saddest events in Roman history. (Beheading moreover is a compelling theme: we have only to think of S. John the Baptist to appreciate this.) The description of the act is, however, fairly unsensational, for Lucan (though Austin in his note to *Aen.* 2.557 speaks of 'horrid details'; cf. Wight Duff 250). What in fact most appeals to the poet's imagination is that a debased Egyptian should carry off the head. Indeed the grisliest line, 672f, is largely a lead-in to the poet's satirical jibe at modern refinements of execution. Even 682f, albeit ugly, can be shown to serve a purpose higher than vivid cruelty.

The section closes characteristically with a denunciation of Ptolemy, delivered by the poet speaking in his own person. He breaks off and rounds upon Fortune, who is at length seen, in a paradoxical way, as helping to deify her abandoned favourite. This rhetorical *indignatio* is admirably discussed in an important article by Konrad Seitz (cf. bibliography).

Throughout this climactic section greater emphasis is laid on certain themes close to Lucan's heart, principally *fama*, and the reputation to be won from loyalty, *fides*. Pompey himself is the conspicuous instance of glory; his reputation, *nomen*, is ever kept before our eyes. And reputation, significantly enough, is his last concern in life – 'nunc consule famae' (624). He is, moreover, in Lucan's hands, aware of the interest his death will command in history. The other characters do not, of course, match Pompey in fame, but loyalty to him assures Cornelia (78-81), and the Mytilenaeans (139) their place in history. Loyalty to Pompey will win Cordus a deathless renown (782), and by contrast even perfidy, with Pompey for its object, will be always remembered (608f). An extreme statement of this paradox comes at 10.377f when Pothinus, urging his troops on against Caesar, says, 'communis gloria nobis,/ nos quoque sublimes Magnus facit.'

577   **ibat** is conative in nuance. Narrative is, as usual, sketchy, for the emotional state is the poet's only concern. At 596, for example, the single word, *salutat,* triggers off Lucan's own reflections upon the depravity of Septimius, and it is not until 612 that narrative of the action is resumed.

578   **hoc** is ablative, the antecedent of *quod* (579).

579   Pompey's speech is not introduced. Though such urgent abruptness is found in the *Aeneid* (e.g., at 1.437, an exclamatory line, 2.657 and 12.871) and at 583 below, as well as 9.122, in all these cases the speaker is at least the subject of the immediately preceding sentence. The present example is unorthodox, but Lucan was right not to weaken the deterrent force of *remane* with a conventional lead-in. It is characteristic that, although Sextus, Pompey's son, is clearly present, Lucan avoids the temptation to put a speech into his mouth; he focusses interest upon husband and wife alone.

581   **ceruice** could mean 'life', but the irony of the word on Pompey's lips is telling, and looks to the approaching catastrophe.

583   **geminas,** used colourlessly of paired parts of the body, is illustrated by Fordyce on Catull.63.75; it is found with *palma* in Varro Atac. fr. 3 Morel.

584   **crudelis** echoes the cry of all abandoned heroines, but here again irony is at work; for Pompey's cruelty is in fact kindness. It is in the same vein that Anna calls Dido cruel at *Aen.* 4.681.

585   **numquam:** like Miss Joliffe in Meade Faulkner's *The Nebuly Coat,* Cornelia 'falls into a common hyperbole in qualifying an isolated action as a habit'. Leo (151f) observed that outside Seneca and the controversialists the abuse of *semel, semper,* and *numquam* is rare; he compares 9.66f below, and 7.602 'uictus totiens' is similar. But earlier abuses are not wanting. Lucretius (1.82) writes *saepius* but he might be hard put to it to find more instances of such crimes in religion's name; *saepe* at Catull. 64.100 makes one wonder how often Ariadne paled; and though Aeneas says at *Aen.* 1.407f 'quid natum . . . totiens ludis' this is the only example of Venus's deceit towards him that Virgil gives us. Even the precise Tacitus falls foul of such exaggeration, for example, at *Ann.* 15.47.1 (see Nipperdey on 13.6.1). It is useful to note such tendencies in an author. Failure to do so has led some editors of Lucan to question the propriety of 'multis . . . lustris' at 2.568f, where reference is

made to Caesar's two lustres spent in Gaul; such proposals as *iunctis* or *geminis* or *castris* (instead of *lustris*) all assume that Lucan is incapable of that particular exaggeration. This is improbable, and for him 'two' is 'many'.

588   **parabas** has a weakened sense, 'intend', as at 595 (*OLD* sv 8).

588-9   **omnibus a terris . . . in fluctus** is a good example of the frigidity that results from mere verbal contrast (see Bonner 262f for further examples). *In* is taken at *TLL* 7.1, 765.37f to mean 'ad maritimum cursum', that is to say that it has a vaguely final sense; but it can mean 'over', and is similar in meaning to 648f 'per undas . . . comes'.

591   **attonito . . . metu**: not surprisingly, the epithet is a favourite of Lucan's. Here, as at 7.779, it is used of something that causes amazement.

592-3   **anxia . . . ad ducis euentum** cohere, a new construction.

593   **arma nefasque** form hendiadys.

594   **sed ne . . .** : for the rhetorical reason see 615n.
        Plutarch records that when Pompey left his ship he quoted two lines of Sophocles's, to the effect that whoever sought a favour of a king became his slave (78); Lucan may here allude to that (so Ehlers 550). At any rate 'summissis precibus' recalls what Ovid says of Pompey at *Pont.* 4.3.41f 'ille rogauit/ summissa fugiens uoce clientis opem.'

595   **sceptra sua donata manu** stresses a point frequently made. On the one hand it implies impiety in Ptolemy and on the other, as *adoret* makes plain, a deep abasement of Pompey.

596   **Romanus Pharia** is a telling juxtaposition to which may be compared 1.105f (both golden lines), 2.137, 3.93, 463, 583, 610, 7.473, 10.343. The deeper principle at work is discussed by Fraenkel on Aesch. *Ag.* 320. Here Lucan is stressing the shamefulness of a free Roman's service to a king; cf. 10.402ff, Hor. *Epode* 9.11-16 and *Carm.* 3.5.5ff, and Tac. *Ann.* 14.59.3.

597-8   **arma . . . regia . . . deformia** is not an infringement of the classical rule that each noun has but one epithet, for *regia*, as a possessive, is felt to be no more than a replacement for *regis*. So at 732 'Romana . . . pia colla' *Romana* stands for *Romanorum* (as Bentley pointed out on Hor. *Serm.* 1.9.30, only to forget himself in censuring 1.655 'saeuum Nemeaeum leonem' as worthier of Accius or Pacuvius). Of the 'double' epithets listed by Munro on Lucr. 1.258, a fair number will be found to be possessive. But Lucan is not always careful of the rule, as D. White points out in *HSCP* 74.1970.187-91; cf. 2.122f and 207f, 3.367, and 6.74f.

599   **inmanis uiolentus atrox** recalls the description of Polypheme at *Aen.* 3.658 (a passage also taken in hand by Statius, *Th.* 8.67).

599-600 **nulla** is a very strong negative, *pace* Fraenkel on Aesch. *Ag.* 186, for it is

155

borrowed direct from common speech; the usage is discussed by J.B. Hofmann, *Lateinische Umgangssprache* (1936), 80, Landgraf on Cic. *Rosc. Am.* 128, Heitland cviii and Haskins's index sv, and Lejay on 1.331. Here as at 5.149 and 649 below the logical elements of the word are distinct, and the phrase means 'inmitior quam ulla fera'.

mitis in . . . seems a new construction (so *TLL* 8.1159.2).

caedes admits perhaps of two interpretations. Usually it is taken to mean 'act of killing'. But, in the light of the sequel (667f), it may mean 'slain bodies', a sense illustrated in *OLD* sv 3.

600   **putasset** is the first example of the pluperfect subjunctive of this verb to be so used; *putaret* had earlier occurred (in Lucan, for example, at 3.447), but generally the indicative is the preferred mood (see Reid on Cic. *Acad.* 2.56).

601   **uacaret** MZV, **-asset** PGU: rhyme is found even in the best classical poets: see Müller 572, Hollis on Ov. *Met.* 8.441f, Austin in *CQ* 23.1929.55. But a triple rhyme is intolerable, and due to assimilation by the scribe of the form of *uacaret* to that of the verbs above and below it. The tenses are mixed indifferently, even in cases where the metre does not require either imperfect or pluperfect, e.g., 1.653-7, 3.315f, 7.860-7, Ov. *Her.* 1.6-10 (with variants) and 6.141-5, St. *Th.* 9.144-7 and *Silu.* 1.1.11-13.

603   **quo** . . . **in orbe** 'in what part of the world', a common use of *orbis*, noted by Haskins and Housman on 5.686 and Klotz on St. *Th.* 10.142; similar is *mundi* at 163 above.

604   **heu**: as might be expected, a sigh of sympathy from the poet is a neoteric device, found in Catull. 64.94, and cautiously used by Virgil in epic, for example, at *Aen.* 4.65 and 12.452 (other examples may represent the sigh of the character, as at 4.283 'heu quid agat?'). Ovid's love of pathos lead him to use the interjection fairly often in the *Metamorphoses* (e.g., 2.447, 612, 3.229, 6.273, 8.85, and 11.562), and Lucan as usual follows Ovid's lead (e.g., 1.13, 2.517, 708, 5.228, 310, 727, 6.303).

605-6   **dedecus et** . . . **fabula** are probably nominatives in apposition to the following sentence; their function is to give the result of the action, or more probably to pass judgment upon it (KS 2.1, 248). Postgate gives examples of the unusual position of the words at the head of the sentence, as does Fraenkel on Aesch. *Ag.* 1645; we may compare St. *Silu.* 2.7.48-51, where the appositional nominative precedes the main verb.

606   **Romanus regi**: the poet stresses his shock by an alliterative juxtaposition.

607   **Pellaeus puer**: again alliteration expresses the poet's contempt for the foreign boy-king.

gladio . . . tuo: Housman alone saw that Lucan alludes to a proverb found in Ter. *Adel.* 958. But this is as close as he comes to saying that Septimius had been a soldier of Pompey's.

608   **in saecula mittet** is echoed at 10.533; Langen collected imitations of the phrase in his note to V.Fl.1.99.

609-10   **scelus hoc:** it is likely that *hoc* stands for *huius* (i.e., 'of Septimius'), a common attraction of the pronoun from the genitive case to that of the governing noun; cf. *TLL* 6.2741.52-74, and in Lucan 2. 474, 3.218, 7.538, and 9.629. This entails that with *Bruti* in 610 we understand *scelus* (Lucan might regard the assassination of Caesar as a criminal act, however laudable). The tone of the question is discussed at 793-4n.

612   **perdiderat iam iura sui** is in contrast to Pompey's freedom of spirit (635), and the physical constraint of his own wife (660): he is being held for death, she for life. The frequency of this and of kindred expressions in Lucan is due to his vision of a world enslaved to Julius Caesar after Pharsalia. A Roman was fully free if *iuris sui*, but in the *Pharsalia* that *ius* is often either lost or handed over to others: so at 2.463, 5.489, 6.302, 7.265, 9.212, 238f, and 560. The sentence is inelegantly written since the reader has to guess the subject from the context.

615   So too Caesar himself fell: 'toga caput inuoluit', Suet. *DJ* 82.2. In this sentence *caput* does double duty as object for both *inuoluit* and *praebere*. L. Håkanson, however, proposes to read *saeuae* for *atque*, a neat improvement; *PCPS* 25.1979. It is not clear that the transmitted text is so unacceptable that emendation, however attractive, is required; the Roman reader (or audience) was perhaps less puzzled by the syntax than we are. In discussing the reason Lucan here adduces for Pompey's action, Cortius noted how common it is for the poet to reject the common-sense explanation and adopt instead a rhetorical reason; he compared 3.296f and 7.233, and 593 above is similar.

617   **uellet** has a weak sense, 'be ready to', as at Catull. 64.138, Lucr. 3.594, Ov. *Am.* 1.12.3, *Met.* 10.132; see Mulder on St. *Th.* 2.182 and Ollfors 2.44f. The sentence is artfully disposed in the chiastic pattern: Pompey closed his eyes so as not to weep, and held his breath so as not to cry out.

619   **consensit ad ictum:** the exact sense of the verb is hard to pin down; it is taken by *OLD* sv 5b to mean 'assent'. *Ad* means 'at the moment of . . . , on . . . ', a usage illustrated by Munro on Lucr. 1.185.

620   The negative notion carries over the first *que*, but the second *que* has adversative force in this context (see 301n). Mooney's *Index* usefully lists instances of both constructions.

621   **probat** 'make trial of' (a sense noted by Housman on Manil. 4.96
addendum). It was a commonplace among the Stoics that the wise man
was unmoved by pain, and smiles for the torturer abound (e.g., Livy 21.2.6,
Sen. *Ep.* 13.5 and Summers on Sen. *Ep.* 78.18). Pompey is in fact carrying out Seneca's prescription in the 78th letter, in that he turns his thoughts
away from his predicament and reflects upon his reputation and its future.
Dido too at her death thought of her enduring greatness (*Aen.* 4.651-62),
but she contrasts what would have been her happiness in this life with her
present wretchedness. Pompey however looks back over a successful career,
undimmed even by this death. Such is the difference between poetry and
dogma. The thoughts of the dying are hard to convey plausibly. But when
Virgil says of the dying Antores at *Aen.* 10.782 'dulcis moriens reminiscitur
Argos', that and no more, we see the master hand (especially in *dulcis*; cf.
Ecl. 1.3 'dulcia linquimus arua'). Here Lucan is too analytical to convey
what wiser heads refused to attempt (cf. Duff in *JPh* 32.1912.125).

622-4   Just as Helen at *Il.* 6.357f knew that she and Paris were destined to be the
future subject of poetry, so Pompey asserts that future ages are *even now*
heeding his actions (cf. Sen. *Thy.* 192f 'fac quod nulla posteritas . . . taceat',
a less bold statement). Lucan gives his utterance a grand vagueness; the
subjects are impersonal generations, *saecula* and *aeuum sequens* (cf. *ueniens
aeuum* at Hor. *Carm.* 3.5.16), while *numquam* and *omni orbe* are comprehensive and admit of no exceptions in time or space. Furthermore, the
juxtaposition of *orbe* and *ratem* stresses the contrast between the world's
gaze and the skiff it looks upon – a typical piece of grandeur (see Introduction p. 24). The sentiment should be compared with 7.205-13, and
374f in the same book.

   Romanos . . . labores: cf.7.312 'Romanus labor' and Housman's 'The
Roman and his trouble/ Are ashes under Uricon.'

626   **ignorant** 'they cannot know' a not uncommon nuance of the present; cf.
1.155 *uetante* 'can forbid', and Juv. 3.260 *inuenit* 'can find'.

627   **scieris** has a long final vowel. The final vowel of the second and third persons singular of the perfect subjunctive was originally long (LHS 1.340),
and that of the future perfect short. Poets soon became indifferent to the
distinction, and lengthened or shortened the quantity of both forms as
metrical need prompted. So at 9.603 *steteris* is future perfect. There are
discussions by Palmer on Ov. *Her.* 10.126 and Owen on *Tr.* 2.323, also in
Neue[3] 3.428-30.

629   **licebit**: the use of this verb in different tenses as a concessive is illustrated
by Owen on Ov. *Tr.* 2.307f. Since Ovid had used the future, followed by

158

tamen as a correlative, in the *Metamorphoses*, its presence in the *Pharsalia* is unexceptionable (*contra* Lease *CR* 12.1898.30f).

630 Pompey consoles himself with the reflection that the past is unalterable. The sentiment is a commonplace: Aristotle quotes the tragic poet Agathon at *E.N.* 6.2, 1139b, and a full list of parallels is given on p. 76 of Wagner's *Poetarum Tragicorum Graecorum Fragmenta* (1848).

631 **uita** is a temporal ablative, as at 9.8, and means 'while one lives'.

632 **fit** has no stated subject, nor does it need one, since the application is general (KS 2.1, 6f). The alliteration of *morte miser* gives vigour to the *sententia.*
uidet: G.B. Conte in his admirable *Saggio di Commento a Lucano* (Pisa 1974), 40, in discussing 6.159f, well observes that Lucan treats death as a spectacle. But Lucan is not alone in this, as Seneca's play *Troades* shows; in the messenger's speeches (1069-1104 and 119-1165) the deaths of Astyanax and of Polyxena are described as staged for the Argive army as audience – *theatri more* at 1126 makes this clear. Doubtless the showy deaths of the amphitheatre in Rome contributed to the sense of staginess. But private life provided instances too of the publicity of death, especially of suicide (see Introduction p. 22). Schnepf has many good observations on the exemplary character of Pompey's death (399-401).

635 **si mirantur, amant**: in the *Life of Pope*, Dr Johnson observed that a hero would wish to be loved as well as reverenced. Pompey's attitude is different (and not for that reason merely rhetorical); he says that reverence, or awe, will be a proof of love. In a sense, personal attachment is of less importance to the public figure than open marvelling. The notions of respect and love are often joined or opposed; cf. Cic. *Fam.* 1.7.9, Lucr. 1.641, Hor. *Ep.* 2.2. 58; Cic. *Fin.* 1.16 and witty Martial 9.1.6.

636 **animi morientis** is not an example of transferred epithet, any more than 1.447 'fortes animas belloque peremptas'. The spirit is only said to die in so far as its body does; cf. St. *Th.* 8.210 'animam tellure reponant', Eur. *Hel.* 52f.

639 Cornelia's speech is partially modelled upon one of Virgil's less convincing speeches, the lament of Euryalus's mother at *Aen.* 9.480-502. At 217 Nisus described her as 'sola multis e matribus ausa/ persequitur', which is recalled here at 648, where *matrum* is equivalent to *matronarum.* The introduction and sequel to both speeches are very similar: 'caelum dehinc quaestibus inplet: hunc ego te . . . aspicio . . . interque manus reponunt' (Virgil); 'aethera conplet uocibus . . ego te . . . peremi . . . interque suorum lapsa manus' (but similarity of situation is bound to entail similar language). Both women moreover close their laments with prayers for death directed towards

the bystanders. It may be suggested that for once Lucan is more credible than Virgil (if anything in speeches of this sort can nowadays be regarded as natural). For Cornelia sees suicide as a possibility; Euryalus' mother ruled it out, but gave no reason for doing so (497).

639   **ego te peremi** voices a guilty sense of complicity in the death of the beloved; cf. Anna in *Aen.* 4.680f.

641   **litora** is here used of a river-bank; see *OLD* sv 1c.

642   **quisquis,** sc. *es* as at *Aen.* 1.330 'sis felix nostrumque leues, quaecumque, laborem' and in the plural St. *Th.* 10.393 'cohibete gradum, quicumque'. The omission of the second person forms of *sum* is illustrated by Housman on 1.441, but most of his examples will be found in Leo 190. Cf. also Fordyce on Catull. 68.28 and Nisbet-Hubbard on Hor. *Carm.* 2 13.2.

642-3 **istud** is culpably ambiguous with a second person verb, for it does not refer to the head of the person addressed, nor even to the head of the speaker. Indeed *illud*, which is what Lucan ought to have written, could be proposed here; but plainly the poet felt it was too tame. (At Persius 4.9 *istud* has expelled *illud.*)

644   **ubi ipsa:** the elision is also found at 2.255 and 558 above.

645   **uiscera** 'his true heart' as at Ov. *Met.* 5.18, St. *Th.* 7.521f, and Juv. 3.72.

645-6 The frequent alliteration in these lines is a sign of heightened pathos.

647   **ante meum . . . caput,** sc. *abscissum;* see 531n.

648   **quae . . . recepi:** the relative clause is here causal, and the indicative is discussed by Austin on *Aen.* 2.539.

649   **per** is commonly repeated in asyndeton, as at 6.639 (see Austin on *Aen.* 2.358, and 263-4n); the copula is exceptional, and the sense of the preposition is different (at least in English) with each noun.

650   **uictum . . . recepi:** Cornelia's loyalty is matched in life by that of the so-called Turia to her husband; cf. CIL 6.1529 d-e, and Val. Max. 6.7.2. Faithfulness of wives to their husbands in exile was a matter of common interest in the early empire; Tacitus implies that it was widespread at *Hist.* 1.3 'secutae maritos in exilia coniuges' (Schnepf has good observations on this, 396-8). The fact, however, that even kings feared to harbour Pompey, is a grandiloquence all Lucan's own.

651   **hoc** is accusative, prospective of the infinitive (so Housman on 675). It is not easy to decide whether *coniunx* is nominative ('Did I, your wife, . . . ') or vocative; in antiquity the vocative was not commaed off, as can now be most clearly seen in the new Gallus fragments (*JRS* 69.1979), in which neither *Lycori* nor *Caesar* are set off in this way.

652	**perfide parcebas** is a neat paradox – *perfide* suggests deceit – and it is stressed by alliteration. The tense is the so-called imperfect of awakening (Gildersleeve and Lodge, 233 n.3).
652-3	**te . . . fui:** *ego* might have been expressed for the sake of the contrast, but this is not invariably the case; see Housman *Papers* 2.884.
653	**nec** adds an afterthought.
654-6	The ancients, lacking barbiturates or gas ovens, had only a few methods of suicide open to them; the three here listed by Cornelia are the commonest, and poets were at pains to vary the descriptions; there is a discussion of the matter by Fraenkel 1.465-7. In Lucan we may compare 2.154f and 9.106f.
654	**permittite** governs a noun, *saltum*, and an infinitive clause, *aptare* etc., a common construction; cf. 1.251-3, 593f above, Housman on Manil. 4.285 (and the *addendum*), *Aen.* 10.758f, and Bo's *Index* to Horace, 268f.
655	**que** effects hendiadys, 'a noose of twisted rope'. Since ropes are made by twisting strands of fibre, poets use *tortus* or a synonym as a standing epithet; see Pease on *Aen.* 4.575. It is important to see a standing epithet for what it is, often a colourless and traditional make-weight. Failure to do so leads to strange imaginings; an object lesson is G. Williams's discussion of 'tortum . . . funem' in Hor. *Ep.* 1.10.48 in *Tradition and Originality in Roman Poetry* (1968), 598.
656	**Magno dignus** is hard to interpret. Postgate took it to imply that the man who kills Cornelia is 'worthy of Magnus' in that he kills Pompey's 'murderess'; but Oudendorp thought, not unreasonably, that Cornelia, after addressing the sailors at 654, now turns to one of her husband's lieutenants as more suitable to kill her. But it seems more likely in the light of 4.542-4 that the phrase means that anyone who can steel himself to the act is thereby worthy of Pompey.
657-8	**praestare . . . inputet** are commercial metaphors, the first meaning 'to discharge an obligation', and the second 'charge to an account'. The man who kills Cornelia will be doing his duty by Pompey, yet the crime of her murder can be charged against Caesar. (Duff's translation, here abandoned, is not impossible; he takes *inputet* to mean 'claim as a service', a meaning common in Silver Latin, and illustrated by Mayor on Juv. 5.14 with *addenda*, p. 418.)
658	This line is an example of how speech is used to continue narrative. Similar is the speech of Eurydice in Vir. *Geor.* 4.494-8.
659-61	The sentences become short and breathless, so depicting Cornelia's near collapse. *et* = *et tamen*, see *OLD* sv 14.

161

660 **prohibent** has for subject *nautae,* addressed at 658. *Accersere* and its past participle are common in expressions of suicide; cf. 4.484, 7.252, and *OLD* sv *arcesso* 5.

662 **rapitur** suggests that she is carried to her bed, violently, as is usual in Lucan, rather than that she is borne along by the ship.
trepida, implying rapid motion as well as agitation, is illustrated by Langen on V.Fl.3.52.

663-91 Some preliminary remarks on this account of Pompey's decapitation are in order (cf. Schnepf 384f). Cornelia's speech separates the butchery from the killing, a device to sustain dramatic tension. Yet even once we are upon the act, Lucan is oblique, and more concerned with ethics than blood. He remarks upon the fixity of Pompey's expression (reminiscent of Ovid's Polyxena at *Met.* 13.478). The reader is undeceived only at 667, towards the close of the sentence, by *lacerum:* Pompey's head is off his shoulders. (This ability to postpone a vital word is one of the blessings of an inflected language.) Only then does the poet account for this condition with *nam.* Even here brutality is not his ruling interest as the closing epigram shows (673). The indignities the head endures are not vividly set forth (no blood), and its abuse is moral, so to say, rather than physical. Lucan seeks pathos, not nausea (676-8). Not infrequently Lucan's gruesome details serve, if only notionally, this ethical purpose. For example, the horrible sea-fight before Marseilles in the third book culminates in the ironic phrase *pelagi decus* in the last line, where Lucan counts the cost of the glory. Likewise Scaeva's incredible prowess, though described to some degree for its own sake, is designed to illustrate the poet's view that fighting in civil war is an expense of spirit in a waste of shame (6.257-62).
And yet it must be admitted that Lucan (and Seneca) love to lavish their descriptive skills upon the revolting for its own sake. Repellent detail is not, of course, unknown in more chaste poets. Sophocles, for example, could not be more clinical in describing the murder of Lichas at *Tr.* 781f, and a passage of *O.R.*, 1276-9, is very like 3.638f above. Virgil, it has been observed, is perfunctory about woundings, and yet Dido's punctured lung at *Aen.* 4.689 or the stricken deer of *Aen.* 7.498f are vivid in a way that Lucan's 'terga sonent et pectora ferro' is not. Perhaps Lucan was shy of going into too much detail in the case of so noble a Roman.

663 **sonent** suggests that Pompey wore a breastplate; Plutarch says he covered his head with the toga (79) – Lucan was unspecific at 614 – and that would rule out any body armour. Once again Lucan has no clear picture of

162

the scene in his mind to convey to the reader.

664 **sacrae uenerabile** prepare the reader for the coming apotheosis of Pompey with which the book closes; cf. 669, 677.

665 **iratamque deis faciem** is hard to explain, because anger implies some disarrangement of the features; *iratam* therefore has been emended, but all such attempts assume that Lucan troubled to see in his mind's eye what he describes. But this is not his way, as the note to 663 and the introduction to 202-55 try to show. At any rate, the conceit that the features of the face were fixed in death is a common one, illustrated by Housman on 2.26, to which may be added Diod. Sic. 17.58 (decapitation), Lucr. 3.654f, St. *Th.* 3.94, and *Herc. Oet.* 1608, 1684, 1726.

666-7 **fatentur, qui . . :** this appeal to historical tradition (if it may be so termed) has an odd ring, set as it is in the midst of a narrative that aims at immediacy. It is not the sort of appeal to authority that is found in the learned poetry of Catullus (e.g., 64.1) or of Ovid (e.g., *Met.* 8.385). It seems to be an apology or even guarantee for a statement that is 'strange but true'; see T.C.W. Stinton, *PCPS* 22.1977.60-89.

668 **sceleris maius scelus** is a word play dear to Seneca's heart, e.g., *Med.* 474 'scelere in uno non semel factum scelus'; more are listed by Canter in *Rhetorical Elements in the Tragedies of Seneca* (Urbana 1925), 151.

671 **obliquo:** the use of this word is discussed by Housman on 1.220.

673 **artis** is commonly used by the declaimers of a wicked skill (cf. Bonner 268). The genitive case is here a predicate (Roby 1282). Commentators have long referred to Caligula's 'miles decollandi artifex' (Suet. *Cal.* 32.1), but the point Lucan is making is that, whereas the axe had once been in common use, the sword came into vogue in the late Republic (see Mayor on Juv. 10. 345), and that Pompey had the misfortune to live during the awkward period of transition.

674 **recessit** in such a context is a *uox Ouidiana*, e.g., *Her.* 16.155, *Pont.* 2.8.65, and *Fasti* 6.708.

675 **hoc** is prospective of the infinitive, *gestare*. But it is worth noting that Housman's objection to referring it to *ceruix* in 674 is not watertight. He felt that it should be *hanc*. But as Munro demonstrated on Lucr. 1.352 and 6.188, adjectives and pronouns do not always agree in gender with the noun to which they are to be referred, but can rather assume the gender of a synonym. So here *hoc* could refer to the idea *caput*, of which *ceruix* is a synonym (see 12n). Housman himself notes the usage on Manil. 2.964 (with *addendum*), 5.181, and above 7.419; similar is 9.285-7 'examina . . . quaeque (apis) uolat'. The metrical advantages are plain, but we encounter the

163

usage in prose, e.g., Cic. *De Or.* 1.197 where *illorum* follows *gentibus* as if it had been *populis.*

676   **degener atque operae . . . secundae:** an adjective and a descriptive genitive are joined at Catull.15.17, Hor. *Serm.* 1.2.10, Sen. *Med.* 21, and Juv. 3.48. *Operae secundae,* as is sometimes the case with such genitives, represents a Greek compound, here for example δευτεραγωνιστής or δευτερουργός (LHS 69). The metaphor is owed to the stage, as at 7.632.

678   **ut non** here introduces a final and not a consecutive clause; in preference to the usual *ne, ut non* is used so that emphasis may fall upon a single negated word, here *ipse.*

679   **inpius** refers generally to a client's failure to help his patron, but it has the added point in the present context that Ptolemy offends against a being almost divine.

680-1   It may be that Lucan knew, either from portrait busts, or from the biographical tradition, that Pompey, like Alexander, had a vigorous growth of hair. This was also pointed out by Pliny, who speaks of Pompey's 'os uenerandum' and 'ipsum . . . honorem eximiae frontis' (*N.H.* 37.14 and 7.53).

682-3   These self-contained lines seem to do little more than break into the sentence with a dash of unpleasantness, not unlike 6.757f. But commentators acknowledge a pathos in the absence of a friendly hand to close his eyes (an action illustrated by Pease on *Aen.* 4.244, p.251). But there is more. While it is true that murmuring heads were part of the poetic furniture of the day (e.g., Sen. *Thy.* 727-9, St. *Th.* 5.236f and 10.517), Lucan is suggesting here that there was no one to catch with a kiss the departing spirit (again illustrated by Pease on *Aen.* 4.684). Both offices are mentioned at 3.739f.

685   **mouebat** here means 'influence' (*TLL* 8.1544.62). By metonymy *Campum* means 'the Roman people gathered to vote for magistrates', a usage noted by Cicero at *De Or.* 3.167; Lucan uses *rostra* to mean either 'the people assembled in the forum' or 'men who address the people from the *rostra,* i.e., tribunes or lawyers'. So far so good. But *leges* is less straightforward. Farnaby took it to be a metonymy for the Senate, and that view is here diffidently accepted. There are no cited parallels for such an interpretation (the line is ignored in Hübner's article on *lex* for *TLL*). It may be that *leges* here means 'the constitution' a sense illustrated in *OLD* sv 3. At any rate Lucan is not aiming at precise language in his eulogy. He only means to show that Pompey was supreme in every department of Roman public life. The three nouns, *Campum, rostra, leges,* plainly refer to home affairs, as *bella* in 684 refers to foreign affairs: a concealed doublet (see 75n).

686   **hac facie:** in other words Pompey was the visible incarnation of Rome's

Fortune; so Ovid calls Augustus Rome visible at *Pont.* 2.8.20 'patriae faciem sustinet ille suae'. Fortune's face is discussed by Housman on Manil. 5.483.

687 **hoc** refers to the whole notion of carrying the head on a pike.

688 **arte nefanda:** pure xenophobia. Embalming was still unusual at Rome, and indeed cremation made it a waste of time. But the passionate prodigality of Nero embalmed Poppaea (so Tac. *Ann.* 16.6.2), and the new fashion for burial in sarcophagi encouraged the spread of the practice; cf. St. *Silu.* 5.1.230 *siccata* and Mau in *RE* 5.2113-4.

689 **capiti** is a dative of 'disadvantage', common with verbs of depriving; see Woodcock 44. The case is generally used of persons; of things it is not unusual in Livy and the poets. Examples in Lucan are 2.156f, 6.724f and 7.233.

690 **cutis** is a word of common speech (*TLL* 4.1578.34). Ovid avoided it in his early poetry, but found a need for it in the *Metamorphoses*, with its descriptions of altered complexions and outer coverings; so he used it of human skin. It may be that Lucan uses it here for its straightforwardness, but it would be hard to deny that it may just be careless.
 ab alto is illustrated in *TLL* 1.1781.41.

692-711 The narrative of Pompey's murder is now over. Before moving on to the burial, Lucan typically takes time out to reflect upon the action in his own person. He mentions the pyramids in preparation for and in contrast to the coming burial of Pompey. A new theme is also introduced, Alexander. This too is prompted by love of pathetic contrast. Both men were called 'The Great', and indeed Pompey modelled himself upon Alexander (Plutarch pairs their biographies); but the Roman's end was tragic, nor was he ever, as Lucan paints him, inclined to tyranny and mass-murder. Starting the Alexander theme now, Lucan will go on to develop it, and compare Caesar to him in the tenth book. For now, he turns to Fortuna and reproaches her for cruelty and bad faith. His final vision is of the surf-beaten trunk.

692 **peritura** hints at Ptolemy's near death; see *Bel. Alex.* 31-6.
 proles was regarded by Cicero as more suited to poetry than to prose (*De Or.* 3.153, and see Norden on *Aen.* 6.784). Lucan's contempt — emphasized by alliteration — is couched in decent language (a point missed by Ahl 223).

693 **incestae** shows in what particular Ptolemy is *degener*.

694-8 Carefully Lucan builds up a vast and resounding structure of words; 696 and 697 have almost the minimum number of words required to compose a line, but their weight, enhanced by the spondaic close in *Mausolea*, is undercut by the short and paradoxical sentence, 'litora Pompeium feriunt'.

694 **Macedon** is only found here for the usual *Macedo*, which was rejected so as to avoid three long open o's in the same line.
antro 'burial vault' at 10.19 as well; see *TLL* 2.192.28ff.

695 **regum** are the Pharoahs. This account is basically correct; cf. P.M. Fraser, *Ptolemaic Alexandria* (1972), 2.35, n.83.
Monte was also used of a building at 463; Seneca uses it of a tomb in *Anth. Lat.* 418.3. These pass unnoticed by *TLL*.

696 **seriem** is used of a family at 4.823. Strabo had remarked upon the steady degeneracy, 17.11.

697 **Mausolea** is used of any vast tomb; see *OLD* sv 2. The spondaic hexameter was a hallmark of the neoteric poets (see N.B. Crowther in *CQ* 20.1970.322, esp. n.2). Lucan allows into his poem some thirteen examples, but they have a shop-worn quality: in only four does he introduce into the fifth foot a word not already there used by Virgil or Ovid; this line is one example, the others being 1.689, 9.297 and 719. There could be no more convincing demonstration of his dependence in technical refinements upon the earlier masters.

698 **litora** here is not so much the shore, as the water on the shore's edge; so at Vir. *Ecl.* 2.25 'nuper me in litore uidi' (see Fordyce on Catull. 63.87 and *TLL* 7.2, 1537.52ff). It is not therefore necessary to see the syntax of the sentence as reversed (a device called hypallage); nevertheless U. Hübner's discussion of hypallage in Lucan, *Hermes* 100.1972.577-600, remains a most stimulating study.

703-4 **in uno ... die**: Lucan uses the masculine in the oblique cases of *dies* with one exception to be mentioned below. In the nominative, the feminine is only used where metrically prompted. The sole exception is 7.254ff; Fraenkel reckoned that this was so because the lines recall Ov. *Fasti* 6.713 (1.70f).

704 **inmunes**: Ollfors treats of the molossus (three long syllables) filling the third foot and first *longum* of the fourth (1.50-7). But only at 747 below and 9.142 is the word not a compound, whose prefix is, metrically considered, separable (so 3.438, 5.44, 715, 9.138). (There is thus no ground for doubting *infelix* at Ov. *Met.* 4.591.) The anonymous writer of an article in the *Quarterly Review* 127.1869.268 got this nice point right.

706-7 **felix** and *miser* ring the chiastically patterned phrase (see 84-5n).

708 **dilata ... manu** alludes to Fortune's keeping her bargain by deferring mishaps. She makes up the tale at a stroke, *semel* (cf.21f).

710 **ludibrium**: just so Dickens called the drowned Quilp the river's plaything in *The Old Curiosity Shop*.

711   Servius knew that Virgil's final vision of Priam at *Aen.* 2.557f 'iacet ingens
litore truncus/ auolsumque caput et sine nomine corpus' owed something
to the fate of Pompey. The pathos of Virgil's description is inherent in the
subject — a mutilated old man, so he keeps the language simple and the sentence structure straightforward so as not to break the spell. Lucan on the
other hand is not content with intrinsic pathos (and neither, we assume, was
his audience). So his final vision of Pompey is not a dignified reflection, but
a teasing paradox. One expects a headless body to be unrecognisable, hence
Virgil's 'sine nomine corpus'; but Lucan fancies that the loss of his head is
the very thing that identifies Pompey (cf. E. Narducci, *La Provvidenza
Crudele* (1979), 44). This, in a nutshell, is the difference between rhetoric
and poetry.

INTRODUCTION TO LINES 712-872

In the ancient world burial was a duty of the first importance. It is of course
just as much a duty in our own day and is enjoined upon us as a corporal work of
mercy; but it is not a function with which we as individuals have much more to do
than assist at interment. Personal attendance to the washing of the body, ritual
lament, and such intimate gestures as a final kiss or the lighting of pyre rarely find
an equivalent in modern experience. But the frequent allusions in classical literature
to the performance of these very acts suggest that conscientious friends might carry
out the duties themselves despite the professional undertakers. The sense of pressing
need or even of desire for burial is eloquently expressed, to choose only two notable
examples out of many, in the *Antigone* of Sophocles and in Horace's Archytas ode,
1.28; Pliny observed that anxiety about burial was a marked trait of the human
animal (*N.H.* 7.1.5). It should be stressed that the urgency to bury was not so much
due to a rational fulfilment of the requirements of public health, but to a feeling,
instinctive and traditional, for the needs of the dead, and surely too of the living.
The spirit of an unburied corpse was troubled, and its friends for their part wanted
to make a parting gesture. Both found a satisfaction and relief in the act of cremation and inhumation. Thus Lucan, when he came to write of Pompey's funeral,
could depend upon a sympathy in his readers which is not wholly absent to-day, but
it is surely less finely tuned and less fully developed.
    The theme with which Lucan is dealing was well-worn, as a glance over the
moving Greek and Latin sepulchral epigrams confirms. Indeed epitaphs for Pompey
were a popular form of literary exercise of which examples remain in the *Anthologia*

Latina, and at Martial 5.74. Since moreover Lucan was writing in the epic tradition he had before his eyes all the grand interments of an imagined heroic world from Patroclus to Misenus and Pallas. Burial as a theme was of great interest to him, as will be shown, but there was a second impulse, namely his desire to counter heroic extravagance with as moving an account as possible of the paltry but all too real burial of a modern hero. Heavy as the literary debt was, there is also to be considered that personal satiric vein which has been noted before in Lucan's verse. So in this section the lavish outpourings of wealth and grief at imperial exequies receive scant respect, and the poet will go so far as to set up Pompey as a deified hero far worthier of worship than a Julius. Lucan's desire to elaborate this part of his book has an additional motive. Pompey's death and burial were an unparalleled tragedy of Roman history. Consider the fate of the other triumvirs: Crassus was far below heroic stature, a greedy man who gambled for military glory and lost, not only his own and his son's life, but Roman honour. Thus for contemporary poets the capture by the Parthians of the standards is as moving a theme as the fate of the general. (This is surprising since the decapitation of Crassus would make for tragic history; but the man himself was not the stuff of heroism or romance.) As for Julius, heroic in life, he met death well, and was honourably interred, soon to be an object of devotion. Only Pompey could stand forth as a example of ruined grandeur (see Shackleton Bailey 170). Lucan saw his chance, and lavished his skill upon the account.

It is interesting to observe how common throughout the poem is the theme of burial, apart from Pompey's. The old man in the second book who recounts the excesses of the social war stresses his own anguish at the difficulty he had in burying his headless brother (169-73). The third book closes with a description of the scene on the beach of Marseilles after the sea battle. The fourth ends with Lucan's laudation of Curio, abandoned to African birds. At 5.278ff Caesar's mutinous troops urge that the desire for a decent civilian burial is one motive of their revolt. And at 6.810f Lucan delivers one of his most telling jibes at the whole war as deciding no more than the place of burial for victor and vanquished. But he will go further and use burial as a linking theme, a structural device that binds together the closing scenes of the seventh, eighth, and ninth books. The majestic reflections on Pompey's dead army make up much of the last lines of the seventh (though it in fact finishes with a curse upon Thessaly). At the end of book VIII their general receives his last honours and Egypt is reviled for her part in the butchery. Book IX opens with a calm and glorified Pompey, but closes with the mockery of an extravagant and useless burial of his embalmed head.

When we consider Lucan's debt to earlier accounts of burial in epic, there is a risk that a modern interpreter will speak of an anti-heroic sensibility. In one way that is what we are dealing with, but not because Lucan faults such descriptions, rather he knows that they are irrelevant to his theme. When we read of the broken bits of boat used to construct the tiny pyre we must recall the great tree-fellings of Virgil and Ennius. (See Norden 185ff and *Herc. Oet.* 1618ff; the Ennian passage may not be in the context of a funeral; Lucan's imitation of the commonplace will be found at 3.440ff.) The feeble flame is so unlike the pyre of Patroclus, at which victims were offered. In fine, the expectation of a reader who is acquainted with traditional epic accounts is baulked at every point, and his pity should be awakened by the sense of contrast. For Lucan makes it clear that Pompey of all men deserved a grand funeral. He consoles himself for its absence with a personal attachment to the hero, and with a belief that the very meanness of the rite will assure Pompey of divine status.

The critical reader must however ask himself if the poet's effort has succeeded. Lucan is moved, but are we? If we are not, then the failure may prove to be ours. But a fair judgment was long ago passed upon him by Horace Walpole, who was prepared to rank Lucan above Virgil: 'Lucan who often says more in a half a line than Virgil in a whole book was lost in bombast if he talked for thirty lines together' (*Correspondence,* ed. Lewis, vol.29 p.256). And the poet won the praise, not unmixed, of Macaulay, who knew rant when he saw it. Regretfully it has to be admitted that the concluding section of the book is obnoxious to Walpole's criticism. Nor is the reason hard to divine. As was said above, the death and disfigurement of Pompey were intrinsically moving to the Roman reader; Valerius Maximus had said that the whole business was 'ipsi Fortunae erubescendus', 1.8.9. The allusion by Virgil to the event, Propertius 3.11.33-6, and Manilius 4.50ff all touch upon a wound nationally felt. Lucan's real sense for this power of Pompey's name led him to rely upon its continuance beyond his own day. But as time passed, Pompey became less of a reality and more of a rhetorical *exemplum,* and Lucan has poured out his enthusiasm upon a *nominis umbra.* Virgil was faced with a different task. Since Camilla, Lausus, and Pallas were not names that instantly set Roman pulses racing, he had to endow these shades with flesh and blood. His sympathetic art quickened his inventions so that their misfortunes and deaths are not without power to move us today.

Virgil had to work to stir up the reader's emotions. Lucan however could still expect Pompey's fate to be moving, and so he expends less time than he might on awakening our sympathy for his hero (or rather, the hero of this book). In the picture of Pompey there are some fine strokes: his last long look at Italy with which the third book opens, his concern for Cornelia at the close of the fifth, and the longing of Rome for him at the beginning of the seventh. But these cannot counterbalance the overall magniloquence; the suggestion of a human being within the cocoon of words is faint indeed. We are not shown the sudden generosity of a Dido, nor the useless tears of her lover, nor the sisterly tenderness of Juturna. Lucan is so sure of his contemporaries' response to his tale that he spends his time on an apotheosis, not without power, but frigid at the last. But antiquity judged differently. For Statius, in his birthday poem on Lucan, *Silu.* 2.7, chose this very section of the eighth book to paraphrase: 'tu Pelusiaci scelus Canopi/ deflebis pius et Pharo cruenta/ Pompeio dabis altius sepulcrum', 70-2. But in the last analysis, a character who has not lived cannot die.

Confirmation of this adverse judgment may be secured by comparing Lucan's poem to Wolfe's *Burial of Sir John Moore at Corunna*, an anthology piece. In almost every respect the similarities are striking. Both poets stress that the usual trappings of military pomp are absent; the funeral is performed in haste and at night. There is no coffin, no shroud. The dead man will be trodden under foot. But there is a consolation, namely that Moore is buried by a British hand (cf. 767). The ceremony must be broken off and no marker is left on the tomb, save the hero's glory. Wolfe, like Lucan, depended upon historical sources for his information, and wrote some years after the event, (and also like Lucan he died young). He relies for fullest effect upon the freshness of the national grief, and focusses upon the pathetic accidents of Moore's burial. But now that Moore's reputation is confined to military historians, Wolfe's poem, though competent, has about it the air of the rhetorical exercise. Lucan has one advantage over his Irish twin, in that the expression of a personal wish to convey Pompey's ashes back to Rome should produce a conviction in the reader of the poet's sincere devotion. But the goal of classical rhetoric was to arouse an emotional response in the reader. And to secure that response in a reader remote from the events narrated requires more work than Lucan was prepared to do.

712   This line is prospective of 10.1f 'ut primum terras . . . attigit et diras cal-
cauit Caesar harenas'. In this context it hints at Caesar's supposed intention
to maltreat his enemy, a theme made explicit at 315f and 765. Lucan's
technique of foreshadowing deserves some notice, for it points to a care in
the construction of the poem which is sometimes denied him. The broad
hint is a useful device for the epic poet. Homer had shown the way by
making Hector conscious of his not far distant death. Dido is described in
the first book of the *Aeneid* as 'pesti deuota futurae' (712). On a smaller
scale Lucan says of the bridge at Ilerda that it was designed 'hibernas pas-
surus aquas' (4.16); only after line 48 does it become clear why he fixed
upon this piquant detail. He can use the device to link books; this book
ends with the poet's hopes for an apotheosis of Pompey, and the next
opens with his spirit in heaven. So too Cleopatra, who will play a large part

in the tenth book, is introduced at the close of the ninth. But of all fore-shadowings the most consistent has been that of Pompey's own death and burial; allusions are made at 1.685, 2.731-6, 5.63, 475, 6.810, 7.704, and in this book at 11, 81, 393, and 436f.

713   **raptim** is a rare word for poetry; it is not found in the *Aeneid*, or the *Metamorphoses*, nor in the tragedies of Seneca. This suggests that it was not felt to be suitable. At any rate, Lucan has it again at 7.330, and all subsequent epic poets admit the word.

714   **uel ne meliore sepulchro**: the point of the remark is as yet obscure, but will be made clear as the narrative progresses.

715   Economy of presentation is here again in evidence. Plutarch recounts that Pompey was buried by his freedman and by an old soldier who chanced by (80). This is touching and romantic, but not good enough for Lucan, who requires a degree of propriety as well. And it is in accordance with the demands of propriety that he had Lentulus rather than Theodotus speak against Pompey's plan to go to Parthia for aid (see 328n). So too now he employs a lone Roman officer to burn and bury his general. This Cordus is an invention of Lucan's (but he is given another name, Servius, at *De Viris Ill.* 77.9). At a stroke Lucan diminishes the number of actors and raises the social status.

716-7   The sentence is by way of parenthesis, brisk but by no means adequate in accounting for Cordus's presence. Granting he joined Pompey at Cyprus, how did he reach the shore of Egypt? Where were his *latebrae* (715)? Lucan is not interested. He wants someone of the proper status to bury Pompey and so produces him like a rabbit from a top hat. Postgate observed how appropriate the rank of *quaestor* was to the situation, for he was sup-posed to stand in relation to his superior officer as son to father; cf. L.A. Thompson, *Historia* 11.1962.339-55.
     Icario remains a baffling allusion, but our continued ignorance is no grounds for emendation. The encrustation of the line with showy, and presumably learned, epithets is somewhat intrusive in what is, after all, no more than a sketched-in background.

718   **ferre gradum** is a characteristic periphrasis of epic; Langen illustrates num-erous others, formed with *ferre*, at V.Fl.2.282.
     pietate ranges Cordus alongside Cornelia, the Senate, and the Mytilenaeans and against Caesar and the Egyptian court. Statius caught the note when he styled Lucan himself *pius* in this very context at *Silu.* 2.7.71, quoted above in the introductory section to these lines.

171

timorem is probably the subject of the verbs in the *ut* clause; it is therefore an example of metonymy, equivalent to *se timentem.*

719   **conpulit ut** . . . is a construction found again at 7.801, but it is far from usual in poetry, which prefers the infinitive, as at 3.144. Here, as in 440f, the word order gives a picture of the sense.

720   It can be argued that two distinct actions are here described, first, pushing the body to land, and then beaching it. But the repetition of the second half of the line from 570 suggests that Lucan was in too much of a hurry to write carefully; nor had he Virgil's craftsmanship, that left half lines where inspiration faltered.

721   Asyndeton, as at 715, marks the resumption of narrative. The scene is romantically coloured, and the moon's sympathy is a fair touch of pathos. (Lucan had noted the sun's sympathy at the opening of the seventh book.) The interest of nature in the action is picked up at 728. It is important to recall that burial at night was common among Rome's poor. *Lucis*. . . *parum* is a construction found in prose, but only here in elevated poetry.

722   **cano** . . . **aequore**: all is vivid and concrete for once. Cordus's use of the waves to help push up the dead weight is particularly well observed.

724   **eripiente mari** is taken by Cortius to mean 'eripere uolente' and Francken and Postgate accept this in principle. But this is unnecessary in the context, for the sea was actually pulling the body away from Cordus. Moreover E. Laughton in *The Participle in Cicero* (1964), 40f argues that many verbs implying a process, e.g., verbs of giving or going, have an inherent sense of attempted or prospective action, and that such a nuance does not reside in the tense of the verb or participle.

726   **sedit** must have Pompey as its subject, an abrupt shift between *inpellit* and *incubuit*. Housman gives examples of sentences which supply their subject word from a different case of that word in a subsequent clause in his note to 9.466-8.

727   **incubuit Magno** describes an ancient gesture of grief. So Thetis found Achilles slumped over Patroclus, *Il.* 19.4.

    lacrimasque . . . **uolnus**: the wounds would be those on breast and back (663) as well as the neck. In the heroic age oil was poured into the wounds, as at *Il.* 18.351. This was too simple for Roman poets; a conceit arose among them that tears were used to cleanse the wounds, a conceit fully illustrated by Heinsius on Ov. *Her.* 11.125. Imagination comes then into play and at *Met.* 4.140f Ovid has the blood of Thisbe drop into the wounds of Pyramus; Seneca took up the notion in his lost treatise *De Matrimonio* (see Bickel, *Diatribe in Sen. Phil. Fragmenta* (1915), 325f and 386). But

for absurdity the palm goes to Statius, who fancies that Hypsipyle drops her
nursing milk into the wounds of the child Archemorus at *Th.* 5.619.

728   **ad . . . sidera fatur**: the stars are addressed because it is their secret influence
which fixes men's doom (cf. Vir. *Ecl.* 5.23 and *Cons. ad Liu.* 192). But even
before the rise of astrology the address to heaven, as the gods' home, was
usual; cf. Carden, *Papyrus Fragments of Sophocles* (1974), 18. It should be
noted that Cordus has three short speeches, of which the third, to the res-
cued corpse, as most important, is last and longest.

729-42   Three points can be made about this prayer as a whole. First, it is cast in
the form of a negative enumeration, as at Hor. *Carm.* 4.3.3-9, Ov. *Met.* 1.91-9,
Luc. 4.299-302 and 5.149-55; in fact the negative enumeration is one of
the commonest devices for filling in a background of foil material. But
Lucan can let it get out of hand, as in the long unwedding of Cato and
Marcia at 2.354-64. Secondly, the content of the prayer contains a hint of
satire, which runs through the whole of the closing section, against lavish
display at funerals, particularly imperial ones (so B.L. Ullman in *CQ* 15.
1921.75). It is not hard to imagine that the poet had in mind just such a
ceremony as was proposed for Augustus: 'funus triumphali porta ducendum
praecedente Victoria . . . canentibus neniam principum liberis . . . senatorum
umeris delatus in Campum crematusque' Suet. *D. Aug.* 100.2-3 and 850n).
Members of the immediate imperial family were also lavishly attended, as
Tacitus records of Germanicus (*Ann.* 3.2-5). Here, at the opening of the
final section of the book, the satire aims at contrast and pathos, but soon
it will turn to paradox: the very meanness of the rite will be its distinction.
Thirdly, the period from 729-35 is neatly turned to prevent tedium. Three
lines only are end-stopped, and they occur in the middle of the sentence as
a whole. Alliteration is frequent, especially of *p* and *t*. At 730, 733, and
734 *ut* is postponed to break up the parallelism of construction.
pretiosa is countered by *uilem* at 736.
sepulchra must here mean *rogus*, for spices were burned with the dead. It
seems to be so used also at Ter. *And.* 128, *Aen.* 6.177, Sen. *Med.* 798f 'de
medio/ rapta sepulchro fax', and 750 below.

730   **Pompeius Fortuna tuus**: it is important to appreciate that Fortuna, though
sometimes seen as a deity with her own personality, is also a personal assoc-
iate of men and families: each has his own *fortuna*. This was, in the case of
a general, of the highest importance, and is tellingly stressed by Cicero in *De
Imp. Pomp.* 47 where he reckons that a man's *fortuna* was as effective as
uirtus in obtaining commands. Mayor's note to Juv. 10.285 'Fortuna ipsius

173

et urbis' illustrates the concept. These two notions were perhaps never distinctly formulated and so we find mixtures that are hard to analyse, e.g., at Hor. *Carm.* 1.35.23f (for which see Nisbet and Hubbard). Thus in the present book at 686 'hac facie Fortuna . . . Romana' the Fortune of Rome is identified with or incarnate in Pompey. And the Fortune addressed at 860f seems to be at once Pompey's own and the abstract divinity. This special link is observed by Florus (1.40.21) 'per quae omnia decus . . . Pompeio suo Fortuna quaerebat'.

729-31   **petit . . . ut ferat** is a construction not found elsewhere in poetry.

730   **pinguis . . . fumus** is like the rich smoke mentioned by Callim. *Hymn.* 4.179f (which is not to suggest that Lucan had read Callimachus); cf. Ov. *Tr.* 5.5. 11 'da mihi tura puer pingues facientia flammas'.

732   **Romana pia colla**: the double epithet is discussed on 597.
      parentem is not an official title. Cicero urged his brother Quintus to be regarded as well as called 'parens Asiae' at *Q.Fr.* 1.1.31, and Lucan styles Cato 'parens uerus patriae' at 9.601; the loose conferring of this honour is illustrated by Mayor on Juv. 8.244.

733   The custom of carrying triumphal insignia at a funeral is mentioned by Horace, *Epode* 8.11f and by Dion. Halic. *Ant. Rom.* 8.59.3.

734   Lucan has lifted the first part of this line straight from the *Apocolocyntosis* (as it is called by some) or *Ludus* of his uncle Seneca, 12.3, 2 'resonet tristi clamore forum'. But is *fora* here simply a metrical eke? In Pompey's own day there was only the *forum Romanum*, but after Augustus there were three *fora,* the *Iulium* and *Augusti* having been added. It is probably therefore an anachronism.
      totus marks the end of an enumeration as at 1.72-80, 2.642, 5.266, above 43-5, 99, 120-3, and 830 below. This technique of closing lists in asyndeta is illustrated by Leo, *Ausg. Kl. Schr.* 1.179f.

735   The custom here spoken of is called *decursio;* its essential features have taken shape in *Il.* 23.13f, and similar rites are attested in all epic or history, even to *Beowulf,* 3169-82. In all accounts one feature stands out, namely, that the troops are armed. And that makes *proiectis armis* so hard to understand. Some suggest that this refers to reversed arms, a symbol of military grief mentioned at *Aen.* 11.93, Ov. *Am.* 3.9.7, and, as a civic gesture, at *Cons. ad Liu.* 141f and Tac. *Ann.* 3.2.2. If Lucan meant that, it is wonderful that he did not write *inuersis,* as he could easily have done. The phrase rather suggests that the men threw their arms upon the pyre. There are three notices of such an event, two historical and one imaginative. Suetonius says that soldiers cast on to Julius's pyre 'arma sua quibus exculti funus

celebrabant' (*D.J.* 84.4). At Augustus's funeral, says Dio (56.42.2), triumphal insignia and imperial awards were offered to his flames. Finally at St. *Th.* 6.244-6 the troops at the funeral of Archemorus cast on his pyre bridle or belt, crest or spear. It therefore seems likely that in this passage Lucan is recalling an unusual act of ritual grief, perhaps associated with imperial exequies. (The phrase *proiectis armis* will also be found at Caes. *B.G.* 7.40.6, where it means 'thrown down'.)

736 Cordus's long preamble is brought up hard against the first four words of this line; the paradoxical effect is enhanced by the sandwiching of *Magno* between *uilem* and *plebei. Vilem* must recall the prophecy of Lentulus at 393 'te parua tegant ac uilia busta'.

arca would shock a Roman reader, because heroes are carried out on *feretra* 'biers', not in *arcae* 'boxes'. The word recalls Horace's grim description of a pauper's funeral at *Serm.* 1.8.8f 'huc prius angustis eiecta cadauera cellis/ conseruus uili portanda locabat in arca'.

737 **effundat**: the box would not be burnt, but used again for another, and so its burden is dumped out. The box itself is said to do this, but this is probably an instance of the active verb's meaning 'allow to be done . . .'; cf.74n.

siccos, because without incense; but the body's fat served as well (778).

740 **subicique facem conplexa maritum** is an allusion, it seems, to suttee (unless *conplexa* means 'after an embrace . . .'). Suttee is mentioned by both Greek and Roman writers (e.g., Strabo 15.1.30, Diod. Sic. 19. 33.3, Cic. *Tusc.* 5.78, Prop. 3.13.15-20, Val. Max. 2.6.14, and Sen. *Contr.* 2.2(10).1; St. *Silu.* 2.1. 24 mentions the desire of a contemporary magnate to be incinerated with his *puer delicatus*); the mythological precedent had been set by Evadne, the wife of Capaneus.

subici: the short u is discussed by Müller 290f; similar is the short o in *obicit* at 796.

742 **nec** = *nec tamen*, for which see *OLD* sv *neque* 5. As Postgate observed, the parataxis stresses the contrast between the clauses, which express the sentiment 'so near and yet so far away'.

743 **iuuenis** well suits the rank of quaestor, and hints too perhaps at the helpless inexperience of youth. (For an address to another corpse to share its fire we may compare St. *Th.* 12.426-8.)

744 **nullo custode** explains in just what particular the unknown corpse is said to be cheap in the eyes of its kin. Relatives were supposed to guard the body till the flames subsided (cf. Dio 56.42.4, Dion. Halic. *Ant. Rom.* 8.59.4, and Prop. 3.16.24). But there were professional watchers, as may be gathered from Firmicus *Math.* 3.9.3.

175

746	The caesurae in this line are at 2 strong, 3 weak, and 4 strong; we should read *quaecumque 's* (aphaeresis rather than elision).
746-7	**ulli . . . tuo** is like 'multorum . . . suorum' at 3.621.
747	**sed Pompeio:** the molossus is noticed at 704; the scansion is not really exceptional here or at 9.142 'an furtiuus', because the monosyllables are regarded as proclitics and closely adhere to the following word.
748	The object clause precedes its main verb also at 1.361f, and for *quod* instead of *ut* we may compare 3.744f. Lucan clearly delights to assert that only by a sacrilege can Pompey be buried, just as it will require a sacrilege to get him back to Italy (845).
750	The present tense assumes the shade's compliance.
751	There ought to be an antithesis in this line: 'you are ashamed at your cremation when Pompey . . . ' what? One would expect something like 'lacks material to be burned'. 'Sparsis . . . manibus' looks back for contrast to *conpositum* (748) rather than to its immediate context. *Manes* is discussed at 844.
752	**fatus** is only a participle as Postgate observed.
	plenus . . . sinus: Cordus' act has not, as usual, been visualised by Lucan, but Farnaby comes to the casual poet's aid by suggesting that Cordus strewed sand in his cloak first. The accusative after the adjective is found elsewhere in Lucan at 2.37, 4.726 and 10.132; a general discussion is offered by Landgraf in *ALL* 10.1898.209f.
754	**pendebat** is discussed on 797-8.
755	The broken timbers of the boat used to burn Pompey appealed strongly to the Roman imagination; cf. Manil.4.55 'eiectae . . . fragmenta carinae' and Val. Max. 1.8.9 'concisae scaphae ligna'. Lucan's choice of *lacerae* (when he could have written *fractae*) suggests a similarity to Pompey's condition (*lacerum* 667).
756	**exigua:** stress is laid upon the smallness of the trench (it was dug in a hurry) to enhance the pathos. Throughout the book in fact this note has been struck (see 245-6n), and it sounds the more clearly for the contrast with *Magnus.*
	scrobe is also feminine in Ov. *Met.* 7.243.
	nobile corpus was used at 4.809 of Curio but there is no point in the repetition.
756-7	**corpus robora nulla premunt** is the reading of all the Mss. with a minor exception. Burman conjectured *premit*, which is accepted here; it also appears as a variant reading in the Ms A (shburnhamensis = Parisinus Bibl. Publ. Lat. Nouv. Acq. 1626). Housman's defense of *premunt* by giving it the sense

'support' is attractive; it would be cogent if there were examples of this verb so used. (His arguments at 5.209 and 9.925 are along similar lines.) But *premit* deserves more attention. For, in the first place, the number of a verb is commonly assimilated by scribes to that of a near noun (e.g., 1.491, 2.13, 218, 4.186f, 620, above 118; Housman collected examples on Manil. 4.890, as did Wagner in *Quaest. Verg.* 8.2a). In the present context, almost every word in the line works against the preservation of the singular form; there is a plural noun immediately before, and the line ends with a plural noun and verb. Textually considered, it is easier to account for *premunt* than for *premit.* Secondly, we read at *Aen.* 10.375 'numina nulla premunt'. Now one of the commonest causes of variant readings in the Mss of Virgil and of other epic poets is the scribe's recollection of the text of Virgil. To take but one example in Lucan, to which Housman drew attention, at 4.48 for the correct 'hactenus armorum' two Mss read 'hactenus aruorum', the result of some ancient scribe's recalling Vir. *Geor.* 2.1. It might be objected that the whole tradition is nowhere so corrupted by recollection. But at 5.137 all the Mss offer 'Cirrha silet *fatique* sat est arcana *futuri*', which Burman corrected to *farique.* That error may be due to a recollection of *Aen.* 2.246 'tunc etiam *fatis* aperit Cassandra *futuris*', suitably altered to seem to construe in its new context. The general effects of recollection are discussed by Willis in *Latin Textual Criticism* (1972), 99f. Here *premit* is not likely to have survived long the two-pronged attack of assimilation and recollection; it should therefore be preferred to *premunt.*

757   **nulla . . . nulla:** for the variation in the quantity of the final a, and in the accent upon the word see Herescu 197-200.

758   **accipit** points up Pompey's helplessness; the fire has to receive him; cf. St. *Th.* 6.220f and *Herc. Oet.* 1484.

759   For the ritual address to the dead see Fraenkel on Aesch. *Ag.* 1489. Here *ille* is somewhat imprecise, for normally it would imply that Magnus, from the previous line, is the subject. But of course the subject is Cordus, last mentioned in 756. Lucan expects the reader to gather the sense from the context, and not from an ordered syntax.

761   **nudo** is found only in G and comm. Bern.; it is acknowledged as a variant by adn. *Nullo* is read in the text of MZV. (There is an erasure in U, and P reads *mundo*, stupidly recollecting 7.617 'in funere mundi'.) *Nullo* is the vulgate, but *nudo* deserves serious consideration. At 6.550 *nuda* of all the other Mss is altered to NVLLA by N, and at 9.64 *nudi* is glossed thus by adn., 'potest legi et *nulli*'. There are no examples in the Mss of Lucan of

177

the opposite change. Three other factors would contribute to the alteration of *nudo*. First, *funere nullo* occurs at 5.668, and so recollection, as
described in 756-7n and as seen here in the reading of P, would prompt a
scribe to alter *nudo*. Secondly, phrases such as 'uolnere nullo' and 'crimine
nullo' are so common as line ends in Lucan that recollection of their pattern would facilitate or even prompt change. Lastly, *funere nullo* is straightforward in sense, but *funere nudo* is less clear since the noun means 'corpse'
as at 7.820 (see *OLD* sv 2) and *nudo* will mean 'unburied', a sense the
scholia usually feel obliged to point out (as at 157 above and at 9.64 in
adn.; see *OLD* sv 5). Postgate admitted the attractions of *nudo* (cxi), and
as *lectio difficilior* it deserves a place in the text.

763   **officiis auerte meis** is a paradox. It was the custom for the living to turn
away their faces when lighting the pyre, 'an handsome symbole', says Sir
Thomas Browne, 'of unwilling ministration'; cf. *Aen.* 6.224 (and the parody by Althaea in Ov. *Met.* 8.511).
    iniuria fati is again used of Pompey at 9.143.

764-5   The expression is comprehensive: there are the three natural elements of
land, sea, and air, and, set against these, the inhuman Caesar.

766   **quantum potes** stresses the dead man's feebleness; there is a remarkable
parallel in *Epig. Gr.* 111: 'By-passer, I once guarded a tower in wartime, and
shall now continue to do so, though a dead man, to the best of my ability
(ὡς δύναμαι)'. (The inscription was found in the Ceramicus at Athens.)

767   **Romana succense manu** offers a small but real consolation; cf. 9.63f
'manus hoc Aegyptia forsan/ obtulit officium graue manibus'.

770   The object of *transfundet* is *te,* a vigorous thought somewhat obscured in
the translation.

771   **paruo** is discussed on 756.

778   **tabe fouens bustum**: similar is Sen. *Med.* 778f 'rogus qui uirus Herculeum
bibit'. The short e of *tabe* is regular; it is only lengthened at Lucr. 1.806
(not necessarily at 3.553 too).

781   An address from the poet to someone in the poem is even more powerful
than the usual figure of apostrophe. But Lucan's hectoring rebuke to
Cordus is unlike anything in previous epics. Lucan is an onlooker of the
action he describes, and personally enters into it with encouragement or
reproach (cf. Seitz 220). *Demens* may be compared to *Aen.* 9.728, where
Servius remarks 'hoc ex affectione sua (his own feelings) posuit poeta'.
    isto pro crimine again points to Lucan's opinion that the world after
Pharsalia is turned upside down, and pious duty has become a crime (see
748n). So at 2.168 in similar circumstances (after Sulla's proscriptions)

'pauido subducit cognita furto'. The theme will be elaborated upon at
840-5.

782   **omnis . . . in annos**: cf. 7.208 'in saecula', and *TLL* 2.117.25-36.

784   **fassus sepulchrum** is somewhat harsh, for the noun is given an unusual
verbal nuance, as if it were *sepultura*.

785   **posce caput** looks forward to the close of the ninth book when the head
receives its honours. (It may also be that Lucan has some sense of the
primal urgency of burying the head especially; cf. Hor. *Carm.* 1.28.24.)

786-7 These details are more in the poet's manner than is the restraint shown in
the description of Pompey's murder and decapitation. But despite their
unpleasantness Postgate saw in them a reference to the injury that was
felt to have been done to the dead by an incomplete cremation. It was for
example proposed that Tiberius be only half-burnt, and that was the fate of
Caligula (Suet. *Tib.* 75.3, and *Cal.* 59; cf. Mayor on Cic. *Phil.* 2.91, p.133).
Cordus's actions, if logically considered, are back to front, what the ancients
called hysterologia; he ought to extinguish the fire before grabbing the
bones. But since the bones are the leading notion in the poet's mind, he
speaks first of them and goes on to add the subordinate notion. Many examples and a clear explanation are given by Page on *Aen.* 6.361. In Lucan we
may compare 2.388 'urbi pater est, urbique maritus', 5.393f and 9.352f.

788   **aequorea restinguit aqua**: in grand funerals, such as Pompey deserved, wine
might have been used (cf. *Aen.* 6.226-8, Prop. 4.7.34, [Tibull.] 3.2.19, and
St. *Silu.* 2.6.90).

788-9 **congesta clausit humo** is verbally echoed by Tacitus in describing Agrippina's
burial at *Ann.* 14.9.2 'neque . . . congesta aut clausa humus'.

789   **parua . . . leuis** both stress the slightness of the remains -- a common sepulchral
theme (cf. Ov. *Met.* 12.615f of Achilles). A pedant might however point out
that a striving for pathos has blinded Lucan to the fact that there was more of
Pompey left after his incomplete cremation than would have remained after a
full burning.

791   Mooring ships to a tombstone on the shore is a commonplace of sepulchral
poetry. We meet the notion at 7.860 and in Leonidas of Tarentum, *A.P.* 7.
264, 266 and 675.

791   **moueret** 'disturb'; see 529n.

792   **sacrum**: the incidence of this and of kindred words now gradually increases.
Lucan prepares the reader for Pompey's apotheosis.

793   **hic situs est Magnus**: the point of this studiedly simple epitaph is that true
greatness needs but the bare name for complete identification. From this

179

point on the tomb becomes Lucan's obsession, as the head has been up to now. At first he will call it a disgrace, and will deliver over it a personal *laudatio funebris*. But from this strain of complaint he will modulate just before the close of the book to the exalted note, that a mean grave will serve Pompey well after all, for it must in time disappear and so contribute to his deification (a sentiment shared by lovers of Mozart). The book can end therefore on a note of calm triumph, which is sustained into the opening of the ninth.

793-4   **placet ... dicere:** this question is similar in tone to the one at 609f, and to 7.739f 'neque enim donare uocabo/ quod sibi quisque dabit'; in all of these the speaker finds fault with a word or notion as being inadequate to express his meaning or sense of fitness.

794-5   **quo ... socer:** this poor burial is worse than no burial at all, a sentiment found at 761f and 9.64-6.

796   For the short o of *obicis* see 740n.

     manes ... uagantis: usually a wandering shade was reckoned to be unhappy, but in the present context it is the form of burial that causes the disquiet.

797-8   Housman elegantly explained this vexed passage. As Mr E.J. Kenney points out, the radical sense of *pendeo* is 'be poised or suspended, hover' in any context; *nare* is 'to float'. The usage of the two verbs can therefore to some degree overlap in such expressions as 'enaret in aeris auras' (Lucr. 3. 591) and 'pendebat in auras' (Ov. *Met.* 8.145). *Pendeo* is the verb of more generalised sense and the context gives it sharper focus. So at 754 *pendet* has the sense 'surrounded by water', as Housman showed on 9.337 and Manil. 4.288 and 595; cf. Ov. *Her.* 19.149f 'natat ille, sed isdem ... spes mea pendet aquis'. The sentence is disposed in a chiastic pattern from 797 to 799: in this context *situs est* and *modus tumuli* come to much the same thing, while the *qua* clause and *Romanum ... imperium* perform similar roles of definition. Lucan's sentiment was earlier expressed by Valerius Maximus, 5.1.10, 'caput (Pompey's) in suo modo terrarum orbe nusquam sepulturae locum habuit'. It is characteristic of a Roman that Lucan sets Fame's boundaries coterminous with those of the Empire (see Costa on Sen. *Med.* 372-4).

799   **obrue,** as Postgate observed, (*CQ* 1.1907.221f), might after a fashion mean 'bury', and he compared Ov. *Met.* 13.446 (quoted at 860n). Lucan's taste for paradox would readily embrace the notion that the rock and not the ashes were more deserving to be covered.

     saxa is not a generic plural; the poet has chosen it, as he chose *corpora* at 2.22f, or *templa* at 3.153, because the form is metrically more manageable (see P. Maas *Kl. Schr.* (1973), 527-85).

800 **crimine plena deum**: the gods were from time to time charged with heed-lessness of the sufferings and death of their favourites. The close of Soph-ocles's *Trachiniae* affords a most notable example of this. Suetonius records at *Cal.* 5 that the Romans stoned their temples at the death of Germanicus. Lucan uses this sentiment at 7.724f and 149 above, but he even goes so far as to impute crime to heaven (or at any rate he indicts it) at 2.288, 5.59, above 55, and 9.144. Statius picks up the notion – languidly – at *Silu.* 5.2. 85. In Lucan's comprehensive imagination neither god nor man is free from guilt of some sort in the midst of civil war (see Heinsius 403f).

800-01 **Herculis . . . Bromio**: Hercules and Bacchus constantly appear together in the eulogies of men. They were mortal and the archetypes of the conqueror and benefactor who, thanks to their services to the rest of mankind, were accorded divine status. So Virgil joins them at *Aen.* 6.801-5, and Horace at *Carm.* 3.3.9-13 and 4.8.30-4 (cf. *Eleg. Maec.* 66-72, Ov. *Am.* 3.8(7).51f and *A.A.* 1.187-90, St. *Silu.* 4.3.155). It was for this reason that the Ptolemies actually claimed descent from both heroes (see Gow *Theocritus* vol. 2, p. 331). So by mentioning them at this point Lucan hints at a fuller sort of comparison of Pompey to them and so paves the way to an apotheosis; the elder Pliny makes much the same comparison at *N.H.* 7.95. For this theme see E. Norden *Kl. Schr.* (1966), 425 and Edwards on Sen. *Suas.* 1.1, p.84.
Oete . . . iuga Nyseia: Servius attests on *Aen.* 11.849 that mountains were regarded as memorials, if notable men were buried on or near them. At *A.P.* 7.390.1f Cyllene in Arcadia is said to be the monument of Apollodorus. (Other landmarks might serve; Greece and Salamis at *A.P.* 7.73, the Carpa-thian sea at Prop. 3.7.12, the world at *Herc. Oet.* 1827.)

801 **vacant Bromio**: Lucan is not asserting that Bacchus died at Nysa or is buried there, only that the place was set aside as his demesne. For the sense of *uacant* we may compare Sen. *Phaedra* 55f 'cuius regna pars terrarum/ secreta uacat', and Claud. 10 *Epith.* 54 '(mons) Luxuriae Venerique/ uacat'. In these lines, as in 110f, an absolute tone dominates: *tota, omnia, nullo* admit of no exceptions. Indeed the contrast between *omnia* and *nullo* shows that the members in which these words occur must cohere, so that Cortius's full-stop after *potest* is rhetorically impossible.
quare: Norden observed (400-2) that Virgil was not scrupulous in avoiding the use of what he rather unfeelingly calls indifferent words at line-end. In *Aeneid* VI there is one in every twenty-two lines. Lucan however is very sparing, and there are but nine examples in this book (192, 350, 382, 444, 742, 746, 764, 786), or one in ninety-seven lines. The close of the line is too

prominent to allow the declaimer to miss the chance for emphasis. *Quare* however, the last word in the line but the first of the apodosis, is clearly not 'indifferently placed'.

803   **tenere** has sacral overtones, for a god is said to possess his special places of worship (cf.3.403 and 9.163f, Hor. *Carm.* 3.26.9f and *C.S.* 69, *Il.* 5.890). But the verb is also used of the dead man's possession of his last resting-place, as at 5.230f.

        caespite: sods of earth were used, heaped up, to form grave mounds (see *OLD* sv 3c), but on the beach Cordus had only sand and rock at his disposal. Lucan, unless he is as usual incautious, is using the word as a pure metaphor. Its choice is however rhetorically generated, so to say, by the preceding *arua.* There is a strong contrast between one lump of turf and all the fields of Egypt.

804   For *populi* see 420n.

805   The prohibition is driven home by the double alliteration at the beginning of the line.

806   **dignaris** refers not to Pompey, addressed in 805, but to Cordus, last addressed at 795-7; cf. 513-5n.

807   **actus** in the sense of *res gestae* is post-Augustan (see *OLD* sv 11). **monimenta maxima rerum** enhances by its alliteration the importance of the deeds. *Maxima* suits *rerum* better than *monimenta*, and should be regarded as a transferred epithet.

809   **reuocato consule** has long been seen to be untrue to history, for Metellus Pius carried on the war in Spain even after Pompey's arrival. (Is it possible that Lucan is recalling the fact that Metellus Numidicus was replaced by Marius in the Jugurthine war in 107 BC?) At any rate the phrase is prompted by the desire to make a strong contrast with *eques* in the next line.

810   **commercia tuta** has no connective to add it to the enumeration, a pattern illustrated by Munro on Lucr. 1.715.

811   **pauidos maris:** the genitive of reference with an adjective is discussed by Woodcock 57, and further examples in Lucan are given by Heitland ciii.

812-3   **in Euro ... Boreaque:** the winds have given their names to the regions from whence they blow; Horace had already used *Boreas* to mean 'the North' at *Carm.* 3.24.38.

813-4   **ab armis/ ciuilem repetisse togam:** the juxtaposition of *armis* and *ciuilem* is designed to heighten the contrast, which is further emphasized by their positions in their lines. *Ab* has its temporal sense 'after'; see *OLD* sv 13b, and especially Munro on Lucr. 6.968, where he observes how common the usage is in Ovid. The metonymy in the sentence recalls Cicero's 'cedant arma togae'.

815   **donasse** 'waive a claim to', and the dative 'denotes the one forgiven or the person or thing in consideration whereof one forgives or forgets' (Summers on Sen. *Ep.* 78, p.266). The sentiment recalls Ov. *Met.* 15.757 'multos meruisse, aliquos egisse triumphos'. The composition of the two sentences from 806 to 815 deserves notice. 806 is a protasis whose apodosis extends over six and one-half lines; indeed, even 813-5 are still logically a part of that apodosis. 807, the first clause of the apodosis, is in content general and unspecific. At 808 we get down to business, and that line, for variety, begins with dactyls, and the sense pauses at 4/1. 809 has no internal sense division, but the next line is brought up sharp again at 4/1. *Commercia . . . maris* is a colon on its own, and the sense pause is at 4/2 (the bucolic diaeresis). 811-3 form a tricolon crescendo, as has been noted, and the sense stops at a strong caesura in 4/1. The phrasing of this tricolon is interesting for it progresses from the vague and depreciatory *barbariem,* to the more specific but still slighting *gentes uagas.* But the last member opens out into a spreading vision of oriental empire. Then a new sentence begins and it also is carried up to 4/1. A second member is added asyndetically, and it fills the last line, 815, in which there is an internal rhyme. At 816 the preceding ten lines are summed up in a pithy question, half a line in length. It comes as a jolt after the long period. The variety of pauses and caesurae is, by Virgilian standards, impoverished, but the writing is undeniably vigorous and smart.

817   **non ullis**: the seemingly contradictory expression finds an analogy at 7:404f 'nulloque frequentem ciue suo Romam' (Dilke).

818   **solitum** is probably a rhetorical exaggeration rather than a considered reference to the temples founded by Pompey (mentioned by Aul. Gel. 10.1.7 and Pliny *N.H.* 7.9.7 and 8.20). The name of the dedicator was inscribed on the architrave of the tympanum, as we can still most memorably see on the Pantheon in Rome (cf. Ov. *Fasti* 5.567 'spectat et Augusto praetextum nomine templum', *Cons. ad Liu.* 288 'nec sua prae templi nomina fronte leget'). Whatever we make of *solitum, super* is indefensible either as Latin or as architecture. As not infrequently happens, Lucan has in his mind a Virgilian phrase (*super alta* will be found at *Aen.* 1.680 and 6.787), which he has not assimilated to its new context. He aims at magniloquence, not precision.

819   **arcus**: no arches are attested for Pompey (see *RE* 7A sv Triumphbogen). Lucan speaks off the top of his head, and from the point of view of his own age, when triumphal arches had become more common. Still, did he never

use his eyes as he walked about the city?

820 **nomen:** the important noun is withheld as long as possible. It is a defect of style, that the obvious halt formed by 'nomen harena' is overridden by an addition two lines in length. The sense of these is however far from idle, and the increased precision of the shift from the vague *aduena* to the particular 'Romanus hospes' is neat (cf.114f). For all that 821f give a strong impression of afterthought.

821-2 The failure to notice a hero's tomb is pathetic; so, for example, Caesar nearly treads on Hector's at 9.975f. For this reason, tombs were meant to be conspicuous to travellers; cf. 854 below, *Il.* 7.86ff, *Od.* 24.80-4 and Beowulf 2803-8. Hence the placing of tombs along the Appian way. *Rectus* is a vivid touch, and seems to be Lucan's own.

822 This line gives the first hint, to be followed up and amplified at 850-8, that Pompey's tomb will be a place of pilgrimage. The theme was started back at 114f. Cf. *Aetna* 568ff, esp. 590, and Prop. 4.6.83f.

The action (such as it was) of the eighth book is now over. The remaining fifty lines are a purely personal reflection. Lucan likes closing books in this way. At the end of the fourth, for example, he comes forward in his own person to praise Curio (Ahl's view that Lucan treats Curio as a degenerate is unacceptable because it leaves out of account lines 809 to 815; p.94). The seventh book ends with a long and personal address to Thessaly. The character and extent of these reflections is unexampled in what is left to us of Roman epic. But it must be remembered that the *Pharsalia* is the first historical epic of any measure of completeness that we possess. And historical epic, especially such as was roughly contemporary with the events described, tended to adopt a note of panegyric. This is evident in the remains of the later books of the *Annales* of Ennius, and praise must have formed some part of the *Bellum Sequanicum* of Varro of Atax, the *Bellum Actiacum* of Rabirius, and the historical poems of Cornelius Severus and Albinovanus Pedo. Now one common strategy of praise recommends that the poet identify himself closely, as a friend say, with the person he sets out to praise (this to avoid the charge of mere hire). The technique is common in Pindar, who, as an aristocrat, probably was the friend of some of his patrons. But Lucan is not writing about the recent past, so flattery cannot be a motive for his personal intrusions into the narrative. But the historical epic encouraged a degree of personal utterance that would be ludicrously out of place in a mythological epic (Virgil's Nisus and Euryalus spring to mind), and it is that encouragement which Lucan here exploits. Also in these closing lines several themes are more fully restated, in particular those of pilgrimage and apotheosis: not for nothing is the last word *Tonantis*. By painting an almost divine Pompey, Lucan prepares the reader for the transformed and majestic hero of the opening of the ninth book, a commendable transition.

There do not seem to be any stylistic traits which elevate the concluding lines of the book. Lucan's favourite devices of alliteration, apostrophe, repetition, rhetorical question and paradox are no more in evidence here than elsewhere. He does venture upon a necessary periphrasis at 854, and at 843 he remodels a common phrase in order to raise the tone of his diction, but such devices are far from remarkable. There is a dearth, common to the later books generally, of some once-favoured patterns, e.g., golden lines and encompassing word order. Still, at 864 and 866 the golden line reappears for the first time since 481, and its lapidary solidity is a contribution to the effect of the close. The alliteration too of the very last line lends vigour to the conclusion.

All taken in all, the great strength of the passage is the poet's own entrance. Lucan is praised (if at all) for his obvious sincerity. Which is another way of saying that his rhetoric succeeds in producing in the hearer an impression of conviction in the speaker. It is just this admission of a personal desire that must enhance, indeed create, the impression of sincerity. This impression is further aided by a distinct incoherence of structure, which is meant to suggest the wayward path of dithyramb. At one moment Pompey's tomb is a disgrace, at the next a glory; now an object of pilgrimage, now lost to sight. These abrupt changes in attitude are meant to seem (and indeed may be) unconsidered. It is as if the poet's words were the exact reflection of his uncontrolled thoughts, pouring out like fused metal. (J. Wight Duff noted and deplored this incoherence (260) and Ehlers suggests that the text represents two alternatives, only one of which would have been published (552); neither view is fair to the daring of the poet.)

823 The address to a land is borrowed by Catullus from the Alexandrians, as Baehrens pointed out on 4.13. By Lucan's time it was a well-established figure.

824 The warning is recorded by Dio 39.56.4, and mentioned by Cicero, *Fam.* 1. 7.4. The Sibylline books are reported only as saying that a large number should not assist the Egyptian king.

cautum has a prosy ring, but it is also found at Ov. *Her.* 18.110.

826 **ripas aestate tumentis:** by the figure synecdoche *ripas* here stands for the river, as perhaps at *Aen.* 9.105 (cited by Håkanson 68; cf. 778n).

827 **precer** is a verb usually used of praying for benefits, but cf. Hor. *Serm.* 2.3.

203 'mala multa precatus Atridis' and Tibull. 2.6.17f 'tu me mihi dira precari/ cogis'. The preceding *saeua* makes the nuance plain. It is at this point that Lucan enters his narrative most openly. To some degree Catullus had shown the way (in a context of praise) at 64.22-4 where he addresses the heroes; Virgil had followed suit at *Aen.* 9.446-9 and 10.791-3 out of a desire to express a kind of lyrical grief for the deaths of young men, and to hold out a promise of immortality. Lucan had prepared the reader for an expression of sympathy; *nostra* at 556 is not lacking in warmth, but it is somewhat generalised ('we Romans'). Here his attachment is more outspokenly personal. Unfortunately he reuses the device at 9.598 where he says that he would rather lead Cato's army in Libya than win a triumph. For other such 'intrusions' we may compare 1.417, 5.610, 7.436, 552-3 and 768.

828   Haskins explains the second part of the curse thus: 'not that rain usually did fall in Egypt in winter, but the poet prays that there may not be that either to make up for the loss of the overflow of the Nile'. Pliny observed that, up to his time, the lowest recorded inundation had occured in the year of Pompey's murder 'ueluti necem Magni prodigio quodam flumine auersante', *N.H.* 5.58.

830   **tota** marks the end of an enumeration; see 734n.

832   The sistrum is discussed by Griffiths on Plut. *De Is.,* p.525.
    iubentia: the participle came to be commonly used to replace a relative clause from the late Republic on; cf. Catull. 64.8, *Aen.* 1.492, Hor. *Carm.* 2.14.15 and 16.23.

834   **tu nostros ... in puluere** carefully balances in contrast *nos in templa tuam.*

835   The cult of Julius in Rome is discussed by Weinstock 391ff, and 399ff. Lucan's denunciation is bold stuff, but it should be pointed out that his antipathy to the imperial cult may not have been to his contemporaries so very shocking. One reason for this is that after Augustus the cult seems to have gone into a sort of decline. Neither Tiberius nor Caligula were deified. Nor was Tiberius in any hurry to complete the temple of the divine Augustus – this was left to Caligula (cf. Suet. *Cal.* 21). Claudius, though deified, is lampooned for that very reason by Seneca in the so-called *Apocolocyntosis*; the publication of this work shows how far the court was prepared to go. Nero himself joked about mushrooms being the food of the gods and he let the new temple go to ruin (Dio 61.35.4 and Suet. *D.V.* 9.1). It would seem that fashionable Romans took the whole business with a grain of salt. Scepticism notwithstanding, it must be stressed that Lucan's invective ('saeuo ... tyranno') goes well beyond urbanity. We may compare 6.809

186

and 7.455-9 (one of Lucan's greatest moments); both passages are taken by adn. to refer to Julius alone (Augustus was untouchable).

837-40 Protases embrace the apodosis at Aesch. *Ag.* 345-7, Lucr. 3.946-9, Ov. *Met.* 3.263-6, Livy 22.60.11, Stat. *Silu.* 2.6.61-8, and 218-25 above.

839 **tui Magni:** so at 730 Pompey is called Fortune's own (cf. 848-50).

842 Tomb-robbing was a sacrilege of the most grievous nature, but Lucan would regard the sin as a 'felix culpa' if it meant Pompey's return (cf. 781n).

843 **satis o nimiumque** is a refashioning of the too prosaic *satis superque* (cf. Ov. *Met.* 4.429f 'satisque ac super'). The interposed *o* heightens the strangeness, as does the omission of *ego.* That the nominative must occasionally be supplied from an oblique case is amply demonstrated by Housman in his note to Manil. 3.158, with the *addendum;* so Manil. 1.893, and 3.398 above; in general, the oblique case precedes so that the reader is aware at a glance what person is in question (as at 636 above; cf. Oudendorp on 2.218).

844-5 **transferre reuolsos:** to end one word and begin the next with the same syllable was seen as a defect of euphony by Isocrates, *Techne,* fr. 6, and Quintilian too speaks against it at *I.O.* 9.4.41. Poets were pretty indifferent to repeating the syllables *re* and *it,* but there are some ugly juxtapositions (if a modern ear may judge) at Ov. *A.A.* 3.315 'discant cantare' and *Met.* 3.213 'nuper percussus', and in Lucan at 6.42 'siluas uasta'. Special accounts of the practice of Greek authors are given by G.B.A. Fletcher in *CR* 52.1938. 164f and J. Diggle in *PCPS* 15.1968.59; for Latin authors Herescu 44-7, Austin on *Aen.* 2.27, Heinze on Hor. *Ep.* 1.1.95, J. Richmond in *Phil.* 112. 1968.135, and Housman's additional note to Manil. 2.242. The special case of cacemphata was discussed at 14 above. (Landor notices the matter in his *Imaginary Conversation* between Chesterfield and Chatham.)
manes has a wide variety of nuances. It properly refers to the spirits of the dead collectively, but comes to be used of an individual. Once this sense is established it is no long step to use the word of the mortal remains, even before burial, as at 9.151 'inhumatos condere manes' and 751 above. Lucan has in mind here the recovery of the bones of Orestes by the Spartans or of Theseus by the Athenians; this hint (noticed only by Guyetus it seems) is evidence of Lucan's subtle skill in raising Pompey to heroic status.

846-7 **poscere . . . uolet** is another instance of the distributional figure ἀπὸ κοινοῦ ; cf. 75n.

847 **feralibus Austris:** the autumn winds blew up over the Pomptine marshes and brought deadly fever to Rome until the marshes were drained in this century (cf. the fate of Daisy Miller and see Mayor on Juv. 4.56). There is a similar list of disasters at 1.645-7.

187

848 **ignibus . . . nimiis** are the heat-waves mentioned at 1.646f and 9.375, as well as at Hor. *Ep.* 1.7.5f.

849 **urbem Magne tuam:** cf. 839, and 7.29 'tua Roma'; Rome, Fortune and Pompey are all intimately linked together (cf. 686).

850 Another case of an exceptional honour. It had been proposed that Augustus' bones be gathered by the chief priests of the most important colleges, though this was not in the event done (Suet. *D.A.* 100.2, Dio 56.42.4).

851 **nam quis** should probably be taken to stand for *quisnam,* a not uncommon usage, illustrated in *OLD* sv *nam* 7. (If this explanation is not correct, it is hard to see what logical function *nam* performs; Ehlers 551 goes so far as to bracket the passage as a doublet of 823-50.)

852 **imbrifera siccas** is an example of the common juxtaposition of epithets of contrasting sense.

853 **spectator Nili:** tourism to the Nile is discussed by Borneau 88.

854 **mercis mutator** is an elegant periphrasis for *mercator.* Lucan's fondness for coinages with the *tor* suffix is noticed by Heitland ci.

855 The *miserabile bustum* of 816 has turned into a *uenerabile saxum.* But Lucan will wish even that stone away in order that the mystery surrounding Pompey's resting place may be complete.

857 **manes tuos placare:** it was customary for travellers to honour the important altars (or tombs) which they met on their journeys; cf. Agamemnon's complaint to Zeus at *Il.* 8.238f, and Suet. *Cal.* 3.2 'sicubi clarorum uirorum sepulchra cognosceret (Germanicus), inferias manibus dabat'.

858 **Casio praeferre Ioui:** Lucan has already said that Pompey may be found more deserving of divine status than Julius at 835; here he more boldly suggests that Pompey's tomb will eclipse the local shrine of the chief of gods. This prepares the reader for the even bolder assertions of 863f, and for the comparison of the final lines of the book.

858-9 Lucan has now resigned himself to the meanness of the tomb, but he proposes to discover a virtue in it yet. The phrase 'templis auroque sepulti' provides a link with the opening of the next book, for it is there recalled in the tenth line, 'auro positi nec ture sepulti'.

templis auroque may be a case of hendiadys, but the point of *templis* is unclear. For Sir Thomas Browne rightly observed in the third chapter of *Urne-Buriall* that 'He that looks for Urnes and old sepulchrall reliques, must not seek them in the ruines of Temples; where no religion anciently placed them'. Kirchmann in *De Funeribus Romanorum* 2.26f speaks of temples believed in antiquity to be tombs, but there is no evidence that ashes were deposited in a temple already built. (Indeed Cornelia's proposal at 9.61f to scatter her

188

husband's ashes in the temples is meant to be an insult, however sacrilegious, to the gods.) If Lucan is not simply saying the first thing that has come into his head, he may be alluding to a popular form of monument, the temple-shaped shrine for ashes, which is discussed and illustrated by J.M.C. Toynbee in *Death and Burial in the Roman World* (1971), 130-2. There may be an allusion to such a container at St. *Th.* 6.243 'templum ingens cineri'.

860-1   Grotius explained that Fortune is in a sense buried with the man to whom she was so closely attached for so long; Housman aptly cited in confirmation of this an epitaph on Ajax by Ausonius, 220, p.73 Peiper, in which Valour bewails her burial with the hero. Somewhat along the same lines is the passage in the funeral oration of Lysias, 2.60, in which the freedom of the dead men is buried along with their bravery; we may also compare Livy 2.55.2 'cum Genucio una mortuam ac sepultam tribuniciam potestatem' and Ov. *Met.* 13.446 'obrutaque est mecum uirtutis gratia nostrae'.

862   **Libyco** is a geographical inaccuracy indulged in by Petronius too, 'Libyco iacet aequore Magnus' 120,63. But Martial, 5.74.2, and Seneca in the epigrams attributed to him, 12, 23, 65 and 66, have a rhetorical point to make when they say that Pompey is buried in Africa.
       in has the sense 'beside' or 'near'. The usage is not well illustrated in *OLD* sv 33d. Cf. Vir. *Ecl.* 7.66 'populus in fluuiis', Prop. 1.3.6 (Shackleton Bailey 80), and Lucan 4.634, 696, and 5.289.

863-4   The explanation of these lines offered by comm. Bern. shows just how much trouble they gave in antiquity. The simplest is the first: some men are repelled by the ritualism of the Capitol and prefer old-fashioned Etrurian rites (in revering the *bidental*, a place where a thunder-bolt has fallen and is buried). All we require to accept this is some evidence that it was so; the life of the poet attributed to Vacca says that Lucan was an augur, so it may be that here he speaks from experience. (The second explanation found in comm. Bern. is fantastic: occasionally men prefer not to go to the Capitol, but to worship Caesar in his mausoleum on the Tiber, Tuscan turf being an allusion to the river's Etrurian headwaters; the third explanation seems to be no more than a variant on the first.) Lucan seems to be suggesting that people who stand apart from grand but meaningless rites preserve a superstitious dread of elemental forces (and heroes, especially angry ones, were just such forces). It follows that such people will disdain the deified Julius but honour the heroic Pompey.
       sua does not refer to the subject of the sentence, but to the gods to whom incense is owed; see LS sv *suus* IA5β.

189

867   **pulueris exigui congeriem** is designed to contrast in each detail with 'ardua marmoreo pondere moles'.

868   **bustum cadet** contrast with *surrexit* at 866. The simplicity of these two words is very moving and there is a calm assurance about these closing futures, uttered by Lucan in his role as *uates*.

871   **populis:** cf. 7.207 'populosque nepotum'; here the word means 'crowds', a sense illustrated by *OLD* sv 4.

872   The Cretan lie is first recorded in poetry by Callim. *Hymn.* 1.8, and in a sepulchral epigram of Gaetulicus, *A.P.* 7.275.

        Tumulo is an ablative of cause; it exemplifies what commentators call 'res pro rei defectu': Egypt lies for lack of the tomb.

        Creta Tonantis finds an echo in *Herc. Oet.* 1882. *Tonans,* a sort of kenning word favoured by Ovid, has, as the last word in the book, powerful overtones (enhanced here by alliteration). In effect, Lucan sets Pompey alongside Jupiter.

APPENDIX I: PARTHIA

This appendix will treat of four lines in the eighth book (217, 292, 315, 337) whose subject matter is largely related. For all four allude to the fundamental otherness of Parthia and its fancied complete isolation from Mediterranean lands. The manner of the expression is linked by two common features: either the otherness is named outright with words of the *al* - root, or Lucan employs astronomical terminology.

217 **totum mutare diem** is expounded by Housman as follows in a note to 7.189: 'diem id nos longitudinem nuncupamus . . . totum mutare diem dicitur qui se ad Parthos confert, hoc est in orientem, mutat enim diei tempora aliasque numerat horas'. Though this may well be true, it is not necessarily what Lucan is getting at. As 'Medorum domos Scythicosque recessus' (216) makes clear, Pompey is urging Deiotarus to pass beyond the Roman world into the completely different eastern one (cf. 312). *Dies* here is a common usage for *plaga caeli*, 'clime', and Haskins rightly compared St. *Th.* 1.200f. *sub omni . . . die* which 'Lactantius' took to mean *sub omni caelo* (cf. *Silu.* 3.3.99f). Here adn. gloss *diem* as *caelum,* which recalls Hor. *Ep.* 1.11.27, also cited by Haskins. Thus Housman's 'longitude' may be too restrictive in general: correct so far as concerns this line, but not 7.189 or the Statian passages.

292 **polus alter** is neatly explained by Housman as 'caelum a nostro diuersum'. Postgate mistakenly took Lucan to be saying that some part of Parthia fell beneath the south Pole. But *alter* here is not 'the other of two' (so also *TLL* 1.1731.54 citing Claud. 15.2) but *contrarius.* The locution is especially common in the phrase *orbis alter* (see *TLL* 1.1736.27-37) where *alter* means 'different', not necessarily 'opposite'. At Manil. 4.674f Parthia is called *orbis alius* and so its heaven also may be called either *alius* or *alter*.

315 **orbe alio** is closely related to the phrase *orbis alter* cited in the previous note, and numerous parallels will be found in *TLL* 1.1627.72-1628.2.

337 **auersos polos,** as Housman saw, confirms his interpretation of *polus alter*

191

in 292. But *aliena sidera* is not perhaps to be taken literally, though Housman so understood it. The whole phrase is said by comm. Bern. to mean 'quasi Parthi in alio orbe sunt et alio sidere utentur'; that is, *sidera* is no more than a poetic plural, and the phrase means 'clime' as at 2.294 'alio sub sidere reges', and 6.816, where again the plural is found. (It is odd that in his note to that line Housman says 'Cortius contulit II 294, VII 189, VIII 337': but the latter two he understands otherwise in the notes he wrote *ad locc.*) Another explanation may be that behind *aliena* lurks the notion of national stars, which Manilius expounds at 4.585 and 696ff; Plautus alludes to it at *Rudens* 8-10 (see Fraenkel 2.37-44). In seeking Parthia Pompey is putting himself at the mercy of their protecting constellations, and, as Lentulus will go on to say, their foreign gods.

Throughout his treatment of Parthia Lucan has been at pains to stress its total 'otherness'; so he rings changes on *alius*, among other devices. To my mind the handling is varied and skilful, especially in comparison with the startlingly similar fragment of Albinovanus Pedo found in Sen. *Suas.* 1.15 (FPL, ed. Morel, p. 115f). There Pedo calls attention to the 'otherness' of the German world and speaks in 18 of 'alio . . . sub cardine gentes', in 19 of *alium . . . orbem* (where his *quaerimus* recalls *quaeris* at 337), and in 21 of *aliena . . . aequora* (where *aliena* is the possessive of *alia;* cf. Ov. *Met.* 7.22 'Thalamos alieni concipis orbis'). All this in four lines is too obvious compared with Lucan's more careful separation of elements. It is not necessary that Lucan knew Pedo's work; both are dealing with a commonplace, the danger and pathos of approaching what is not one's own, so it is not surprising that both hit on similar means of expression. It may however be the case that some readers find both poets mechanical on such a point.

APPENDIX II: VIRGIL AND OVID RECALLED

This appendix lists Lucan's straightforward recollection (or theft) of phrases from Virgil and Ovid; in only a few cases is the wording less than exactly reproduced. It should be well known that such plagiarism was the life blood of Latin poetry; the young poet's mind is full of the work of his predecessors and he acknowledges his debt to them openly by imitation (a process noted in the work of the young film directors of our own day). A sympathetic analysis of the psychology of frank and audacious borrowing will be found in Ruskin's *The Seven Lamps of Architecture* 5.5.

Virgil Recalled

2. Ecl. 6.80
7. Aen. 2.729
8. Geor. 1.402, Aen 7.512
28. Geor. 4.83
29. Aen. 2.324
118. Aen. 3.104
132f. Aen. 8.65
138. Aen. 11.694
143. Aen. 2.431
171f. See note
195. Aen. 3.285 (and Ov. Met. 5.7)
202. Aen. 6.867 (or Ov. Met. 1.329)
261. Geor. 4.452, Aen. 3.457
271. Aen. 8.333
272. Ecl. 2.21
307. Aen. 7.293
316. Aen. 9.391
391. Ecl. 1.66 (or Ov. Pont. 1.9.48).

399. Geor. 1.60
453. (also 2.490) Aen. 7.599
536. Aen. 2.130
638. Aen. 7.395
680f. Aen. 1.589ff
717. Aen. 6.166
759. Aen. 10.409
776. Aen. 1.176
777. Geor. 3.281
818. See note.
867. Geor. 4.87, not Hor. Carm. 1.28.3

Ovid Recalled

5. Met. 8.167
6. Met. 2.275
(16. Met. 7.614)
31. Met. 10.384
(44. Tr. 3.1.54)
48. Her. 5.63
51. Met. 11.719
75-6. Tr. 4.3.71-80, 5.5.50

78. Her. 12.76
79. Tr. 5.3.47 and Pont. 4.9.17
86f. Met. 6.246
87. Met. 11.420
99. Tr. 4.3.14
103. Met. 8. 125
104. A.A. 1.321
132. Met. 11.618
134. *Caesaris ira* in last poems
143. Tr. 3.10.1
161. Met. 3.396
174. Pont. 3.7.27
182. Met. 1.274
189. Her. 2.19
199. Met. 4.245
201. Tr. 1.9.1.
202. See Virgil
208. Pont. 2.8.26 (not Hor. Carm. 1.1.6)
209. Met. 3.26, 701
210. Met. 3.17
224. Met. 2.662

238. A.A. 1.666
260. Am. 3.14.31
304. Tr. 4.1.77
313. Met. 5.73
334. Rem. 48
391. Pont. 1.9.48
432. Tr. 3.10.63
447. Met. 2.731 (and often)
480. Met. 5.151
503. Tr. 3.1.50
524. Met. 8.10
528. Tr. 1.6.5, Pont. 2.3.60
557. Met. 1.514
560. Met. 11.487
630. Met. 6.193
639. Met. 4.110
640. Met. 3.468
668. Met. 10.315
782. Pont. 2.9.3, Met. 9.137
865. Am. 3.11.7
869. Met. 14.142

INDEX

(Numbers in italic refer to pages. Numbers in ordinary type refer to the Commentary by lines of the text.)

194

haplography 88, 506
recollection 9, 395, 567, 756f, 761
Corneille *142*

damno 'reject' 126
dative case
    agent 301, 370
    disadvantage 689
    goal 456
    predicate 31
death, love of 364
decursio described 735
'do' for 'allow to be done' 74, 137
dux replaces *is* 14

ellipse
    of idea 'only' 51f
    of idea 'news of' 473
    of idea 'thought of' 45, 285f
    of participle or defining word in
        prepositional phrase 531
emphasis (figure) *23,* 80, 215
emulation 471
enjambment 24-7, 371, 390-4
enumeration (negative) 729-42
epanalepsis 556f
epithet
    balancing 283, 372f
    constant 13, 40, 62, 564, 655
    contrasting 57
    transferred 807
era in epic 66
euphony 14, 200, 844
exaggeration 585

fas 'loyalty' 142
figura etymologica 46
final clause 414, 498
Florus 273f

genitive case
    descriptive 21, 158, 374, 676
    equivalent to adjective 676
    object 61
    predicate 673
    reference 811
geographical inaccuracy 245f, 260,
    540, 862
hendiadys 1, 541, 593, 655, 858f
heu 604
hic 'yours' 75f
historical inaccuracy or invention *5-9,*
    57, 79f, 133f, *112,* 211-38, 227,
    302, 359, 416, 507, 715, 809
hypallage 698
hyperbaton (see word order)
hysterologia 786f

imperfect tense
    of awakening 652
    conative 577
imprecision of language 45, 75f, 204f,
    272f
in 'beside' 862
incest 404
indicative mood
    deliberative 349
    irrealis 522
infinitive (explanatory) 314-6, 345-6
ingens 28
is avoided 14, 198, 255
iste = hic 545
iugulum 'slaughter' 11
iura, cura confused 75f

juxtaposition (see word order)

kenning word 3, 872
κυκλός (figure) 492f

leuior, melior confused 395
litus 'water on shore' 698

magniloquence *20-4*, 20, 138, 140,
    274-6, 335, 650
materia 'opportunity' 76
mens = animus (76), 331
metaphor
    commercial *100*, 657f
    legal 332f
    theatrical 676
metonomy 161-7, 471, 685, 718, 813f
metre
    aphaeresis 746
    elision of *ae* 40
metrical convenience or exigency 12,
    60, 66, 78, 213, 288, 338, 381,
    394, 627, 703f, 734, 799
mons 'vast building' 695
moralising 241-3

ne 125-6
nec, neque 'also not' 503
    = *et ne* 498
    = *et non* 250f, 303
    = *ne quidem* 'not even' 206, 497
negative idea
    carried over *aut* 378
    carried over *que* 554f
    overlogical 125-7
    resolved 599f
nominative case (apposition) 605f

omissio (figure) *18*
omnis (conclusive) 43-45, 734
ora 'head' 12
Ovid 40-62, 46f, 66f, 75f

paradox *24*, 37-9, 94, 125-7, 137,
    207-9, 237f, 269-71, 356, 537, 547,
153, 652, 694-8, 711, 736, 748,
    763, 781, 799
participle replaces relative clause 832
pendeo 797f
perfect tense
    altered to present 108
    gnomic 30, 404,
    infinitive (timeless) 381
    instantaneous 60, 108
personification 40, 197-9, 303-5
Petrarch 85, 90
pleonasm 71, 105, 142, 372f
Plutarch *81f*, 37-9, 70-85, *100*, 158,
    274-6, 328, 332, 397-404, 594, 663,
    692-711, 715
populi 'Romans' 'Italians' 420
prepositional phrase (adnominal) 430
proclitics 747
pronouns omitted 97, 137, 652f, 843
prosaic language (and colloquial) *14,*
    66, 335, 385f, 438, 690, (713),
    (719), 721, 729-31
prosody
    subici 740
    tabe 778

que
    adversative 301
    explanatory 148, 190
    'or' 46f
    reduplicated 260
question, rhetorical 31f
quidquid = in quantum 179
quodsi 311

Racine *82*, 70-85
regna = reges 278
relinquo 'leave alone' 244
repetition of syllable 844
    of words *13f*, 388, 475

Printed and bound by CPI Group (UK) Ltd, Croydon, CR0 4YY

09/06/2025

14685959-0001